Education management in managerialist times

Education management in managerialist times

Beyond the textual apologists

Martin Thrupp and Robert Willmott

Open University Press
Maidenhead · Philadelphia

Open University Press
McGraw-Hill Education
McGraw-Hill House
Shoppenhangers Road
Maidenhead
Berkshire
England
SL6 2QL

email: enquiries@openup.co.uk
world wide web: www.openup.co.uk

and

325 Chestnut Street
Philadelphia, PA 19106, USA

First published 2003

A catalogue record of this book is available from the British Library

ISBN 0 335 21028 7 (pb)   0 335 21029 5 (hb)

Library of Congress Cataloging-in-Publication Data
CIP data applied for

Typeset by RefineCatch Limited, Bungay, Suffolk
Printed in Great Britain by Bell and Bain Ltd, Glasgow

For Chris, Sophie, Paul, Tracy, Margaret and Phil

Acknowledgements

As well as building on their published work, this book has benefited greatly from informal conversations with many of the 'textual dissenters' mentioned, some of those more clearly 'within' the education management arena, and many other colleagues and students as well. Although responsibility for the text remains ours, we especially want to thank Alan Cribb, Alma Harris, Carol Vincent, Clementina Marques-Cardoso, Dave Baker, Dave Gillborn, Deborah Fraser, Diane Reay, Gill Crozier, Helen Gunter, Hugh Lauder, Les Bell, Mark Olssen, Marny Dickson, Miriam David, Nick Foskett, Pat Thompson, Peter Duncan, Philip Wood, Richard Hatcher, Richard Smith, Sharon Gewirtz, Stephen Ball, Terry Wrigley, Thanos Fragos and Tom Gordon.

Contents

PART I
Background

1 Introduction: What's wrong with education management?

Since the late 1980s there has been a phenomenal increase in the publication of educational (especially *school*) management books. Arriving at a rate that no one can really keep up with, academic bookshop and library shelves now groan under the weight of recent texts on school self-management, school change, school leadership, school improvement, strategic human resource management in education, educational marketing and the like. The remarkable growth of this literature, what Helen Gunter (1997) refers to as the 'education management industry', reflects at the most immediate level the desire by school leaders and others for practical guides to running schools in an era of devolved management. More generally, it reflects the dominance of managerialism in education and wider public policy (Clarke *et al.* 2000). Management has clearly become *the* solution of our times.

Yet despite the apparent popularity of education management texts, in this book we argue that this literature is harmful because of the way it fails to challenge existing social inequalities and the way it chimes with managerialist policies that will only further intensify existing inequality. This is by no means a new argument: work on this theme has been done by other academic writers like Lawrence Angus, Stephen Ball, Jill Blackmore, Gerald Grace, Helen Gunter, Richard Hatcher, Roger Slee, John Smyth and Gaby Weiner as well as ourselves.[1] However, this book builds on this corpus of work to rehearse the argument against the education management literature more comprehensively than ever before. In essence, we see much of the education management literature helping to redefine school management and leadership along managerial lines and hence to build the inequitable, reductionist and inauthentic 'managerial school' (Gewirtz 2002) and 'performing school' (Gleeson and Husbands 2001). We think this is barking up the wrong tree and that much of the literature should be permanently retired. Instead, what is needed are education management texts which are more genuinely educational, more politically astute and more committed to social justice and which send those messages unambiguously to both practitioners and policy makers.

Our general starting-point is a distinction between what we call *problem-solving* and *critical* perspectives on education, although much the same difference has been noted elsewhere as that between 'policy science' and 'policy scholarship' (Grace 1995) or 'sociology for education' and 'sociology of education' (Moore 1996). Problem-solving perspectives reflect 'common-sense', functionalist, ahistorical, individuated and often monocultural views about the purposes and problems of schooling. Crucially, even when 'quick fixes' are not seen as realistic, there are always thought to be school-based solutions to school problems. Such perspectives dominate the media and policy circles and problem-solving perspectives on education are also widely found among teacher educators, headteachers and teachers themselves, even those with considerable experience. By comparison, critical perspectives on education are less common but more searching. Drawing on sociologically and politically oriented educational research and scholarship (for instance, Halsey *et al.* 1997; Ball 2000), they hold that schools play a key role in perpetuating social inequality through reproducing the values and ideologies of dominant social groups (for example, middle class, white, male) and the status rankings of the existing social structure. From this understanding, the problems faced by schools are often seen as deeply rooted in their social context. As a result, those holding critical perspectives tend to be much less convinced than problem-solving colleagues that technical, school-based solutions hold the answers to educational problems.

Of course, all this is to greatly simplify the state of play because in practice there is a complex and sometimes contradictory spectrum of educational perspectives. Nevertheless, our concern about the education management literature is that it is far too problem-solving in orientation and that this has many unfortunate consequences. Our response in this book is a critical one and has three main elements:

- We start with what we believe are well-founded social, political and educational concerns about managerial schooling.
- We demonstrate that the education management literature generally fails adequately to reflect or respond to these concerns but rather, in subtle or more overt ways, acts to prop up recent managerialist reform. Or as Ball (1993a, 1994) has put it, we think too many education management texts are engaged in an ideological process of 'textual apologism'. This is illustrated by drawing both on our own fresh reading of the education management literature and on the arguments of other 'textual dissenters' like the authors listed above.
- Our argument reflects the belief that there has to be a better way to manage, even in managerialist times. We are not against management *per se* but against managerialist conceptions of it, and a further aim of the book is to set out some alternatives while being realistic about the

context within which those who lead and manage schools currently have to work.

Organization of this book

The organization of this book reflects the three aspects of our argument signalled above. Chapters 2 and 3 provide the necessary theoretical, historical and policy background for illustrating why most current education management literature may be inadequate and, indeed, harmful. Chapter 2 summarizes the nature and limitations of neo-liberalism and managerialism. Chapter 3 focuses more directly on educational inequality, educational reform and the rise of the education management 'industry'. It also illustrates early instances of education management writers brushing off political and sociological concerns about problem-solving approaches to education management, a process that continues today. Chapter 4 provides a different kind of background by introducing the education management literature and outlining our approach to reviewing it.

Part II of the book (Chapters 5–9) does the substantive work of critically reviewing the work of recent textual apologists. There are chapters on educational marketing, school improvement, school development planning/ strategic human resource management, school leadership and school change (the reasons these particular areas were chosen are discussed in Chapter 4). By discussing a range of recent texts written by both well and lesser known authors, these chapters explore the concerns that we have long held about the education management literature based on our own reading, on the accounts of the textual dissenters already mentioned and on a few previous critical reviews (for example, Ozga 1992; Fitz 1999; Thompson 2000). Put frankly, our key concerns have been:

- that the politics of the education management literature are mostly too opportunistic, offering glib accounts that gloss over contradictions within government policy and thus provide overt or more subtle support for the neo-liberal political project;
- that education management generally promotes the decline of the teacher as a professional educator. Given that the current policy environment is undoubtedly one where virtue ethics (making sure people are well trained then leaving them to get on with the job) have been ruled out of contention, the concern here is that education management has colluded with the growing control of teachers by promoting their compliance with reform;
- that education management is mostly informed by positivist social science so that while it is poorly theorized in terms of explicit social

theory, it in fact has an implicit secreted theory which is individualist, ahistorical, monocultural and functionalist;

- that education management is an area which usually 'bleaches context from its analytic frame' (Slee and Weiner 1998), being too technicist and too generic to take much account of the social dimensions of education;
- that education management is primarily regarded as a male activity;
- that education management usually fails to meet the empirical test because it implies predictability when in reality many educational activities have quite unpredictable outcomes;
- that education management too often borrows indiscriminately from general management literatures which are themselves deeply problematic;
- that education management is generally pathologizing, since by underplaying the importance of social context, it assumes that failure is located in institutions and their staffs;
- that education management is often illusory because it offers the promise of autonomy for education managers but neglects the problem of governments 'steering from a distance' and the ways that education managers may be victims as well as beneficiaries of reform;
- that education management is usually anti-educational by not focusing enough on pedagogy and curriculum and by encouraging inappropriate links to business;
- that education management distracts from more important educational and social justice issues, and
- that education management fails to reflect on all of this as it pursues a too hurried and unquestioning approach to school management issues.

If these were our key concerns at the outset, the purpose of the extensive reading that underlies the Part II chapters was to find out just how problematic the education management literature really is. Inevitably, the picture that emerges from these chapters is more complex and nuanced than the generalizations above can portray. Nevertheless we will show that there are serious problems, and so each chapter also concludes by suggesting alternative strategies for those managing and leading schools in the area under discussion, alternatives that may help to challenge the current politics of education but are realistic about what schools and school leaders are often up against in managerialist times. The focus here, then, is on what Cockburn (1991) in relation to gender reform has referred to as 'tactical' work – that which is do-able in difficult day-to-day circumstances rather than what is necessarily ideal over the longer term (which she calls 'strategic work'). In some cases these tactics involve doing nothing – refusing to engage in compromising activities – but in other instances more active responses are suggested.

Part III (Chapter 10) concludes the book by summing up the findings of the Part II chapters, engaging with some of the normative policy implications of our analysis, sketching ways in which policy could and should be refashioned to enhance social equity and develop individuals' intellectual, social and moral capacities. This chapter also considers how education management writers might begin to shift towards a more socially and politically critical stance, and the costs and benefits of doing so.

Our motives and intended audience

Before turning to our substantive arguments, we want to explain why we have written this book and for whom it is intended. One reason why it is important to do this is that even those who take a critical perspective on education do not always see the work of critiquing textual apologists as a worthwhile activity. For instance, Ozga (1992) undertook a review of education management texts in the *British Journal of Sociology of Education*, which was perhaps mostly noteworthy for the fact that she did not actually review any education management books because she considered they were not worth it. Similarly, we have both had comments about the book from academic colleagues along the lines of 'why are you bothering?' or 'rather you than me!'

These are perspectives with which we have some sympathy. After all, sociologists like Ozga typically start from such different theoretical premises from those of most education management writers that her impatience with their texts is easy to understand (see also Ozga 2000a). Moreover, Ozga does at least raise the problem of the education management literature – many holding critical perspectives on education do not so much criticize it as ignore it altogether. (This is not as hard as it sounds – the textual apologists and their critics generally have different networks, attend different conferences and read different books and journals.) Similarly, the 'rather you than me' comment is one we can certainly identify with since this was a book we both found rather painful to research and write. As will become apparent, the remarkable proliferation of education management texts has been accompanied by a lot of very pedestrian writing and, as we pored over the kind of literature which has been well described as 'vast, repetitive and intellectually stultifying' (Ozga and Walker 1995: 37), it did become frustrating to find so little of critical potential and depressing to have to document more of the same, time and time again.

Nevertheless, we have persevered because, as the saying goes, 'it may be dirty work but someone's got to do it'. To us the limitations of the education management literature need to be continually highlighted because while the literature may be deeply problematic, its impact on research, policy and practice has become considerable. Taken as a whole, the education manage-ment literature has come to constitute a large proportion of academic and consultancy activity around education. As Angus (1994) argued in response to Ozga's review:

> I cannot stress too strongly that the influence [of education manage-ment] texts in the area of educational practice is profound. Social critics need to understand that these books address very real problems as experienced by school administrators, their staff and their school communities. That is why the texts are popular and publishers are happy to produce a stream of them. To the extent that they engage with and offer solutions to what participants perceive to be practical problems, they cannot be dismissed out of hand.
>
> (Angus 1994: 78)

We would go further and suggest that the dominance of the kind of simplistic problem-solving perspective exemplified by the education management litera-ture has become a major obstacle preventing socially critical perspectives on policy and practice from becoming more influential. Given this, dealing with the way the academic 'community' sends out distinctly mixed messages is not a waste of time but a key agenda for those who want to address social justice concerns in education. Yet, as already noted, it is apparent that most critically oriented academics in education have not engaged with this literature. Some may be busy producing important findings about the limitations of recent education policies but not recognize that these are being marginalized by problem-solving accounts which provide support to the same policies. Others are probably just adopting the 'high ground' strategy of never getting 'bogged down' in arguments with those holding entirely different points of view from their own (many academics have this down to a fine art).

Partly, then, this book has been written to help provide a critical introduc-tion to the education management literature for those who already hold critical perspectives on education but who have yet to grapple with this vast literature. We have also wanted to celebrate the work of those who have already acted as textual dissenters. Their willingness to take issue with the direction and politics of educational scholarship substantially different from their own is admirable, and while there are limits to the energy anyone would want to put into this kind of activity (and we have already reached those limits in some places – see below), it is still unfortunate that so much problem-solving work has been allowed to go unchallenged by critically oriented researchers.

If the book has been partly written for a critical audience, it has been written even more for the textual apologists it criticizes and for those who employ their arguments in one way or another. However, our motives are even more likely to be misunderstood amongst this group. This problem has been underlined by some of Martin Thrupp's exchanges about textual apologism with leading proponents of the school effectiveness movement through the pages of its journal *School Effectiveness and School Improvement* (*SESI*).[2] These exchanges have taught us that if motives are not clearly established, those criticized will often be dismissive, for instance attributing criticisms to ignorance or arrogance:

> Maybe the criticisms reflect, firstly, simple ignorance. Many of them appear to come from people who have read very little school effectiveness research.
>
> (Reynolds and Teddlie 2001: 104)

> It may be that school effectiveness is simply victim to academic snobbery.
>
> (Reynolds and Teddlie 2001: 105)

> Much of the criticism of the school effectiveness research is that it doesn't seem to take into account what the critics are interested in. Many of the suggested ways forward seem to be along the lines of: why don't you do things like we do?
>
> (Townsend 2001: 125)

The *SESI* exchanges have also taught us that it is necessary to assume that academic criticisms will often be taken personally. Perhaps in an ideal world, academics and researchers could separate personalities from substantive issues, but in the real world they often cannot or do not. For instance, one researcher forwarded a draft response that included the comment:

> I would prefer to debate the issues, leaving out the perceived motivations of my critics, or the methodological flaws of their research. Nevertheless, the distinctly personal criticisms of many comments in the Slee et al. (1998) and Thrupp (1999) volumes leaves me with no recourse than to make similar rejoinders.

We want to clear up these distracting possibilities so that the authors criticized in this book can concentrate on our substantive arguments. First, it will have to be up to the reader to judge whether or not our account is well informed. We have studied numerous education management texts in order to develop our argument (see Chapter 4 for a discussion of our approach), but obviously it has not been possible to read all the outpourings of the education management industry. However, it is unlikely that our critique here would have looked much different had more literature been studied. This is both because the literature on the whole shares similar assumptions and because it will become apparent that we have set out to illustrate the diversity of perspectives that does exist in the areas under discussion.

Second, what about the claim of arrogance? Raising concerns about textual apologism can easily be seen as a puritanical activity – and, indeed, Teddlie and Reynolds (2001), have described some of Thrupp's criticisms of school effectiveness research (SER) as 'paranoid and meddling' (p. 52). Similarly, Hopkins (2001) sees 'exercise[s] in critiquing and debunking the research and practice of others' as a 'form of intellectual narcissism' (pp. xi–xii). Nevertheless, in line with the discussion above, our perspective is that the messages sent out to practitioners and policy makers are important (in fact more may often rest on them than on a lot of academic debates), so that where they are considered seriously problematic they must be challenged. It is not helpful – or fair – to leave practitioners and policy makers wallowing in a sea of competing perspectives because academics will not debate the issues. Yet this position should not be confused with intellectual arrogance. In fact, like Ball (1997a: 258), we accept that

> Critical researchers, apparently safely ensconced in the moral high ground, nonetheless make a livelihood trading in the artefacts of misery and broken dreams of practitioners. None of us remains untainted by the incentives and disciplines of the new moral economy.

We would also not want to understate the challenge of maintaining academic quality in such an 'applied' and policy-influenced area as education management. Ours is no simple case of 'academic snobbery' or 'ivory tower elitism'. We firmly believe that teaching and managing schools well is deeply important and essential work and, indeed, our own lives are not as disconnected from the messy realities of running schools as some might imagine.[3] Nevertheless, an orientation to textual dissent is much more likely where authors have been exposed to critical understandings of education through some background in foundational education disciplines like philosophy, sociology or history. Yet many of those who teach, consult in, and write books about education management do not have this kind of background. Moreover, managerialist education policy does not encourage this kind of thinking, and it is becoming increasingly lacking in initial teacher education or in teacher or headteacher in-service programmes too (for example, Snook 1998; Thrupp 1998). As a result, a vicious circle is set up where those writing books about education management often lack much critical awareness, and the practitioners they are dealing with often do not expect or value it either.

Finally, what of the concern about writing as personal attack? In the instance noted above, the author was from the USA and part of the problem may be that what represents a healthy argument in one national or scholarly context will be considered beyond the pale in another. In the event the comment was dropped, but we want to make it quite clear that our concern is with criticizing arguments and the social and political work those arguments do, and not with attacking individuals. Indeed, we know and regularly meet with some of those we criticize here and, in most cases, have a perfectly amicable personal relationship despite our academic differences. Nor are we interested in ascribing personal motives for why individuals choose to write in textually apologetic ways; indeed, we would prefer to believe the damage done by textual apologism is usually unwitting. So our request to the textual apologists discussed here is to not be defensive – please engage with our substantive arguments.

Overall, then, this is a book that has been written as much for academics and practitioners who have yet to be convinced there is any problem with education management as for those who already act as external critics or who have chosen to keep their distance. Having said this, we realize that our chances of being heard by some in the education management arena may be quite slim. For instance, by the end of the *School Effectiveness and School Improvement* exchange it was apparent that the critical viewpoint was being systematically misinterpreted, perhaps deliberately so (see Chapter 6). In this situation it really does become pointless to continue and, indeed, this is one of the reasons this book focuses on school improvement rather than school effectiveness.[4]

Yet other areas of education management might be more open to critical challenge than school effectiveness research has proven to be. For instance, school leadership is one area where the textual dissenters have already made considerable inroads. Moreover, there is unlikely to be any education management area where *everyone* involved is comfortable with dominant assumptions or the arguments of leading proponents. For instance, launching the *International Journal of Leadership in Education,* Waite (1998: 92) noted that

> Like it or not the area of educational leadership (aka educational administration) has a reputation for being deeply conservative. But conservatism is not the path to renewal. New and different voices are required . . . the time is ripe. The voices have become a chorus.

At the very least, then, we expect this book will be read by those individuals or groups who are more open to alternative education management perspectives or already trying to act as internal critics. We hope they find it useful. We also hope they can persuade some of their less searching colleagues to read our arguments as well since there is a definite wake-up call here for many involved in education management.

2 The market, neo-liberalism and new managerialism

In the mid-1990s, Gewirtz and colleagues wrote that the 'market solution (to just about everything) currently holds politicians around the world in its thrall . . . Schools in England are now set within the whole paraphernalia of a market system' (Gewirtz *et al.* 1995: 1). Five years on, Bottery (2000) has highlighted the development of global markets and concomitant restructuring of education systems geared to economic and technical imperatives. He warns that now 'nation states are in danger of becoming the servants of global markets, their education systems providing the human resources to feed them' (Bottery 2000: vii). Bottery discusses 'managerial globalization',[1] where in the past two or three decades, education managers in the developed world have been urged to look at management literature along two separate dimensions.

The first dimension is that of the public/private/voluntary sectoral divide. Here, it is argued that there are practices from other sectors of which those in the public education sector would do well to take note. Bottery notes that this has manifested itself in a number of ways. One is through the use of a pervasive managerialism, commonly referred to as New Public Management (NPM). NPM is characterized by a more directive and assertive management and the use of more private sector practices. Another is seen through the exhortations by politicians and businesspeople for educators to read the guru management literature, such as Peters and Waterman's *In Search of Excellence* (1982). Such exhortations have not fallen on deaf ears in influential educational circles; hence part of the reason for this book.

The second dimension involves looking beyond educators' own shores and examining management practices in other countries. As Bottery notes, the first port of call continues to be the USA, but increased interest has been seen in Japanese management and interest in management practices now transcends traditional borders. 'As writers feed off one another's experience, as multinationals get into bed with one another and borrow each other's practices, so they begin to define what looks like a global picture of management practice' (Bottery 2000: 13).

However, the use of managerialism has been consolidated globally, especially in England following the 1997 Labour election victory. In the English context, such consolidation is inextricably bound up with the continued acceptance of quasi-market mechanisms and the increased emphasis on performance management in order to enhance national competitiveness. For instance, the rationale for learning in the 1998 Green Paper *The Learning Age* is 'openly technical-rationalist, economic and reductionist and provides no reasons why learning might be a good other than its economic usefulness' (Bottery 2000: 19).

This brings us to the argument of this chapter, namely that education is a public good that is undermined by marketization and (new) managerialism, in turn (and with depressing irony) undermining the very national competitiveness such processes and mechanisms are meant to enhance and encourage. In order to provide a robust critique of marketization and (new) managerialism, we need to spell out in detail the nature of 'the market', new managerialism and the contradictions inherent in the neo-liberal or so-called New Right (ideological) justification of the latter. Part of our discussion in this chapter is at an ontological level which may not be familiar to some readers.[2] Nevertheless we want to stress that this and the rest of the chapter is important because it provides the conceptual underpinning to our critique of textual apologism and hence the backdrop to each of the other chapters.

The market: Hayek, contradiction and the transcendental argument

It is important to make clear, briefly, what we mean by 'transcendental'. Transcendentalism may be defined as (a) Kant's philosophy of the transcendental; (b) a mode of thought that emphasizes the intuitive and super-sensuous; (c) a form of religious mysticism. This book is concerned with definition (a). In essence, a transcendental argument answers the question: of a proposition known to be true, what conditions must be fulfilled? In other words, we are going beyond experience in order to establish conditions of possibility. So, for example, while we experience buying in a market, we may not be terribly interested how it is possible that such transactions can take place. Here, our argument is that markets, in order to function, need or require extensive regulation, that is, institutions that determine rules, apply sanctions, delimit activity.

Gewirtz *et al.*'s (1995) *Markets, Choice and Equity in Education* recognizes that the market is intended as a 'policy solution' to problems of cost, control and performance and is to be driven by self-interest and a global phenomenon. We want to add to this by more clearly explaining what we mean by 'the market', delineating its various meanings, and, at the same time (transcendentally), argue for its untenable transposition to the public sector. However, as Ball (1990) notes, the neo-liberal and neo-conservative elements of the New Right 'display a number of *vital* contradictions' (p. 41, our emphasis). Ball is quite right not to lose sight of the contradictory mixture that is the New Right philosophy, that is, between the neo-liberal and neo-conservative constituents.

The origins of the neo-liberal conspectus can be traced back to the collapse of Keynesian social democracy, particularly the oil crisis. The temporal coincidence of such neo-liberal ideas as the need for the state to withdraw from, rather than continue to inhibit, the spontaneous workings of 'the (capitalist) market' and the oil crisis provided the necessary (but insufficient) conditions for the imposition of managerialist (or business) models on to the public sector as a whole. The Black Papers in England contributed to the anti-statist thrust of the neo-liberal critique of the state. In contrast, the neo-conservative strand of New Right philosophy underscores the need for 'strong' state involvement. As Gamble (1988) notes, the conservative element is characterized by its emphasis upon the *conditions* that are required for the establishment and maintenance of social order, namely

> the need for authority, hierarchy and balance. Conservatives have generally been fierce critics of liberal doctrines of individualism which justify the removal of all restraints . . . Both [the neo-liberals and conservatives], however, regard the trends established by the growth of public sectors and the kind of government intervention practised since the 1940s as pernicious. Both focus on the rise of a 'new class' of public sector professional employees who come to staff the agencies of the public sector and who have a vested interest in its continued growth.
>
> (Gamble 1988: 54–5)

Jonathan (1997) has convincingly argued that the populist appeal of the New Right agenda for restructuring – or the quasi-marketization of – the public sector needs to be traced back further than the oil crisis. It stems more from the liberal promises of equality following the Butler Act 1944. She argues that New Right attacks on education tapped a reservoir of popular unease. Such unease was not surprising since, 'despite reformist measures over three decades, the post-war education project of individual emancipation for each and simultaneous social progress for all had failed to deliver to many what they had hoped for from it' (Jonathan 1997: 57). Indeed, it was the failure of Keynesian social democracy that resonated well with 'liberal' thinking that dates back further than the oil crisis. One of the key arguments of this chapter is that the New Right panacea was both misconceived and contradictory. Such contradiction and misconception will be teased out via an analysis of the ontological underpinning of the neo-liberal project whose aim is to inject the competitive nature of 'the market' into what is seen as a stifling, inefficient and expensive public sector.

Part of the process of systematization of the New Right philosophy places a premium on a (potentially rewarding) search for congruent (complementary) ideational items. Hence the selective use of arguments from Mill, Hume, Smith *et al.* during the 1980s by such organizations as the Centre for Policy Studies, the Adam Smith Institute and the Institute for Economic Affairs. The Centre for Policy Studies was founded by Margaret Thatcher and Keith Joseph and quickly became a focus for the ideas of such right-wing thinkers as Milton Friedman and F.A. Hayek. The underlying theme for the ideas systematized by the sections of the New Right was the alleged superiority of market mechanisms and the need for sound money. Such cultural embroidery was carried out against the backdrop of the Black Papers, of which the last was published in 1977.

> [Henceforth] the discursive cudgels of the conservative educational offensive were taken up by a variety of related and overlapping New Right agencies and groups . . . What makes them markedly different from the rather informally produced *Black Papers* is the degree and sophistication of their organisation and strategies for dissemination . . . By the 1980s . . . neo-liberal texts, particularly the work of Hayek, and monetarist theories like those of Friedman, are paraded as a basis for social and economic policy making.
>
> (Ball 1990: 34–5)

However, as Gamble (1988) notes, the call for the restoration of sound money has been the New Right's centrepiece and is the issue on which the New Right first made a major impact. Despite continuing disagreement about the nature of the economy, the widening of divisions between competing macro-economic perspectives and the undermining of the theoretical underpinnings of monetarism, it was the marked deterioration in economic performance in the 1970s that accounts for its ascendancy. Monetarists argue that, among other things, the control of inflation should be prioritized, irrespective of any increase in unemployment. New Right economics decries state intervention because it is held that administrative and bureaucratic structures are inherently inferior to markets as a means of allocating resources. With regard to public expenditure and taxation, New Right economists assert that market solutions would in every case be superior to the established public provision. At the same time, there evolved the contribution of 'public choice theory' (see also Chapter 9), which argued against the notion that public bodies were disinterested and enlightened, while private individuals and companies were self-interested and avaricious. The argument here is that the pursuit of self-interest by private bodies is licensed by the existence of a competitive framework of rules that does not exist in the public sector. Consequently, many in the New Right concluded that 'markets were much superior to democracy in representing and aggregating individual choices. It was only a short step to arguing that democracy needed to be hedged around with restrictions to ensure that it did not permit encroachments upon the private sphere' (Gamble 1988: 52).

The 'moral argument' proffered by New Right thinkers will not be addressed here (but see Gamble (1988) and Jonathan (1997)). Rather, we want now to focus on the social ontology that underpins the quasi-marketization of education. We have briefly looked at the need for 'sound money' embodied in the monetarist doctrine, whereby taxes and public expenditure should be as low as possible and that its institutions be subject to the competitive ethic of the market. New Right thinkers and politicians alike readily adopt the rhetoric of the so-called *free* market and how its wealth-generating, dynamic properties should be transposed to the public sector. In brief, the argument that an objective contradiction underpins the Education Act 1988 (and all other public sector policies that have introduced quasi-market principles) is a transcendental one. In other words, such legislation decries excessive regulation but, because it does not recognize the need for any degree of regulation, ends up excessively centralizing the education system.

Hayek's catallaxy: the denial of social structure

The key thinker used by the neo-liberals in their unrelenting drive towards the quasi-marketization of the public sector is Hayek. As already mentioned, neo-liberalism – and the New Right generically – is also employed as a portmanteau, which embraces Friedman's economic liberalism, Nozick's libertarianism (the advocacy of the minimal state) and Hayek's Austrian economics. Hayek lends support to the *sui generis* properties of the division of labour. He distinguishes between catallaxy and economy. His conception of economy is a restricted one, referring to clusters of economic activities that are organized for a specific purpose and have a unitary hierarchy of ends, in which knowledge of how to achieve ends is shared. A catallaxy, on the other hand, has no unitary hierarchy of ends, but a mass of innumerable economies without a specific purpose. As Hayek has famously pointed out, it is the product of *spontaneous* growth as opposed to design. One of Hayek's central arguments against state socialism is that the catallaxy eludes regulation by central control. This is because of the extraordinary division of knowledge required by any advanced industrial economy. Thus *the* fundamental economic problem is not calculational but epistemological, namely how to coordinate the actions of innumerable agents without the possibility of any adequate centralized knowledge of their needs and resources. Consequently, competition operates as a discovery procedure and the main role of markets is in generating information, through the price mechanism, as to how economic agents who are ignorant of each other may best attain their equally unknown purposes (Sayer 1995).

The salient point, then, is that the complex and evolutionary nature of the catallaxy makes its qualities unknowable to any single mind or organization. Hayek correctly takes to task the socialist vision of a collectively controlled and planned advanced economy – a 'fatal conceit', which he terms 'constructivism'. As Sayer points out, many Marxist positions have failed to acknowledge the fundamental difference between running a technical division of labour for producing a particular type of commodity and coordinating a social division of labour involving millions of different commodities, thousands of enterprises and billions of customers. This is not to license chaos, for although catallaxies are unplanned, they are ordered. Yet, for Marx, the only good order 'must be the product of conscious collective purpose, a Hegelian legacy of humanity rising to consciousness and control over itself . . . Marx is resistant not only to actions having bad unintended consequences, but to unintended consequences *per se*' (Sayer 1995: 76). However, Hayek adopts the extreme counter-position to Marx. In brief, he reasons that because unintended consequences of actions are central to the functioning of catallaxies, one must not intervene. This simply does not follow and, among other things, excuses problems that can – and should – be confronted and removed (ecological problems, poverty and so on). More crucially, Hayek denies that catallaxies possess emergent properties:

> Absent from Hayek's image of capitalism as an unimaginably complex mass of individuals responding to one another through markets is any notion of major social structures . . . while modern societies and advanced economies are indeed catallaxies, they are *also* systems with grand structures . . . his celebration of the miracle of the market simply ignores the temporal and spatial upheavals associated with the creative destruction of capitalism. Hayek's exaggeration of 'order' is the complement of Marxism's exaggeration of 'anarchy'.
>
> (Sayer 1995: 77–8, emphasis in original)

It is thus not surprising that the erasure of relatively enduring social structures leads to an emphasis on 'the market' as a sphere of freedom. Yet a market encompasses not simply commodity exchanges and associated transfers of money, but also enduring organized practices that facilitate such exchanges on a regular basis. It is worth briefly discussing the different types of market and the multiple meanings of 'the market'.

The nature of 'the market'

In essence, markets differ according to the way in which transactions are organized, particularly with regard to pricing. 'Spot markets' are those in which prices are flexible and relationships between actors ephemeral. Spot markets approximate economic models. Yet most real markets do not fit this type of market. Instead, fixed prices provide a stable environment for calculating costs and organizing production and distribution. Economic models tend to assume the universality of 'arm's length contracting', whereby little information other than price is provided and buyer–supplier relationships are minimal. 'Relational contracting', by contrast, involves the sharing of information, the careful building of trust and collaboration between buyer and seller, before and after the transaction. However, neo-liberals wrongly contend that markets work best 'on the spot', at arm's length, and thus discourage information sharing. Hayek *et al.* overestimate the sufficiency of price as source of information for buyers and sellers in markets. Prior to commodity exchange, non-price information normally has to be exchanged and is usually provided at no extra cost to the buyer.

The New Right is well known for its trumpeting of the 'free' market, in which all that exists (or, rather, matters) is spontaneous exchanges between individuals who have something to sell. The role of the state is thus held to distort this smooth-running, spontaneous gathering of free individuals. 'Yet far from being an unnecessary interference, *the state is a normal feature of real markets, as a precondition of their existence.* Markets depend on the state for regulation, protection of property rights, and the currency' (Sayer 1995: 87, our emphasis). We will return to the latter shortly. Clearly, markets are not 'free', since their regulation does not benefit all. There are enduring *structured* power imbalances. However, Sayer points out that the conceptual slides endemic to employment of 'the market' are a feature of both lay and academic uses and are found in right/left-wing, liberal and economic theory. The Right proffers idealized models of markets as descriptions of *de facto* markets; the Left avoids any rigorous scrutiny of their properties. Sayer argues that concepts of markets differ according to (a) their level of abstraction; (b) their inclusiveness; (c) whether they are couched within a 'market optic' or a 'production optic'; (d) whether they refer to real or imaginary markets.

Real markets may be conceptualized at different levels of abstraction. One can talk about the local fruit-and-vegetable market concretely (who the sellers and buyers are, what is sold, and so on) or more abstractly, namely in terms of the exchange of commodities and property rights for money or as a mode of coordination of the division of labour. At the same time, concepts of markets also differ in inclusiveness. Markets may be defined narrowly in terms of routinized buying and selling, or inclusively to cover production and consumption of exchanged goods and the particular property relations involved. Restricted concepts exclude major contextual influences that explain behaviour. As Sayer (1995: 99) puts it: 'The dynamism of capitalist economies is not simply a consequence of markets in the restricted sense, but of capital, obliged to accumulate in order to survive, and liberated from the ties which bind petty commodity producers.' What is included on the Left is determined by a 'production optic', in which markets are marginalized. For the Right, what is included is determined by a 'market optic', whereby production is conflated with exchange. For our purposes, we are concerned with the 'market optic' of the Right. The market optic ignores production and its social relations. Indeed, in mainstream economics, the whole economy becomes *the* market (in the singular) and almost invariably counterposed to the state.

The key point here is that *markets are not an alternative to production, firms or hierarchies* [our emphasis] (Sayer 1995: 101). Instead, they are a mode of coordination of the division of labour. Furthermore, one can distinguish among literal concepts referring to real markets, those referring to imaginary markets, and those that use market metaphors that have limited similarity with real markets. As Sayer argues, it is not the level of abstraction used in metaphorical approaches, but their quality, that is important. Indeed, what is often lost is the social relations that underpin real markets. Thus the notion of latent markets

> which only need freeing figures strongly in neo-liberal rhetoric, and contrasts strikingly with the view . . . that markets are social constructions whose birth is difficult and requires considerable regulation and involvement by the state and other institutions to achieve . . . The liberal underestimation or denial of this institutional support is partly derived from the elision of the difference between potential or imaginary and the actual in its concept of 'the market'.
>
> (Sayer 1995: 104)

The rest is supplied by the effacement of organizations and the relations between them.

The transcendental argument

Transcendentally, the neo-liberal social ontology cannot be sustained: market exchange requires state involvement. In other words, state involvement is a *necessary precondition of market exchange*; this is what we mean when we talk transcendentally. By corollary, the existence of schooling is equally necessary, since without adequate educational provision, there could be no sustained level of skills and knowledge for the exchange of sophisticated goods, services and consumer products. Given that the market is not 'free' and is necessarily subject to some form of institutional regulation, then

> deregulated governance of education loses its justification, and the [neo-liberal] project loses its rationale even on its own terms . . . If this line of reasoning can be sustained when elaborated, it would provide

a transcendental argument against the existence of principles of free-market exchange into the governance and distribution of education ... Furthermore, if neo-liberal principles can be shown to be incompatible with the governance of that social practice without whose alignment no vision for the ordering of society can be realised, then the vision itself is called into question, not only on grounds of equity ... but on grounds of coherence.

(Jonathan 1997: 25–6)

There are two distinct issues here. First, there is the transcendental argument that markets – or Hayek's catallaxy – are regulated by institutions that are irreducible to individuals. Second, Jonathan's argument is that the very institutions that underpin market relationships themselves require an educated workforce, in turn negating the neo-liberal project of subjecting the education system to market disciplinary mechanisms. However, what is important for our purposes is that the neo-conservative element of the New Right corpus contradicts the Hayekian contention that 'free' markets do not require regulation. Moreover, neo-liberals themselves could not avoid the fact that the education system is state-run and did not appear out of thin air. The argument for reconcilability is centred on the short-term need for the state to establish the conditions for a market-based education system. Yet the fact that the state *has* to regulate belies the neo-liberals' atomistic social ontology that is central to the argument for state non-intervention. However, of course, the devolution of control to individual schools contradicted the neo-liberal corpus since such devolution was done at the behest of central government. Any notion that such centralized control was to be ephemeral, a necessary prelude to complete deregulation, is simply to conceal the contradiction: the need for state control ever remains while we have an education system, and while we have an advanced economy the need for state education equally remains.

Finally, what now needs to be hammered home is the fact that precisely because the market is corrosive of the conditions of human well-being it should never be used as a model of restructuring our social institutions generically, not just education. Human autonomous development is undermined by market colonization. The point here is that 'the market is compatible with the good life only to the extent that it is hedged and bounded, such that non-market associations and relations can flourish' (O'Neill 1998: 62). However, defenders of the market argue the opposite, namely that the market fosters the development of the autonomous person. Following O'Neill, there are two counter-arguments here. First, the value of autonomy requires the existence of valuable options over which autonomous choices can be made. Such options are necessary conditions for autonomy, since autonomy is in part constituted by the existence of significant options. Autonomy requires a variety of adequate options, which, in turn, require boundaries on the extension of markets. The existence of such options calls for the existence of educational, cultural, familial and associational spheres in which the prospects and relationships that constitute the valuable options can be pursued. As O'Neill puts it:

> These are undermined if they are colonised by markets, either directly by being transformed into commodities that are subject to sale in the market, or indirectly by being subject to the norms and meanings of the market. Hence autonomy requires, at the very least, the restriction of the entry of the market into those non-market spheres.
>
> (O'Neill 1998: 70)

Second, even if it were to turn out that the market was a necessary condition for the development of autonomy, it is insufficient. Autonomy requires individuals who have the capacities to exercise rational judgements and choices and those capacities require *non-market domains of informal and formal education, and material, cultural, familial and working conditions that develop the capacity for self-determination, which a 'free' market will fail to deliver*.

Furthermore, the dynamics of the market are not conditions for an autonomous character able to form his or her identity, but those for the dissolution of any settled identity. O'Neill notes here that this is not to assent to the conservative's claim that change and identity are not compatible, since some change is developmental and, as such, forms part of what it is to have an identifiable character. To have a character is to be the subject of a life that has some narrative unity, from childhood through to adulthood, and the realization of projects and of failures that lead to reprioritization of one's ambitions. Change is incompatible with identity where it consists of a series of disconnected changes. Thus, the conditions that the defender of the market offers as conditions of autonomy, that is the constant development of new and previously unknown desires by the entrepreneur, the mobilization of labour, its movement for movement's sake, can be conditions that undermine character. This applies with equal force to education: unremitting competitive pressures, predicated upon market norms, are inimical to the development of children or older students as independent critical autonomous people. The concrete reality of quasi-marketization does not help children: on the contrary, it serves simply to disrupt, even damage, their education – spiritual, moral and social – and to engender fear and stress in educators and parents alike. Indeed, while the fortuitous and accidental underpin any person's narrative, the sort of fantastical 'continuous change' conjured up in the educational change literature (see Chapter 9) is clearly contrary to autonomous development.

New managerialism

Exworthy and Halford (1999) note that, traditionally, the public sector has been characterized by Taylorist management, i.e. bureaucratic, inflexible and mainly concerned with control and cost cutting. By contrast,

> The *new* managerialism emphasized innovation, creativity and empowerment. The new managers are policy 'entrepreneurs', highly motivated, resourceful, and able to shift the frame of reference beyond the established norms and procedures. In addition, the new managers enable staff to make their own contributions and, in doing so, to generate greater identification with, and commitment to, the corporate success of the organization.
>
> (Exworthy and Halford 1999: 6)

Drawing upon Pollitt (1990), Flynn (1999) argues that the new managerialism embodies a number of different assumptions and values, which are assumed to be unproblematic and include 'the idea of progress through greater economic productivity, technological innovation, worker compliance and managers' freedom to manage. It is a diffuse ideology which privileges commercial models of organization and management practice and insists that these can (and must) be transplanted to public sector services' (Flynn 1999: 27).

Equally, Ball (1994) distinguishes between management as theory and management as practice. Furthermore, he argues that it is not a unitary whole.

> There are at least two, perhaps three, discourses of management in play here within the reform process in the UK. They have different effects. One is what might be called 'professional management'. This is articulated around a development planning perspective and relates particularly to the production of school management plans . . . it is a 'clean' (context-free) management insofar as it treats the school in isolation and concentrates upon the business of *education* rather than education as *business* . . . It divorces management practices from values and from politics . . . It is technically oriented, rational and apolitical . . . The second discourse I would term 'financial management'. It begins from a concern with balancing the books, with maximizing the budget, and with doing educationally what can be afforded. This is for many practitioners the unacceptable face of management . . . There is a close relationship between the discourse of financial management and the third discourse, which I call 'entrepreneurial management'. Here the market is to the fore; image, hype

and PR, and competition, diversification and income generation are prominent in the managers' lexicon.

(Ball 1994: 67–8)

Let us now examine more closely the nature of the new managerialism. Given that one significant dimension of the reconstruction of the welfare state has been the process of managerialization, it is hardly surprising that public sector management was one of the significant growth areas of employment and education during the 1980s and 1990s. A variety of studies have discussed the emergence or rise of what we have already referred to as the New Public Management (NPM) (see, for example, Hood 1991; Dunleavy and Hood 1994; Butcher 1995; Boston *et al.* 1996; Ferlie *et al.* 1996). Clarke *et al.* (2000) note that the NPM is usually taken to refer to some combination of processes and values that was developed in the 1980s as a distinctively different approach to the coordination of publicly provided services. Although there are variations, typical characteristics ascribed to the NPM include:

- attention to outputs and performance rather than inputs;
- organizations being viewed as chains of low-trust relationships, linked by contracts or contractual-type processes. The separation of purchaser and provider or client and contractor roles within formerly integrated processes or organizations;
- breaking down large-scale organizations and using competition to enable 'exit' or 'choice' by service users;
- decentralization of budgetary and personal authority to line managers. (Taken from Clarke *et al.* 2000: 6.)

Equally, as Elliott (2001a) points out, performance management presumes that the performance of core activities can be made transparent to the public's gaze on a continuous and sustainable basis through audit. Here, there is a sustained attempt to provide perfect information about the workings of the organization through highly selective objectifications of performance known as performance indicators (PIs). PIs wrongly presume that the relationship between cause and effect can be captured in a timeless form. Thus, to Elliott, 'Information about performance is supposedly perfect when it is shaped by timeless propositions about the relationship between inputs and outputs. PIs therefore leave little room for a view of causality as a time-dependent phenomenon, the understanding of which changes over time and is never perfect' (Elliott 2001a: 194). At the same time, there is an intolerance of time, which is discussed more fully in relation to Fullan's work on school change in Chapter 9. In essence, 'Performative cultures are intolerant of time because disaster is always imminent and things have to be done now to ward it off. People within the organisation therefore have to be kept in a continuous state of activation'

(Elliott 2001a: 198). This constant state of activation engendered by Ofsted has now been reinforced by performance management in schools, especially the linking of teachers' pay to their performance.

However, Clarke *et al.* (2000) note that such views of the NPM have some limitations. Among these is

> a tendency to a rather over-unified or over-coherent view of the NPM as a form of co-ordination. For example, Ferlie and his colleagues have suggested that a singular view of the NPM disguises the existence of four overlapping, but separate, models of the NPM. They distinguish between the 'Efficiency Drive', 'Downsizing and Decentralization', 'In Search of Excellence' and 'Public Service Orientation' models . . . There are other difficulties, too. The NPM is too often treated as a coherent whole of global significance and force despite the fact that comparative studies have tended to show wide national divergences in reform programmes, albeit often utilizing the language – or discourse – of New Public Management as a means of legitimation and institutionalisation.
>
> (Clarke *et al.* 2000: 7)

However, Clarke *et al.* rightly imply that confusion surrounding the status of NPM is immediately dispelled if we resist conflating or eliding the ideational and practical levels. As they point out, many examinations of the NPM conflate the politics and practice of public service reform, treating the NPM as though it has been installed as the only mode of coordination. Such examinations also conflate the descriptive and normative aspects. Instead, Clarke *et al.* (2000: 7) suggest that the impact of NPM has been 'more uneven, contested and complex than can be accounted for in a view of a simple shift from public administration to New Public Management or from hierarchies to markets or networks'. Furthermore, they argue that accounts of the NPM tend to focus on management as activity and occupational group, in turn occluding the more complex social, political and economic organizational changes. Indeed, when talking about managerialism, we are talking about more than just 'the work of managers', for managers can and do work in a variety of ways, depending upon what they are asked to do, which necessarily includes the value and political framework within which they manage (Bottery 2000: 62).

Clarke and colleagues argue that a more productive starting-point is to recognize, at the outset, that management is not a neutral, technical activity; any such invocation of neutrality lies at the core of managerialism. They go on to write that managerialism

> defines a set of expectations, values and beliefs. It is a normative system concerning what counts as valuable knowledge, who knows it,

and who is empowered to act in what ways as a consequence. Indeed, a central issue in the managerialization of public services has been the concerted effort to displace or subordinate the claims of professionalism. It can no longer be assumed that 'professionals know best'; rather we are invited to accept that managers 'do the right thing' . . . we see managerialism both as a 'general ideology' . . . that legitimizes and seeks to extend the 'right to manage' and as composed of overlapping, and sometimes competing, discourses that present distinctive versions of 'how to manage'. Its natural home has been the corporate capitalist organization that provides the reference point for claims about 'behaving in a businesslike way'.

(Clarke *et al.* 2000: 9)

Taylorism: the Revised Code of 1862 and payment by results . . . *déjà vu*

It was mentioned earlier that traditionally Taylorist management has characterized the public sector, which was contrasted with the new managerialism. It must be emphasized, however, that the new managerialism does not dispense with Taylorism. On the contrary, in education especially, managerialist restructuring is Taylorist: the 'new' inflection must not detract us from this. The system of payment by results that was introduced by the Revised Code of 1862 represents a chilling precursor. In essence, it consisted of a payment to inspected elementary schools for each child, one-third of which was for attendance; the remainder was a payment that was reduced by one-third in each of the three areas of reading, writing and arithmetic if the child failed to satisfy the inspector. The children had to be presented for an examination in set 'standards', and the regulations also provided for further grant reductions if the buildings were inadequate or if there were insufficient pupil teachers (Silver 1994: 32). At the same time – and in a manner congruent with Ofsted philosophy – each school's religious and moral tone was to be taken into account by the inspectors. Silver quotes Fitch, who wrote in 1901 that payment by results is 'a business-like and sensible plan for apportioning the public grant among school managers, and . . . a satisfactory assurance to the taxpayer that he was receiving a good educational equivalent for his outlay' (1994: 32). This comment, made more than a century ago, could easily have come from the past decade too. At the time there was strong opposition to the system of inspection, which proved equally ineffectual. Matthew Arnold, one of the inspectors, rejected the payment-by-results system on the grounds that it would result in a mechanistic preparation of children for examination.

The crucial question is whether such mechanistic preparation was an unintended consequence or a necessary constituent of the philosophy underpinning the payment-by-results system. In fact, the mechanistic ways in which children were taught as a result of the payment-by-results system were inextricably underpinned by managerialism. As Fitch makes quite clear, the focus was on examination results, which were held to be attainable independently of any reference to, or consideration of, children. The impetus was on what should be achieved in relation to a specific amount of cash spent; as if a cash-value could be readily placed on a child's achievement of a specified number of examination passes. The payment-by-results system thus predates Ball's (1990) argument about the commodification of education brought about by the Education Act 1988, since here the system likewise excluded the human element, namely that children were (and are) part of the examination process. The fact that a retired Inspector of Schools for the London County Council, G. A. Christian, wrote in 1922 of the reactionary influence of the 1862 Revised Code, which resulted in 'at best a pernicious influence on education', is attributable to the technicist or technocratic philosophy of the Revised Code. Michael Barber, former head of the Department for Education and Science's Standards and Effectiveness unit and a key textual apologist in the English context has written:

> There are many recent examples of technocratic influence on the curriculum. The GCSE [General Certificate of Secondary Education] general and subject criteria are strongly influenced by this approach. However, the best example is the pre-Dearing National Curriculum which set down in great detail, through Programmes of Study, Attainment Targets and Statements of Attainment, what both the content and proposed outcomes of the curriculum at every level should be. The most enduring image of the pre-Dearing National Curriculum – a primary teacher ticking boxes – is a testament to technocracy gone wild ... *It seems likely that, as long as we have a national curriculum, an element of the technocratic approach will be with us. It has, however, been subjected to some important criticisms. One is that it purports to be value-free. In other words, it is an approach to planning a curriculum, but it assumes agreement about the goals of the curriculum.*
>
> (Barber 1996a: 13, our emphasis)

It is a *non sequitur* to assume that an element of the technocratic approach is an inevitable accompaniment of any (national) curriculum. More importantly, the 1988 Act, as with the Revised Code of 1862, did not purport to be value-free: it was value-free in that, among other things, values about children, more specifically about the 'good life', could not be entertained because of its managerialist underpinning. The criteria of managerialism are palpable in the Revised Code: efficiency, productivity and cost-effectiveness ('value for money' in Ofsted terminology).

What needs to be emphasized is that the technicist core remains firmly in place; the 'newness' of current managerialist approaches stems from its additional accentuation of 'entrepreneurship', the 'right to manage' and the maximization of group commitment to 'total quality'. As noted earlier, Ball distinguishes between the business of education (in essence an intra-school affair) and education as business. The latter is technicist in orientation and underpins the SATs-cum-league-table philosophy. Clearly, the payment-by-results system is managerialist in Ball's latter sense of education as business. The precursory effects of the National Curriculum and testing arrangements are reflected in Silver's reference to an interview with a teacher conducted by the Cross Commission in 1887 on the working of the elementary education Acts. The teacher commented that the payment-by-results system had 'a very harassing effect upon the teachers' and that the teaching of children was 'very much pleasanter' prior to the Code. At the same time, the Code encouraged such fraudulent activities as fixing attendance figures.

The progenitor of Taylorism is Frederick W. Taylor. Taylor was the founder of 'scientific management'.[3] Taylor assumed that people are intrinsically lazy and will thus attempt to get away with doing the minimum amount of work. Taylor was opposed to any form of group activity, maintaining that group involvement resulted in a decline in productivity. The reasoning behind this stemmed from his belief that self-interest was an overriding human characteristic. For Taylor, work tasks were to be well planned in advance and the worker was to be given written instructions. He operated bonus schemes and was not in favour of trade unions, mainly because he believed that the principles of scientific management would considerably attenuate conflict between employees and management. Moreover, he advocated authoritarian methods of management. As Clegg and Dunkerley note, Taylorism offered the most thorough dehumanization of work ever seen under capitalism:

> Taylor presents the individual in the same way as he would an item of machinery. The worker thereby is perceived as a means of production. In just the same way that management's task is to maximize output from capital equipment, under the principles of scientific management it is also part of the managerial task to maximize the output of the human component. Pursuing this analogy, in the same way that there is no psychological involvement with capital equipment, under the principles of scientific management, similarly there is none with human assets; as machines are fuelled by coal, gas or petrol, so humans are regarded as being fuelled by money.
>
> (Clegg and Dunkerley 1980: 96)

This applies with equal force to the current examination and league table regime, which focuses solely on the 'output', negating the 'input', that is the children and their intrinsic cognitive and emotional capacities. Moreover, the imposition of competition via league tables enjoins that children's different and distinctive cognitive capacities are ignored at a stroke, since the pressure to reach high scores ultimately means that any actual understanding (or lack of) be at best played down. The 1862 Code was underpinned by the same managerialist considerations that currently underpin the National Curriculum and testing arrangements, whereby children as children are negated (yet necessarily cannot be). The payment-by-results system, like the Local Management of Schools (LMS) and league table mechanisms, necessarily excludes reference to the human (child) element as part of its ideational underpinning: the rationale focuses on pecuniary matters, namely the (impossible) requirement that ever-improving results be obtained at the cheapest possible cost. Hence the contradiction between child-centred philosophy (or, indeed, any reference to children *per se*) and the managerialist accountability regime because of the Taylorist negation of the human and the concomitant reduction of learning to ostensibly valid measurable outcomes, which are the result of the drive for cost-effectiveness and efficiency.

New managerialism and necessary contradiction

For Bottery, managerialism

> does not only feed back into the workings of the state to influence the actions and thought of policy-makers: it also has wider, more pervasive and therefore probably more damaging effects on society at large. In particular, in the pursuit of management objectives, it reduces first-order social and moral values to second-order values. By doing so, managerialism not only achieves a hegemony within organizations; it also parasitizes and weakens those values upon which the wider society – *but also its own existence – depend* . . . Now it is accepted that wherever managerial and non-managerial relationships and values exist side by side, there will always be a tension between them. Yet wherever managerial values achieve hegemony, these wider values are cheapened and debased.
>
> (Bottery 2000: 68, our emphasis)

It is precisely the *necessary dependence* of managerialism upon such 'first-order' values that Willmott (2002a) has trenchantly argued for: managerialism denies that which it depends upon in order to work. The point here is that any action in invoking managerialism also inevitably invokes its antithesis. Such first-order values include autonomy, criticality, care, tolerance, equality, respect and trust. As Bottery notes, the key words in the managerial mantra are economy (curbing the amount being spent), efficiency (getting the most out for the money being spent), and effectiveness (achieving as near as possible the aims designated at the beginning of the process). The quantifiable has taken precedence over the qualitative. Thus, such values as caring have tended to be sidelined in the pursuit of monetary considerations.

> Yet, perhaps even more importantly, where care is espoused, it tends to be regarded as a value-added component to a service, rather than as an integral and primary feature of any human relationship. In other words, because it is assigned this second-order status, it is conditional upon managerial calculation rather than being an unconditional ethic, and this leads to all human relationships being treated as means to ends rather than as ends in themselves.
>
> (Bottery 2000: 70)

Thus, at the ideational level, managerialism cannot work without the values it tries to strike out; at the practical level, its structured manifestation (LMS, SATs, league tables) cannot eschew the reality of children and teachers. Both in theory and in practice, human beings cannot be expunged. Bottery rightly argues that managerialism in education is anti-humanitarian:

> Just as in much modern business, where targets are set beyond the reachable, so they are increasingly set in education, and (of course) by those who do not have to reach them. Stress is then caused, not only by the pressure this puts on the teacher to try to achieve them; it also causes untold stress in that they have to reach these targets with children who have no hope of attaining them, and for whom they are equally stressful and anti-educational.
>
> (Bottery 2000: 78)

Of course, in theory anti-humanitarianism presupposes some notion of humanity and in practice it deals with real human beings. Managerialism erases such values as caring since it is value-less; yet in the very process attempting to be value-less it is inevitably value-laden. It is not at all surprising then that advocates of managerialism in education are constrained by such ('practical') values as caring. This is the result of a necessary contradictory relation: child-centredness *per se* does not presuppose managerialism, yet managerialism (and managerialization) in education cannot eschew child-centredness (however crudely defined). The former is necessarily dependent upon the latter – it cannot work without it.

New Labour, new managerialism: 'modernizing' managerialism in education

We want to end this chapter by highlighting the fact that, in the UK context, New Labour has actually *intensified* managerialization in education, thereby indicating the increased stringency of constraints that educators now confront and underscoring the urgency of our text. Indeed, as Husbands (2001: 8) notes, over the past two decades, the imperatives on schools to respond rapidly to imposed change from central government have markedly increased: 'the introduction of performance management from 2000 represents the culmination of increased policy, public and research interest in the quality, effectiveness and measured improvement of schools over some three decades'. This book thus subjects to critical scrutiny some of the more recent 'fads' in the education management literature such as school leadership (which has received prime ministerial recognition for leading headteachers and a national college), school change (where Fullan's maxim about the significance of both pressure and support has been influential, especially the need for both restructuring and reculturing) and strategic human resource management (which now extols performance-related pay and the move towards a 'hard' as opposed to 'soft' approach).

As Clarke *et al.* (2000: 1) put it, New Labour has 'proved to be just as enthusiastic about the reconstruction of welfare as a major political task, seeing it as a means through which a distinctively "modern" British people might be constructed'. In essence, New Labour in education, as in other spheres, has adopted most of the premises of neo-liberalism, many of its objectives and nearly all of its methods of delivering them. As Fergusson succinctly puts it:

> Competition, choice, and performance indicators remain the unchallenged totems of policy, not in overt policy statements but simply by being left untouched by New Labour reforms. Structurally, little that is fundamental is changing in the ways in which schools and colleges are run. Markets and managerialism hold sway. Structures and methods remain largely unaltered. Only the rhetoric of what schools and colleges can and should produce changes. The commitments to excellence and diversity are softened in favour of raising standards for all. The projects of the New Right and of New Labour begin to look ideologically consonant. The point of difference is not whether schools should be better, but which ones should be made better first. And what counts as 'better' remains largely locked inside the black box of the National Curriculum, testing, and how to teach more effectively.
>
> (Fergusson 2000: 203)

Indeed, the emphasis on performance has not supplanted the competitive model of separate self-managing schools with devolved budgets. However, there is an important difference between the New Right model and New Labour's modernization strategy. As Fergusson notes, the New Right model was outcomes-focused, and precisely how those outcomes were achieved and who benefited was of little concern. The skill of individual teachers in improving pupils' achievements was implicitly viewed as a kind of enterprise, underpinned by mechanisms of promotion and demotion. In contrast:

> New Labour's version is *much more interventionist*, and *considerably more managerialist*. Outcomes remain the focus, but they are now constituted as targets and benchmarks, rather than just comparisons with other institutions. And once criterion referencing has eclipsed norm referencing in this way, externally determined performance indicators are necessary . . . the imposition of numeracy and literacy hours is an attempt by government to shape the processes that improve performance.
>
> (Fergusson 2000: 208, our emphasis)

Indeed, the modernizing process by the state takes the pursuit of improved performance much further than the marketized version. As Husbands (2001) emphasizes the sharpness of focus on performance management, the range and depth of statistical and comparative data on which analyses might be based, and the centralization of the management of school, teacher and pupil achievement:

> What is imposed is simultaneously limited and expansive. It is limited in the extent to which performance management focuses school leadership on to the core tasks of enhancing pupil progress against measurable criteria; but expansive in the extent to which the language and assumptions of performance management describe a cultural refocusing of schooling.
>
> (Husbands 2001: 10)

3 Inequality, education reform, and the response of education management writers

Following on from the discussion of neo-liberalism, the market and the new managerialism, this chapter provides additional background to our Part II review of the education management literature because it helps to further highlight what education management authors too often leave out of the picture. The first part of the chapter rehearses in more detail why post-welfarist education reform[1] is likely to have such harmful effects. Many of the most important accounts of the nature and impact of education policy over the past decade have come from sociologists or policy sociologists (for instance Ball 1993b, 1998a; Hatcher 1998a; Gewirtz 2002; Willmott 2002a). This is not surprising, because at the heart of the critique of post-welfarist education reform is a sociological critique of the way it is likely to be reinforcing, rather than diminishing, social inequalities in education. This critique is in turn based on sociological analyses of the enduring relationship between education and social structure, that is the way that education is thought to *reproduce* social inequalities in education from generation to generation, thus these analyses need to be our starting-point too.

In the latter part of the chapter, we begin to chronicle the seeming indifference of education management academics to the risks of market and managerial policies as they were developing in the late 1980s and early 1990s. The point here is to illustrate that the risks associated with the policies *were* being highlighted by critical researchers but were often ignored by those in the education management arena at the time. We consider some likely reasons why this was the case and note the rise of what Helen Gunter (1997) has called the 'education management industry'.

Social inequalities in education

Since the landmark Coleman Report of the 1960s (Coleman *et al.* 1966), many statistical 'origins and destinations' studies have demonstrated the relationship between students' social origins, their levels of academic achievement at school and their level of further education or occupational destinations (see, for instance, Jencks *et al.* 1972; Halsey *et al.* 1980; Lauder and Hughes 1990; see also Halsey *et al.* 1997). What such studies have shown, time after time, in many national settings, is that middle-class students tend to achieve much better academic results than students from working-class backgrounds and that this pattern is remarkably resistant to educational intervention.[2] Indeed, despite the well-publicized school effectiveness research (SER) argument that 'schools can make a difference', the findings about the powerful relationship between family background and student achievement highlighted by Coleman and colleagues have never been overturned. SER has typically continued to find only small school effects of around 8–15 per cent (Teddlie *et al.* 2000), even if both larger and smaller effects have sometimes been claimed.[3] Yet this should not be understood as an argument that schools cannot make any difference as it has sometimes been characterized (Barber 1997). Rather, the sociological issue has always been whether or not schools can make a *substantial or important* difference relative to the impact of family background.

Sociologists have developed a considerable body of theory and empirical research to explain the relationship between social structure and student achievement. The best known theories are those of the late Pierre Bourdieu who argued that there is an organic or interconnected relationship between the culture of schools and the culture of middle-class families which they can use to their advantage in retaining or improving their advantaged social status (Bourdieu and Passeron 1990). To Bourdieu, 'cultural capital' inherited from middle-class families through socialization is confirmed, legitimated and reproduced within schools through both the formal and 'hidden' curricula. On the other hand, students who lack the appropriate middle-class cultural capital are disadvantaged because their speech, thought patterns, attitudes and behaviour are devalued and marginalized. In the process, schools do 'symbolic violence' when they take the cultural capital of the dominant group and treat all students as if they have equal access to it:

> The culture of the elite is so near to that of the school that children from the lower middle class (and *a fortiori* from the agricultural and industrial working class) can only acquire with great effort something which is *given* to the children of the cultivated classes – style, taste, wit – in short, those attitudes and aptitudes which seem natural in members of the cultivated classes and naturally expected of them precisely because (in the ethnological sense) they are the *culture* of the class.
> (Bourdieu 1974: 39, emphasis in the original)

Bourdieu's theories draw our attention to important class biases of language, curriculum and pedagogy within schools, and these have also been highlighted by empirical studies in many settings (for example, Jackson 1968; Anyon 1981; Jones 1989, 1991; Reay 1995; Grenfell 1998). For instance, in a study of language used in classrooms, Grenfell (1998) illustrates how teachers' pedagogical discourses can deny those of students and exclude them. In another study, Jones (1991) suggested that the social class characteristics of teaching groups end up determining the pace and nature of instruction. Her study illustrated how a group of working-class girls encouraged their teachers to give copying work by working silently and discouraged them from asking substantive questions by failing to cooperate. On the other hand, a group of middle-class girls reinforced teachers who gave project work and frequently asked questions of the teachers. Jones argues that both groups of girls were producing classroom practices according to their class cultural conceptions of what it was to 'get the teacher's knowledge' and 'do school work'.

The processes Bourdieu theorizes are relatively subtle but there are also more obvious ways in which social inequalities in education are perpetuated. One is through initial choice of school, and here research shows how middle-class parents usually choose advantaged school settings for their children. In part the preference for schooling at high SES schools (schools with a high socio-economic status intake) is likely to reflect the ideological assumption of a relationship between high social status and quality but it also results from the importance of high SES education as a means of social mobility. By keeping out the children of the working class and ethnic minorities, high SES schools serve parents seeking relative advantage (Ball 1997b). That is, parents use socially elite schools to advantage their child's future prospects. Another way to think about this is to see schooling at a high SES school as a *positional good*. Marginson defines positional goods in education as 'places in education which provide students with relative advantage in the competition for jobs, income, social standing and prestige' (Marginson 1997: 38). The point about positional goods is that they are scarce in absolute terms so that only some people can benefit from them. If they were available to all they would lose the relative advantages they bring and hence their positional value. The fact that high SES schools are seen to offer positional advantage helps to explain why such schools are nearly always more popular than low SES schools which have little positional value almost irrespective of what they do.

Although the class intuition of parents about the superiority of high SES schools may be considered unfair to staff and students in low SES schools, it is not necessarily irrational. From a critical perspective, high SES schools really may be advantageous to attend because they provide their pupils with extra material resources, better pathways to elite tertiary institutions and the effects of the 'old school tie' in the labour market (Connell *et al.* 1982; Kozol 1991; Ball *et al.* 2000; Davies 2000). There are also likely to be compositional or 'school mix' effects which push up student achievement.[4] The significance of these have been highlighted by studies of school processes which suggest numerous advantages that accrue to students who attend middle-class schools over those going to low SES schools (Metz 1990; Gewirtz 1998; Thrupp 1999). These advantages include contact with friends and classmates who have a wider range of curriculum-relevant experiences, higher levels of prior attainment, more experience of school success, more regular attendance, higher academic goals, higher occupational aspirations and less involvement in 'alienated' student subcultures. Students in middle-class schools are also likely to be taught in classes that are more compliant and more able to cope with difficult work so that middle-class schools are able to support more academic school programmes. Finally, it is easier to organize and manage middle-class schools than low SES schools. Day-to-day routines are more efficient and more easily accomplished. They have less pressured guidance and discipline systems with higher levels of student compliance and fewer very difficult guidance/ discipline cases. Their senior management teams have fewer student, staff, marketing and fundraising problems and more time to devote to planning and monitoring performance. The net effect is that solidly middle-class schools allow their staff to teach an academic curriculum and organize and manage their schools much more easily than their counterparts at working-class schools can (Thrupp 1999).

The key point to grasp about such advantages is that they do not reflect the calibre of teachers and senior management *per se* but either stem directly from the other students in the school or from the way school policies and practices of many kinds are supported by high levels of student compliance, motivation and 'ability' which are in turn class-related.

Research also shows that once their children are at school, middle-class parents are more likely to strategically intervene in the trajectory of their children's schooling to further ensure their success. Lareau (1989) has argued that this is because working-class parents see teachers as professionals to be deferred to whereas better educated and more confident middle-class parents regard the teacher–parent relationship as more of a shared responsibility between equals. They also take advantage of their greater disposable incomes, more flexible work schedules and middle-class networks to advantage their children. Nash (1993) has demonstrated how working-class parents are likely to be more happy with 'average' school performance whereas middle-class parents see this as inadequate and are more likely to approach the school with their concerns or buy extra tuition. Vincent (2000, 2001) has also illustrated important class differentials between parents in terms of their relationships with schools and has been exploring the practices of different fractions within the middle class.

Now, if social inequalities are understood to be generated in education through these kinds of processes, what would a good policy response look like? To start with, it would need to be far-reaching and accept that schools will hold only *some* of the answers to social inequalities in educational achievement and see the problem in a broader social and political context. As Anyon has noted in the US context:

> We are aware – and over 30 years of research has consistently demonstrated – that academic achievement in US schools is closely correlated with student socio-economic status. To really improve ghetto childrens' chances then, in school and out, we must (in addition to pursuing school based reforms) increase their social and economic well-being and status before and while they are students. We must ultimately, therefore, eliminate poverty: we must eliminate the ghetto school by eliminating the underlying causes of ghettoization . . . Unfortunately educational 'small victories' such as the restructuring of a school or the introduction of a new classroom pedagogical technique, no matter how satisfying to the individuals involved, without a long-range strategy to eradicate underlying causes of poverty and racial isolation, cannot add up to large victories in our inner cities with effects that are sustainable over time.
>
> (Anyon 1997: 164–5)[5]

Nevertheless, in as much as schooling plays a role in creating inequalities, it can also partly help to undo them. Within schools a critical response would therefore seek to disrupt forms of curriculum (and pedagogy and assessment) which privilege the cultures of some social and ethnic groups over others. This is what Connell (1994) calls 'curricular justice', a fundamental shift in curriculum, pedagogy and assessment to suit groups other than the white middle class. A British example might be a programme which provided an authentic history of African Carribean people, was taught and assessed in a way which gave genuine weight to the language and culture of African Carribean students in the UK today, and where (crucially), the qualification gained was seen to be of equal standing to that gained in other kinds of course. This is not an entirely utopian vision: a critical movement centred on 'race', gender and social class curricular issues developed in the UK over the 1970s and 1980s and remains an important strand of teacher culture today despite pressures against a progressive curriculum (Hatcher 1998b).

A critical approach to addressing social inequalities would also seek to limit middle-class advantage in both choosing schools and intervening in their children's trajectory through them. This could occur through approaches to school choice and grouping which prioritize the reduction of both between-school and within-school segregation. However, it would be neither reasonable nor realistic to ask individual families to exercise responsibility for choice of school since the concern of parents to advantage their children is so strong. Rather, state intervention is required to bring about change in much the same way as people often need to be forced out of their cars and into public transport to prevent urban traffic congestion and pollution.

Of course, this kind of agenda is at odds with the individualistic neo-liberal policy environment currently prevalent in the USA, UK and elsewhere. Years of living within that environment has now also raised middle-class anxiety around social mobility or reproduction for their children so that policies which reduce individual rights around choice of schools will often not be considered politically feasible if votes are to be maximized and political power retained. But we want to raise this agenda at the outset here *because it is this kind of far-reaching policy agenda which the sociological literature indicates would really be needed to remove social inequalities in education.* Moreover, we are not trying to argue a case for all or nothing: less far-reaching but more politically feasible policies and practices could work in the same direction and have *some* impact on reducing inequalities. On the other hand, policies could also maintain or indeed intensify inequalities and this is the problem with post-welfarist educational reform. As discussed below, drawing on the case of England, this set of policies is heading in the wrong direction if we are serious about reducing social inequalities in education.

The impact of post-welfarist educational reform

Post-welfarist educational reform in schools typically involves:

- more open school enrolment policies intended to allow quasi-market competition;
- self-management;
- changes to teacher and school leaders' pay, conditions and training;
- curriculum prescription;
- external evaluation of schools through inspection or review;
- an emphasis on testing, target-setting and performance management, and
- numerous interventions into 'failing' schools.

We focus here mostly on the impact of English policy because it is the paradigm case of the set of neo-liberal, managerial, performative and prescriptive policies we are concerned about. We will not try to describe the reforms themselves (for good overviews see Docking 2000; Tomlinson 2001; Ball *et al.* 2002), but instead try to summarize what we see as their collective impact. However, it is necessary to enter a few initial caveats. First, it has to be stressed that some of the issues discussed here will be either absent altogether or manifested differently in other national contexts (Whitty *et al.* 1998; Levin 2001).[6] Second, even within England the situation is usually more complex than can be portrayed in the space available here. For instance, Ball *et al.* (2002: 19) comment that, 'almost every generalisation about the enactment and effects of Open Enrolment involves some kind of significant inaccuracy'. Third, there is also clearly a risk of both 'golden-ageism' and overdeterminism here. In no way do we want to imply either that the welfarist schooling of previous decades was just and equitable or that managerial reforms have been simply taken up and 'implemented' in any straightforward way. Yet a continuing values 'drift' in education has clearly gone hand in hand with the racheting up of managerial, performative and prescriptive policy and practice. What this means is that what was considered unacceptable yesterday has often become less so today.[7]

Despite these caveats we think the picture painted here is a fair reflection of the available evidence. Taken together, the policies clearly have many harmful effects. They include polarized schools and communities, a narrowed educational focus and the loss of authenticity, a reduction in the sociability of schools and communities, the commodification and marginalization of children, the distraction of existing teacher and school leaders, the discouragement of potential teachers and school leaders, and the undermining of more progressive policies (see, for instance, Gewirtz *et al.* 1995; Woods *et al.* 1997; Jeffrey and Woods 1998; Helsby 1999; Davies 2000; Gillborn and Youdell 2000; Tomlinson 2001; Gewirtz 2002; Willmott 2002a). These problems are all discussed below. It will be apparent from this discussion that it is often the combination of policies which is harmful – the fact that self-management is occurring in a market context, for instance. It will also be clear that many of the reasons why the policies are harmful are related to the sociological roots of inequality already discussed. Nevertheless, the reader might well ask, 'What about the benefits of the new order like greater autonomy for schools? And what of claims that the policies are getting results in terms of reducing student and school failure, better employment prospects and reduced social exclusion?' The difficulty in all of these areas is that there is likely to be considerable mismatch between the rhetoric and what is probably going on, and this problem will be considered too.

Polarization

The market-based approach to education brought in by the Conservative government after the Education Act 1988 was centred on the idea that popular schools were good schools which deserved to thrive while unpopular schools were bad and could safely be allowed to go to the wall (Gewirtz *et al.* 1995). While New Labour has subsequently backed away from such an overt emphasis on educational Darwinism (the 'survival of the fittest' school), it still emphasizes the importance of parents being allowed to choose the best school to suit their child's educational needs as well as their need for information on student achievement to inform that choice, and it is also increasingly opening up 'diversity' through specialist and beacon schools (DfES 2001; Tomlinson 2001).

Yet, if as argued earlier, parental decision-making around school choice is often dominated by concern about social mobility and positional advantage, it is not surprising that studies which have investigated parental choice of schools in educational markets have found that, among the public, low SES schools are widely considered inferior to middle-class schools (Gewirtz *et al.* 1995; Lauder *et al.* 1999). Overall it seems that most parents, regardless of ethnic or class group, believe that attending high SES schools advantages children, even if their own children are not able to attend such schools (Reay and Ball 1997; Lauder *et al.* 1999). The consequent effect of policies which open up choice and diversity is that high SES schools tend to become thoroughly over-subscribed and can choose their students, whereas low SES schools struggle to maintain their rolls and have to take all students to survive. Those high SES schools which get to choose their students tend to favour white, middle-class, able students who will enhance the positional standing of the school. Less favoured schools become dominated by the students left behind – those from working-class backgrounds, minority and indigenous groups, recent refugees, those who have been previously excluded and those with special needs. As a result, the development of school quasi-market relations is likely to intensify the social polarization of school intakes (Lauder *et al.* 1999; Noden 2000).[8]

Like 'choice', self-management is a quasi-market policy in as much as it is intended to allow schools to respond to market imperatives and the incentive to do this is per capita funding which ties school funding to the numbers of students on roll. Because of this, and differential contributions from families in rich and poorer areas, schools also become polarized between those which are well resourced (in terms of material resources, physical plant, staffing levels and so on) and those which are not. For 'unpopular' schools with low positional value, 'self-management' can become a matter of serious and continuing budget constraints. Schools are also polarized in terms of academic status as reflected in league tables and Ofsted inspections because of the differential impact of family background, school mix, school resources and staffing. This then generates inequalities in the ability of schools to attract staff. Apart from a desire to 'make a difference', why would teachers want to work in schools which are badly resourced, under surveillance as 'failing' and perhaps likely to close?

These forms of polarization are mutually reinforcing so that, as the quasi-market develops, it may be difficult for unpopular schools in working-class areas not to enter a spiral of decline (become 'sink schools') or indeed for middle-class schools not to be popular and successful. Of course, the increasing number of interventions directed at 'failing schools' are intended to solve this problem and they do provide extra resources (DfES 2001; Thrupp 2001c). However, the impact of such resources is likely to be limited so long as policies of choice and per capita funding remain in place. Moreover, polarized schools may also help to create more unequal societies by having an impact on residential segregation as, over time, people increasingly choose to live away from schools that have become unpopular.

The effects of the 'diversity' policies also often add to the problem of polarization. This occurs between schools as a result of moving away from a comprehensive model to the establishment of specialist or charter schools which have a selective element. Differentiation also occurs within schools though the promotion of setting and gifted, able or talented programmes which are usually disproportionately taken up by white middle-class families who can exercise their cultural and material advantages in pursuit of a 'better education'. Meanwhile, the market discourages within-school programmes for students who are a liability in market terms such as those with special educational needs.

Narrowing the educational focus and the loss of authenticity

Post-welfarist educational reform has reduced the educational breadth of schools both directly through curriculum prescription and indirectly through its emphasis on outcomes, the intensification of workloads and the impact of market pressures. First, there can be little doubt that curriculum prescription geared to white middle-class interests helps to foster rather than reduce inequality. For instance, Helsby (1999) found that the introduction of the National Curriculum in England led to a reduced teacher autonomy with change away from child-centred approaches and negotiated teaching to didactic pedagogies, traditional whole-class methods and strongly classified subjects. Alternative approaches to teaching which might better suit groups other than the white middle class get squeezed out. However, it is not just marginalized groups which suffer. A highly prescriptive focus, as illustrated by the literacy and numeracy hours in England, reduces time spent not only on subjects often regarded as curriculum frills (for instance art, drama, physical education) but also on subjects long regarded as curriculum basics, for instance science and geography.

There is also much evidence to show how increased emphasis on assessment against narrow criteria – whether through testing, target-setting, inspection or review or performance management – also reduces the curriculum as the 'tail wags the dog': schools and teachers are encouraged to teach to the test/target/inspection/performance management appraisal. Thus Helsby (1999) discusses how ever-present accountability demands have brought a focus on summative assessment, while Reay (1998a) found that pressures to increase attainment have resulted in increased emphasis on the academic over the pastoral, and thus a shift in the values underpinning comprehensive education. Gillborn and Youdell (2000) discuss what they call the 'A-to-C economy' in which 'almost every aspect of school life is re-evaluated for its possible contribution to the headline statistic of the proportion of pupils attaining at least 5 higher grade GCSE passes' (p. 12).

The pressure to perform also leads to impression management by way of fabrication. For instance, prior to Ofsted inspections, teachers create artefacts and ritualistic displays of their work and have begun to internalize a new set of teaching and assessment values and practices led by Ofsted requirements. Ball (2001a) illustrates many other forms of fabrication which occur in the 'performing school' through the routine selection (or manipulation) of statistics and indicators, the stage management of events and the kinds of accounts that schools and individuals construct around themselves.

With lots of administration related to accountability, post-welfarist educational reform also leads to intensification of workloads and this in itself reduces the curriculum. An important loss is the informal activities which lead to mutual learning and improved relationships between teachers and students and which can therefore be 'traded on' in delivering the formal curriculum. We are talking for instance about teachers sitting on a desk during a lunch hour just 'shooting the breeze' or 'having a laugh' with a group of students, or running an after-school club for students centred on some personal enthusiasm such as chess or painting. Post-welfarist educational reform has led to a decline in such 'organic' extracurricular activity as teachers struggle to find the time to manage their formal workloads, let alone anything extra (Gewirtz 2002).

Another indirect pressure to narrow the curriculum comes from the market. Schools may be self-managing but if they do not keep up their market share they can be in trouble. Consequently even the autonomy experienced by more popular higher SES schools will be limited to paths which are likely to reinforce their continuing popularity. Indeed, because so many parents are looking for the style of education associated with the socially elite, the market often has a conservatizing effect in the direction of a traditional grammar school model rather than encouraging exciting innovations as is often theorized (Glatter *et al.* 1997). Thus diversity tends to be of particular kinds which still largely fit this traditional model, for instance the curricula foci associated with the specialist schools programme. It is very difficult in a market context to pursue genuine alternatives.

All of this limits what teachers do and what students learn. Thus Woods and colleagues (Woods *et al.* 1997) report an overall 'foreshortening of choice' for teachers in resolving the day-to-day dilemmas of teaching, and Gewirtz (2002) reports a general decline in the vitality and creativity of teaching and less opportunity for progressive practices. Precisely what the cost of this narrowing of the curriculum in terms of personal creativity and health, society and the economy is going to be for this and future generations remains to be seen. However, a recent survey describes England as 'the most over-tested nation in the world' (Hutchins 2002), and Ball argues that 'the overdetermined

New Labour classroom may well produce a generation of young people marred by what Hugh Lauder calls "trained incapacity" ' (Ball 1999: 202).

Reducing the sociability of schools and communities

At various levels, post-welfarist educational reform also reduces the sociability of schools and communities. To begin with, relationships between heads and their staffs have become more bureaucratic and distant (Reay 1998b; Helsby 1999). There are various reasons for this: greater pay, power and status differentials than under the welfarist order, a managerial shift in the kind of work and intensification of workload for heads, and the more hierarchical relationship encouraged by current management models. Helsby (1999) suggests that increased divisions between management and classroom teachers were often seen by heads as necessary to 'protect' staff from administration. However, Reay (1998b) examines staff relationships across a number of London schools and argues that managerialism has brought a shift in values in which principals have become more powerful and controlling and teachers are increasingly viewed as just a means to the end of increased student performance. She points in particular to headteachers engineering teacher compliance, and reducing dissent through the use of staff appointments, staff training, reference to school effectiveness literature, and in some cases, more overtly aggressive approaches such as bullying tactics in meetings. While there was strong senior team collegiality, the social distance between this group and teaching staff was growing. Reay (1998b) also points to strong regulation and surveillance of teachers, and of relationships between junior and senior staff being 'pared down and perfunctory' within the new managerialism:

> Communication between staff is increasingly dominated by top down, vertical interactions in which junior staff are informed about decisions rather than being part of them and cursory consultation rather than negotiation is increasingly the order of the day.
>
> (Reay 1998b: 188)

As noted above, intensification is also likely to lead to a deterioration in the quality of relationships between teachers and students. Post-welfarist educational reform also leads to increasing tensions between teaching staff. Gewirtz (2002) found a decline in sociability because of time shortage and because teachers were meeting less about teaching matters and more often about management concerns. Reay (1998b) found that the schools were marked by increasing interdepartmental competition, with an ethos of divide and rule created by competitive bidding and intense competition for success. To Woods *et al.* (1997), teacher collaboration has become increasingly contrived. Menter *et al.* (1997) argue that the new managerial discourses 'manufacture consent' to reform and suggest that this makes it increasingly difficult for teachers to talk about loss of control over teaching, and leads to an under-reporting by researchers of feelings of alienation and deskilling. They point to a gap between 'the model of the responsible, accountable professional on public display and the private experience of bitterness, anxiety and overload' (Menter *et al.* 1997: 115).

Meanwhile the market also generates the view of parents as 'consumers' rather than 'partners' and that creates anxiety among teachers about satisfying parents and among parents about their children's education. The anti-social nature of educational quasi-markets extends into communities and cities. As parents drive their children to schools across town, cities become less pleasant places to live with more traffic congestion and air pollution. And in some neighbourhoods children now go to many different schools rather than just one or two, and the notion of the local school as a centre of community has all but broken down.

The commodification and marginalization of children

One of the most disturbing aspects of post-welfarist educational reform is the way it has encouraged those in schools to think of children not in terms of their own needs but in terms of what advantages they can bring to the pos-itional well-being of the school. This commodification occurs both in the initial recruitment of students and in the management of them once in the school. Post-welfarist educational reform encourages schools to recruit bright, middle-class 'able' children and to avoid taking on 'expensive' special edu-cational needs (SEN) and excluded students wherever possible (Gewirtz *et al.* 1995; Bagley *et al.* 2001). This reorientation of schools is encouraged by government schemes which are aimed at offering special programmes for the 'gifted and talented'. To Bagley and colleagues these developments produce a 'pronounced misalignment between the policy emphasis and market strat-egies of schools and the consumer interests of, in particular, parents of chil-dren with SEN' (Bagley *et al.* 2001: 306). Yet it is probably difficult to overstate the importance of intake 'massaging' to the management of schools today. Indeed, Gewirtz (2002: 116) argues that

> Within the context of the market and a performance-oriented educa-tion system, management, I would suggest, is severely limited because what it is effectively doing is producing a redistribution of students amongst schools. It cannot address the root causes of educational underattainment.

Once in schools, children are commodified and some are marginalized through decisions around setting and testing. For instance, Gillborn and

Youdell (2000) note the occurrence of 'educational triage' where decisions are made to focus on some students at the expense of others depending on whether they are seen to have the potential to enhance their school's position in the examination league tables.

Distracting existing teachers and school leaders

Quasi-markets and managerialism often distract from both an instructional and social justice focus. For instance, Woods *et al.* (1997) found that the managerialist discourse which teachers were experiencing was forcing them to focus more on organizational matters than on teaching and learning, and had led to the inflation of these roles. Gewirtz (2002) also points to resentment and accumulated stress among teachers because of an increased emphasis on recording and monitoring student progress, which they perceived as a distraction from the real work of teaching. Managerialism is often forced on self-managing schools by central dictate, for example the requirement in England for schools to undergo Ofsted inspections or to adopt performance-related pay. Managerial solutions can also be promoted in education by central government, for instance through the content of school leader training. More generally, however, self-management opens up schools to managerialism because school leaders and others need to find ways of managing schools and selling potentially unpopular reforms to their staffs. In casting around for ideas, they are inevitably exposed, along with more clearly educational thinking, to generic managerial ideas which flow from the wider policy and business environment: the head as chief executive.

Schools have become more concerned with institutional survival and thus issues around budget, roll size and make-up, and school image. This preoccupation is not limited to working-class schools where survival is a genuine problem: even privileged middle-class schools are preoccupied with a concern to retain and enhance their position in the league tables. They may be seen to suffer from the institutional equivalent of the middle class 'fear of falling' as described by Ehrenreich (1989: 15)

> If this is an elite then it is an insecure and deeply anxious one. It is afraid, like any class below the most securely wealthy, of misfortunes that might lead to a downward slide. But in the middle class there is another anxiety, a fear of inner weakness, of growing soft, of failing to strive, of losing discipline and will. Even the affluence that is so often a goal of all this striving becomes a threat, for it holds out the possibility of hedonism and self-indulgence. Whether the middle class looks down towards the realm of less, or up towards the realm of more, there is the fear, always, of falling.

From a critical perspective, market and managerial distractions, however important for institutional survival, represent an opportunity cost in terms of expense, time and energy which could be used on instructional and equity concerns. For instance, it has been estimated that an Ofsted inspection costs a school £20,000 and there are further costs related to local education authority inspections and school marketing (Hood *et al.* 1999; Gewirtz 2000). Meanwhile many teachers clearly find Ofsted inspections and key stage testing time consuming and stressful (Jeffrey and Woods 1998; Troman and Woods 2001). Gillborn and Youdell (2000: 222) conclude that 'it is time this level of activity was refocused towards the achievement of social justice'.

Discouraging potential teachers and school leaders

Another insidious effect of the post-welfarist educational reform is the discouragement of potential teachers and school leaders and consequent recruitment problems. While it would be inaccurate to see post-welfarist educational reform as entirely responsible for teacher shortages in the UK (other factors such as the nature of the graduate labour market and changing student cultures also come in to play), there is no doubt that the intensification of workload, increased accountability and perceived deprofessionalization of teachers' work have made teaching a less popular graduate occupation.

To some extent the same is true of school leadership. Because of managerial changes in the role of heads and their increasing distance from staff, it seems that most teachers cannot see themselves in the role (Thornton 2002). On the other hand, those of managerial leaning may find the role more attractive. Both trends may help to bring about a new breed of predominantly managerial heads to replace the welfarist heads who have retired or left as post-welfarist educational reform has gathered momentum.

Undermining more progressive policies in schools

One irony of self-management is that it leads to new forms of steering from a distance which result at the school level in over-the-top forms of managerial accountability. Yet this focus also leads to the crowding out of central steering of the 'right' kind, in other words that which could have an impact on social justice. For instance, Gewirtz (2002: 139) notes that, until recently, there was 'little explicit expectation within Ofsted's documentation that schools would attend to social justice issues'. Governments can now use the excuse that schools are self-managing in order not to intervene on equity grounds. Privatization also clearly limits the ability of the state to intervene.

Another difficulty is that strong acknowledgement of the impact of schools' social contexts is impossible within the terms of the post-welfarist educational reform because it collides with its central tenets. It is the state's ability to hold that school staff are clearly responsible for the success or failure of schools which supports its use of quasi-markets and forms of managerial accountability. Yet a key problem is that generic market and managerial frameworks do not adequately capture the impact of social context on schools in a way that can produce more useful and progressive policy, for instance policy that is really attuned to the needs of working-class and minority students.

Greater autonomy?

Moving now to the supposed benefits of post-welfarist educational reform, on the face of it school self-management does not seem to be such a bad thing. It conjures up images of more autonomy and better decisions about the purchase and use of resources in schools rather than such decisions being taken by faceless bureaucrats elsewhere. But while schools are certainly able to take more control over their resources and staffing, this control depends considerably on the position of a school in the local market, and related to this, its financial position as discussed earlier. Moreover, there is continuing, indeed enhanced, control from the centre through various forms of monitoring and other means of control such as the eligibility criteria for bidding for targeted funds (honey-pot management). Schools are so often having to jump through hoops that autonomy – in any important sense – is illusory. Ball (1994: 82) sees the school leader as 'both beneficiary and victim' of reform, both 'in and out of control':

> The head is freed and constrained within the management role . . . Indeed it might be more appropriate to conceptualize school managers not as more autonomous than before but as having been recast as 'the agents of central Whitehall control' . . . with the result that education is both much less subject to local democratic controls and generally part of a more 'state centric' system of public services.
>
> (Ball 1994: 83)

Foreshadowing our argument later in this chapter, Ball (1994: 83) also notes how this points up the 'conceptual and empirical simplicities of the devolution and school based management literature' and cites Caldwell and Spinks (1989).

Improved results?

It is often claimed that, despite any misgivings about the policies, post-welfarist educational reform is producing results in terms of reducing educational underattainment. However, it has to be appreciated that there are intense political pressures on governments to talk up the successes of post-welfarist education policies. Because of this, claims of improved achievement are not always what they seem and need to be interrogated carefully. Take, for instance, the case of what are called in the UK 'failing schools', schools with many underattaining students (see Thrupp 2001c). There are impressive claims made about their improvement in recent Green and White Papers (DfEE 2001; DfES 2001), but there are also important problems. First, some of the percentage gains being trumpeted are actually very modest and in many cases unlikely to be significant. Second, the claims have to be seen in the context of wider problems with using National Curriculum assessment to measure standards over time (Wiliam 2001). Third, the claims have to be seen in the context of wider evidence that national test gains have largely resulted from 'teaching to the test' and (to a lesser extent) various kinds of cheating (Davies 2000; Cassidy 2001; Henry 2001). The key point here is that it can be safely assumed that such fabrication of test gains will be even more marked in 'failing' schools because of the more intense performative pressures on them. Fourth, some of the evidence for success comes from Ofsted data but it is apparent that Ofsted's assessments of schools have been highly politicized, socially decontextualized and methodologically flawed (Boothroyd *et al.* 1997; Mansell 2000). Indeed, Fitz-Gibbon and Stephenson (1996: 17) have argued that Ofsted's methods have 'failed to meet even the most elementary standards with regard to sampling, reliability and validity'. Finally, official case studies of improving schools are usually just too tidy to ring true. They provide little sense of the day-to-day struggles and messy tensions which more independent accounts of 'failing schools' point up (see, for example, Davies 2000; Wallace 2001a,b).

Better employment prospects and reduced 'social exclusion'?

Brown and Lauder (forthcoming) suggest that little is known about the impact of repeated testing on students' motivation or their desire for further education after compulsory schooling. However, they argue that because the government's own targets allow 20 per cent of students to perform below the expected average of each age group tested, the effect of this target alone is likely to ensure that 20 per cent with few skills will become part of a group of early school-leavers classified as neither in education nor in employment. They point out too, as discussed earlier, that schools are rationing their efforts with such students in order to concentrate on 'borderline' cases who can improve their position in the examination league tables (Gillborn and Youdell 2000).

As noted above, the improved results trumpeted by New Labour will be at least partly a matter of teaching to the test, cheating and so on. (Dramatic increases at primary level have also not been sustained at secondary level.)

But however genuine or otherwise, it should not in any case be assumed that any overall increase in the education levels of a population will lead to better employment prospects for those most at risk of 'social exclusion' (or anyone else for that matter). As Alison Wolf (2002) illustrates, this is because of the positional nature of education within the labour market. She concludes:

> Clearly, people without good levels of basic academic skills are at a permanent disadvantage in our world. But if there is one thing which . . . [is] clear, it is that education is a 'positional good' (as the economists call it) – one which gains much of its value from whether you have more than other people – and is not just about acquiring skills in some absolute way. The rewards your education bring are as much to do with being labelled a 'top' or a 'near-the-top' sort of person as they are to do with the sort of curriculum you studied. *And not everyone can be top*. So . . . secondary education becomes segmented as it becomes universal; universities form themselves into even clearer hierarchies; and fourteen year olds who are failing academically quite rationally lose motivation. Pile more and more education on top of what is already there and you end up with the same segmentation, the same positioning and even greater problems of cost and quality.
>
> (Wolf 2002: 251, emphasis in original)

Wolf also argues that vocational education is both expensive and inefficient in terms of promoting social inclusion. One reason for this, raised by Brown and Lauder (forthcoming), is that training for those in the poor work segment of the labour market occurs in a vacuum since firms that make their profit out of cheap labour are unlikely to embrace vocational training because they do not need it. They cite Crouch *et al.* (1999: 75) who note:

> Studies of the effect of employees' initial education on access to employers' internal training procedures usually show that firms' resources are usually concentrated on those already highly educated.

The indifference of education management academics to the emerging limitations of post-welfarist educational reform

Although the preceding discussion has noted numerous problems with post-welfarist educational reform, education management writers did not generally see these problems coming. Rather they embraced the new reforms and sometimes snubbed those who raised critical concerns about them. Viewed in hindsight, what seems to have happened within the education management arena is that policy entrepreneurship, which to Ball (1998b) 'rests primarily on the proselytising, and in some cases the sale, of "technically correct answers" ', led to the promotion of ways for schools to respond practically and uncritically to the emerging post-welfarist education policies. Moreover, while there were plenty of critics in other education disciplines, education management academics lacked a sufficiently socially critical perspective to take their warnings seriously.

The early work of Brian Caldwell provides a good example. Caldwell has been a classic policy entrepreneur, someone described by Whitty *et al.* (1998: 52) as a 'key missionary' of education management. Caldwell's books with Jim Spinks *The Self-managing School* (1989) and *Leading the Self-managing School* (1992) were international best-sellers.[9] With the 'needs of practitioners foremost in [our] minds' (1989: ix), *The Self-managing School* argued for a 'collaborative school management cycle' involving an 'ongoing management process of goal-setting, need identification, policymaking, planning, budgeting, implementing and evaluating' (1989: vii). The cycle is described as 'similar to others which may be found in general texts on management and administration' (p. 23) but one which 'organises planning activities around programmes which correspond to the normal patterns of work in the school'. The core chapters of the book describe the processes in the cycle and they are also framed within a discussion of the case for self-management, examples of its emergence and an argument about what makes for an effective school, and further guidance for getting started and making the process of collaborative school management work. *Leading the Self-managing School* followed up by updating the model of self-management and outlining a transformational model of leadership 'within which the model for self-management can proceed' (p. ix).

Despite the evident appeal of these books to neo-liberal policy makers and practising school leaders, there were important critical responses from other academics. Most substantially, Smyth (1993) edited *A Socially Critical View of the Self-managing School*. Many of the 13 contributors to this collection commented directly on Caldwell and Spinks's *The Self-managing School* and *Leading the Self-managing School*. For instance, Angus (1993b: 11) argued that 'far from challenging New Right themes, *The Self Managing School*, perhaps unintentionally, provides a spurious legitimacy to the New Right educational project'. The book did this, he argued, because of its

> functionalist orientation and its separation of policy and implementation, its advocacy of a particular style of hierarchical leadership and its assumption of very limited and controlled forms of participation [and most fundamentally . . . a total lack of awareness of the profound

shift to the right in the educational policy context within which school selfmanagement is to be exercised.

(pp. 19–20)

What follows was a quite detailed critique, one elaborated in Angus (1994).

Another contributor, Walford (1993), noted that the model for *The Self-managing School* was developed in an isolated school in Tasmania where market competition was hardly an issue. He took issue with Caldwell and Spinks's stated belief that 'We do not believe the equity issue is any longer a valid argument against self-management' (Caldwell and Spinks 1992: 195–6), suggesting that it was a

> sad reflection on their depoliticized view of educational administration that, even by 1992, they have not recognized the underlying purpose of the 1988 Education Reform Act in England and Wales. They seem to assume that all governments will 'naturally' want to promote equity, and that it is only administrative difficulties which stand in the way of such ends.
>
> (Walford 1993: 240)

Demaine (1993: 40) described Caldwell and Spinks's argument for school self-management as 'Non-Right' rather than New Right but suggests that Caldwell and Spinks are 'politically coy rather than naïve . . . they have nothing to say about the politics of the New Right or about the extensive criticism of right-wing education policy in Britain'. Kell (1993: 218) described *The Self-managing School* as 'a curious blend of technicist management and . . . participatory processes'. Finally, in the same collection, Ball also noted that Caldwell and Spinks's model of financial management 'is a far cry from the "what-we-can-afford" world of cuts in public sector spending in which most schools currently find themselves', and it is his chapter which also raises the notion of textual apologism:

> The textual apologists of selfmanagement provide a professionalization and legitimation of selfsubjugation in articulating an idealised technology for reworking the cultural and interpersonal dynamics of schooling. These texts are firmly imbricated in the construction of new forms of control, and concomitantly the reconstruction of teachers' subjectivities, relationships and careers, and thus also the possibilities of their efficacy and autonomy.
>
> (Ball 1993: 79)

In a number of these chapters there is discussion of the slippery use of language in *The Self-managing School*, and in general we can see those of critical orientation coming to grips with the way that seemingly 'non-political' techni-cist perspectives which are not obviously from the New Right nevertheless easily lend themselves to neo-liberal ends. Meanwhile other contributors to *A Socially Critical View of the Self-managing School* offered more general arguments against managerial models of school management, as did other books published at the time by Bowe *et al.* (1992) and Bottery (1992, 1994). The latter also argued:

> Whilst very clear, and persuasive of the need and benefit of the whole school participatory planning, it [*The Self-managing School*] fails to locate such planning within a context which in many countries, has been described as an agenda of budget cuts, and power held by central government, with only participation on tactics possible at the school level. By failing to discuss this wider picture, I would argue, the book obliquely provides support for this pattern of events.
>
> (Bottery 1994: 142)

There is no doubt, then, that education management writers of the early 1990s could have tapped into critical perspectives on self-management in gen-eral, and about Caldwell and Spinks's books in particular – had they wanted to. Unfortunately, most chose not to. A flavour of what was going on is provided by editorials in the 1994 issue of *Educational Management and Administration*, the flagship journal of the British Educational Management and Administra-tion Society, BEMAS (now the British Educational Leadership, Management and Administration Society, BELMAS). The editorials were written by Peter Ribbins, a leading figure in the British education management scene, and in one of them he describes attending the 1993 annual conference of the Australia Council for Educational Administration held jointly with the Australian Secondary Principals Association in Adelaide. He was obviously impressed by Brian Caldwell's keynote lecture at the conference:

> In the paper Caldwell identifies and challenges a number of received wisdoms. In a crucial part of his argument he claims that devolution (or 'decentralisation') can be made to square with the principles of equity . . . what he had to say generated a lot of interest both at the conference and more generally.
>
> (Ribbins 1994a: 2)

Smyth gets a mention too:

> Several keynote speakers were unsympathetic or sceptical about the idea of devolution. One of the most critical was made by John Smyth . . . [His] most recent book is *A Socially Critical View of the Self-managing School*.
>
> (p. 3)

Yet Ribbins was seemingly not concerned about the kinds of problems Smyth was raising, as his next editorial muses on possible titles for books on decentralization and he suggests a good title would be 'Mostly Harmless' (Ribbins 1994b: 75). Reflecting the instrumental nature of the education management literature discussed further below, Ribbins tacitly gives the pragmatic interests of practitioners weight over critical academic concerns too:

> If I heard them correctly, many of the principals present were saying that it was time the focus of debate changed and greater emphasis given to the possibilities and successes of devolution and to institutional and curriculum issues.
>
> (Ribbins 1994a: 3)

Although few cases of education management writers disregarding the critics of post-welfarist education reform are as obvious as this, Ribbins' perspective was probably quite typical of the time since we can see very little engagement with the arguments of the critics of reform. Post-welfarist reform enthusiasts like Caldwell and Spinks were able to continue the process of textual apologism without much challenge, at least from within the education management arena.[10] This begs the question: why were academics in the area of education management not more critical?

Why education management academics were not more critical

One reason why education management academics were not more searching about the nature and impact of post-welfarist education reform in the late 1980s and early 1990s was the limited theoretical roots of the field. Although there are texts on education management theory (for example Bush 1995), and Gunter (2001: 39) contrasts recent instrumentalism with 'the pre-1988 period . . . where there was an interest in describing and understanding organisations through the use of social science theories', it would be incorrect to describe the education management literature as ever being rooted in social theory. In fact, from its beginnings in the USA, education management has tended to use relatively weak forms of organizational theory which are largely individualized despite schools being inherently social places. Fitz (1999: 318) has put the problem thus:

> EMS [education management studies] looks like a field without an 'ology', that is, many studies are not intellectually underpinned by explicit social theory. Thus it is difficult to see that 'management' is about relative distributions of power and authority and that there

are fundamental questions about who holds legitimate authority (and on what basis), if you haven't read your Lukes, Foucault, Weber, Durkheim, Marx, Talcott Parsons, Bernstein, Bourdieu or Giddens, to name just a few.

This lack of a socially theoretical orientation to issues of power and politics would have left education management writers unprepared to critique the nature of the post-welfarist educational reform or even to pick up on the concerns of those who were critiquing it elsewhere, like Smyth and colleagues (Smyth 1993). This is not to say that border trading/boundary crossing between management and policy writers does not occur, for instance Fitz (1999) found 58 articles in the 1986–1997 issues of *Educational Management and Administration* which were 'policy focussed or were written by authors with a presence in the policy field' (p. 317). Yet our own reading suggests only a handful of these could be described as critical in orientation; moreover Fitz also found these articles overwhelmed by almost three times as many (144 articles) describing programmes or procedures where education management was being seen as the kind of 'narrow technical activity' that Glatter (1987: 10) was concerned about.

Another reason for the uncritical nature of the education management field would have been its entrepreneurial and problem-solving nature, with this in turn related to the relatively immediate relationship between education management academics and the needs of practitioners. As Fitz (1999: 315) again points out:

> EMS discourse [is located] in a material base in which knowledge has a generally recognised exchange value. In this field, for example, it is not unusual for relations between field occupants to involve a cash nexus. Indeed . . . academics and entrepreneurs are expected and/or required to offer practitioners 'practical' guidance on how to make their institutions more effective and productive. This advice is in turn, taken as evidence of their utility and expertise. I have little doubt that many practitioners suggest they benefit in numerous ways from the advice. Many do, after all, sign up for the myriad of management courses we offer. In these conditions however it is extremely difficult to develop conceptual frameworks or a language that is critical of the field's specialised discourse and its associated discursive practices.

To be critical, the accounts of education management writers would have risked becoming less immediately 'useful' for practitioners and policy makers and thus less popular and less well-funded.

The growth of the education management industry and the collusion of education management academics

Our concern in this book has so far largely been with the more 'serious' end of the education management field. But since the mid-1980s there has also been a phenomenal growth in the education management literature at the more obviously problem-solving end of the spectrum of education management. This is what Helen Gunter refers to as the education management industry.

> The Education Management Industry has grown very rapidly since 1988 and is concerned with the identification, marketing and selling of products such as books and folders, courses, videos, and multi-media packages. What these products have in common is that they are concerned with do-it-yourself guidance on how to solve manage-ment problems within educational institutions. Some are presented in the traditional book format, others are presented in a folder and are often called handbooks or manuals. It is what Halpin has called man-agement by ringbinder' (1990, p.474) and Angus (1994, p.79) labels 'survival guides' . . . Books and folders contain proformas to fill in, checklists, key questions for action, does and don't, simple diagrams showing clear relationships and new competences are presented through narrative descriptions, case studies and exercises. The busi-ness of managing a school, a school or college is all pervading and you can purchase handbooks that are generic or sector specific; or that are more specialised: appraisal; budgets; inspection; the law; marketing; planning; selfmanagement; senior management; special needs; teams and time [numerous references to particular texts punctuate this list]. Educational management is doing for education what Haynes man-uals have done for home car maintenance, and Doctor Hessayon has done for amateur gardening.
>
> (Gunter 1997: 4–5)

Gunter well described the technicist and uncritical emphases of the literature she is talking about:

> What characterizes the educational management product is the emphasis on so-called good practice, common sense and how useful the strategies are. A useful metaphor is that of *recipes* in which the products are lists of ingredients plus a method which, if followed, will delight your staff and customers . . . Some products do accept that you might want to alter the ingredients or change the order of the method but this is left to you to experiment with and perhaps seek additional

training. Alternatively we could see the product as maps, in which the terrain of management problems has been discovered for you and the solutions to keep you on the right road and heading in the right direction are presented in a neat, easy to follow package. Whichever metaphor is used, what is central to these products is the portrayal of certainty. If the strategies are followed then problems will be avoided or solved according to your management needs. The reader or course participant is often told that the author or trainer is at the 'leading' or cutting edge of new strategies for the educational institution of the next century. The beliefs of the authors tend to be explicit so that you know what type of product you are buying, and the whole tone evinces confidence and you are exhorted into trusting the systematic processes described.

(Gunter 1997: 4–5)

Such problem-solving literature is part of what is examined here, but we are interested too in whether over the past few years the more 'serious' education management literature has distanced itself from the education management industry. Has recent education management literature become any more critical than it was in the early days of devolution and choice? Such questions are explored in the Part II review of the education management literature. The next chapter discusses how we went about that review.

4   Reading the textual apologists

The education management literature today

The education management literature is vast and because one cannot always judge a book by its cover, characterizing particular texts requires careful reading. Certainly some texts have clearly problem-solving titles: *A Practical Guide to Fundraising for Schools* (Morris 2000), *500 Tips for School Improvement* (Horne and Brown 1997); however, the degree to which particular books take a problem-solving or more critical line is usually less obvious. Nevertheless there are clearly important buzzwords such as 'strategic', 'quality' and 'improvement', which in various combinations make up the titles of most education management books. (An 'ideal' title within the literature might read something like 'Strategically Managing the Reengineered Quality School: Leading Towards Improvement and Effectiveness'.) The general nature of most education management texts is also striking. To be sure, the difference between primary and secondary schools is often reflected in the literature, and there are a few books on the management of other kinds of specific contexts such as special schools (Rayner and Ribbins 1999) or schools with ethnic minority populations (for instance Reyes *et al.* 1999). Nevertheless, most titles suggest that the arguments apply to all schools, that education management is in essence generic.

Publishers' catalogues offer another way into the education management literature.[1] There are normally several pages of books on education management in the catalogues of publishers of academic books on education, and while none that we have seen list mostly critical education management texts, they do vary considerably in the range of books they offer. Open University Press, Teachers College Press and RoutledgeFalmer offer mixed lists of problem-solving and more critical books. Corwin Press focuses on the problem-solving end of the market with lots of workbooks and practical guides. Eye on Education offers a series of problem-solving books in its School Leadership library. Allyn and Bacon has a separate 'educational administration' catalogue which features a small number of education management texts which have gone through multiple editions. Jossey Bass takes the generic nature of the literature further than most by interspersing general business leadership and management offerings among its education management titles. Here among the more usual education-oriented titles can be found *The Passion Plan, Leadership A to Z* and *The Five Practices of Exemplary Leadership*.

Perusing the literature from a critical perspective, it is also apparent that even particular education management series or collections often fail to discriminate between more and less critical offerings. For instance, Cassell (now owned by Continuum) had a large series on education management where critical books by Bottery (1992), Silver (1994) and Gunter (1997) sat oddly among predominantly problem-solving texts. The same tension often occurs within edited collections. A good example is the 1366 page *International Handbook of Educational Change* (Hargreaves *et al.* 1998) which offers an extraordinary mix of 'critical' and 'problem-solving' perspectives. Yet it seems that this looseness is often regarded as a celebration of the diversity of the field while the implications raised by the more critical accounts included are ignored.

The challenge of reviewing the education management literature

Our critical review of the education management literature had to take into account its sheer size and many other considerations. To begin with, there was the problem of simply finding our way around the literature. The education management offerings of just the 1990s potentially constitute thousands of books and journal articles. Furthermore, as implied by the 'ideal' title suggested above, it soon becomes clear when you get into the education management literature that it does not easily divide up into neat areas. Rather, there is nearly always some crossing over. For instance, the Jossey Bass reader on leadership (Jossey Bass 2000) includes a reading from Deming's 14 points of total quality management (TQM) (Deming 1986), and the Davies and Ellison (1997a) text on school leadership includes two chapters by Caldwell of self-management fame (Caldwell 1997a,b). Indeed, some books bring together the literature from numerous areas. For instance, *Leadership and Strategic Management in Education* (Bush and Coleman 2000) involves discussion of strategic management, self-management, leadership, vision, organizational theory, effectiveness, improvement, TQM, re-engineering, strategic planning, and development planning. All this interrelatedness was challenging for us in terms of grouping texts for analysis but had to be dealt with.

There was also a tension between covering such a big literature in a comprehensive way and examining aspects of it in enough depth to provide an effective critique. We were conscious that, on the one hand, it could be claimed that we did not know the overall literature well enough, and on the other hand, that our argument in relation to particular texts was too superficial. Our account could also be dismissed if it did not acknowledge variation in the degree of criticality within the education management literature. We knew that some education management writers were more critical than others and that if our account did not acknowledge this diversity we risked overgeneralizing about the nature of textual apologism and not celebrating a small but important group of 'insider' critiques. In a similar way we knew that many education management writers would argue that the education management literature has evolved over time to become more critical. Moreover, the fact is that through the generally barren desert of the education management literature we did find oases. Some were relatively critical texts or parts of texts we had not known about (for example, Tomlinson *et al.* 1999) whereas others were not very critical but could be put to critical use (for instance Sergiovanni's many leadership texts – see Chapter 8). There was also the problem of the 'messiness' introduced by the lack of discrimination between critical and problem-solving perspectives. This is particularly a problem with edited collections, where it would be easy to overgeneralize about the perspective the collection as a whole is putting forward. We also felt it important to cover a spectrum of more and less research-based offerings, although this was not necessarily a guide to textual apologism since research can be as easily framed by problem-solving assumptions as less research-based scholarship.

Another consideration was that some areas of education management would not be as challenging or interesting to critique as others. For instance, there had already been considerable critique of the problem-solving and managerialist orientation of self-management and school effectiveness texts and we often would not be able to add much to what had already been said. Moreover, within the development of education management over the 1990s, these were older literatures and we thought that education management writers would typically see these literatures as outdated, superseded by what would be regarded as more sophisticated literatures, those on leadership, improvement and educational change for instance. We also considered there might be *relatively* ready agreement in the education management arena over the problematic nature of these older literatures, and wanted to concentrate on literatures which were very much 'live' within the education management arena. We could then assess if they really were any better than earlier work or were just continuing to provide textual apologism in more subtle ways.

Our approach

In the event we have chosen to:

- focus on literatures considered interesting in terms of textual apologism and ones which were clearly ascendant rather than fading;
- give different areas individual attention as chapters while acknowledging their interlinkages;
- look for an accommodation between general discussion of the literature and more detailed analysis of the work of specific authors;
- establish some broad categories to indicate the degree and nature of textual apologism or otherwise, and
- limit our analysis mostly to singly or jointly authored texts written after 1995.

The literatures we have focused on

There are chapters in Part II on educational marketing, school improvement, school development planning/strategic human resource management (HRM), school leadership and school change. These areas were chosen as 'rising' literatures and because we thought they would raise various kinds of important issues in relation to textual apologism.[2] There is also some purpose to the order in which the areas are discussed here. Marketing, improvement and development planning/strategic HRM can be seen to involve more specific bodies of knowledge or 'technologies' which are then taken up by the wider literatures of school leadership and change. Hence the first three chapters help to build towards the latter two chapters, which are also our most substantial.

Educational marketing interested us because given the problematic nature of educational markets as already discussed, we wanted to see what arguments texts in this area employed to retain their intellectual and ethical respectability. *School improvement* was another deeply problematic but important area, this time because it has tended to play down social context and because of its extraordinarily close links to recent English education reform, or what Hatcher (1998a) calls 'Official School Improvement'. The inseparable areas of *school development planning* and *strategic HRM* are also closely linked to policy (for instance, performance-related pay), provide key technologies for managerialist restructuring of education and incorporate relatively recent general management fads such as business process re-engineering. *School leadership* yet again has close links to English education reform, or what Ozga (2000a) calls 'Official School Leadership'. Leadership writers often distance themselves from management and managerialism but as far as we could tell this literature was not really in any position to take the high ground. Finally, *school change* seemed to be popular, a kind of mega literature which incorporated aspects of many other education management literatures. However, collections like Hargreaves *et al.* (1998) left us unsure whether school change mostly celebrated post-welfarist educational reform or commented critically on it.

Researching individual areas while acknowledging interlinkages

We have found it easiest to use an organizing framework of chapters on each of the literatures indicated above. At the same time links to other chapters as well as to education management literatures which are not the focus here have often been indicated.

General and specific

Each chapter begins in a general way by giving some kind of broad description of the area being considered, an indication of what is considered the key problem or problems in that area and generalizing about the spectrum of perspectives which characterize it. Particular texts are then analysed, with more detailed analysis of the work of a few major writers in each area. The end of each chapter returns to a general discussion which offers critical recommendations for those in schools about how to respond to management issues in the areas examined.

Kinds of apologism

Our discussion is tailored around three broad categories of texts which reflect varying kinds and degrees of apologism. Discussed first in each chapter are texts which are *primarily problem-solving*. The point about these texts is that you would barely know from them that schooling occurs in the context of post-welfarist education reform and structural inequality as they contain little reference to either. In this sense these texts are 'apolitical', but of course avoiding a concern with politics or the social context is itself a highly political position, one which fits easily within a technicist and managerialist approach.

Next are texts written by *overt apologists*. Compared with texts which are primarily problem-solving, texts which are examples of overt apologism bring post-welfarist education reform into the frame more but their stance is uncritically supportive and barely acknowledges the social justice concerns associated with it. For overt apologists the problem is generally how to restructure the school so that it fits with the ideologies and technologies of neo-liberal and managerial reform; it is certainly not how to contest that reform. These texts rarely examine in any depth the issue of structural inequality in relation to schooling although authors of these kinds of texts would no doubt often argue that they regard post-welfarist education reform working towards social justice as well as effectiveness and efficiency.

The third group of texts focused on are those which exemplify *subtle apologism*. In their discussion of management issues these texts indicate more concern about the context of post-welfarist education reform and social inequality, and indeed they may include elements of textual dissent – see below. However, they still provide support to market and managerial education either because their critique is insufficiently critical or because their dissenting element is not emphasized enough within their overall account to provide any serious challenge.

The limitations of primarily problem-solving accounts are pretty obvious and although it is the overt apologists to which we most object, there are relatively few of them. Rather, the biggest group, the one most likely to argue that their work is already critical enough, and hence the group which gets most attention from us, are the subtle apologists.

In some areas, especially leadership, there is also a substantial critical literature and we are able to refer to the relevant *textual dissenters*. These either challenge the textual apologists directly by critique of textual apologism (for instance Ball 1994; Thrupp 1999), or more indirectly by providing an alternative account (for example, Grace 1995; Blackmore 1999), but the key point about these accounts is that one is left in no doubt that the authors are seriously concerned about challenging post-welfarist education reform and structural inequality. In areas where textual dissenters are less common (such as marketing, and school change), we substitute our own discussion of the theoretical or empirical limitations of the area. In some cases this involves going back to the business management literature to show the weak foundations on which the education literatures are built.

These categories of apologism and dissent are extremely broad and not in any sense rigidly bounded or intended to portray perspectives which are fixed or static. Within the same category will be writers of somewhat varying perspectives, and writers may often write differently for different audiences or move between perspectives even for the same audience, or just write in equivocal ways which are hard to pin down. Indeed, we shall see that 'slippery' is a good way to describe the accounts of some of the writers examined here. Individual outlooks can also change markedly, perhaps as a result of some incident which prompts a rethink or sometimes just a dawning realization that something different needs to be done. For instance, someone who has had an important shift of perspective in the school effectiveness area is Janet Ouston (see Ouston 1999) while Helen Gunter's book on school leadership also describes her 'intellectual journey' from the 'common-sense problem-solving agenda' to that of critical studies (Gunter 2001: 4). Of course this can work the other way as well when writers who start out taking relatively critical perspectives become more problem-solving over time: the work of David

Reynolds (Reynolds *et al.* 1987; Reynolds and Teddlie 2001) provides one example. All of this means that our categories should be regarded as a useful starting-point, a way of getting some initial purchase on the education management literature – but always needing to be further informed by specific arguments about particular writers.

Authored texts written after 1995

Our analysis is limited mainly to authored books written after 1995 although we have included a few earlier books where they are of interest as well as some edited collections when we think there is some kind of generalizable theme or picture being offered. By taking this approach we have reduced the sheer amount of literature we have had to deal with, dealt with the problem of improvement of the field over time by concentrating on the recent books, and side-stepped the problem of what to do about overgeneralizing about edited collections. It might be argued that to leave out edited collections and journals is to disregard much important material, and in some respects we would have to agree. To take the school leadership literature for instance, we would have liked to have commented on the edited collections of Leithwood *et al.* (1996), Crawford *et al.* (1997), Brundrett (1999), Jossey Bass (2000), Riley and Seashore-Louis (2000) and Wong and Evers (2001) among others. Nevertheless, we have browsed these collections and are confident that, with the exception of a few individual chapters (for example, Grace 1997), they are not very critical in orientation and would tend to support rather than challenge the arguments being pursued here. For several reasons we also think authored books probably offer a better guide to textual apologism than other formats. Their extended treatment of topics provides the scope for authors to make their points clearly, whereas journal articles and edited collections are necessarily denser and more cryptic so that it is often harder to make accurate judgements about what precisely is being said. Furthermore, books more often allow us to see the messages projected by education management academics and consultants to practitioner audience whereas journal articles, being often refereed and intended mostly for other academics, will usually be more careful in tone. Finally, the fact is that even by limiting our analysis to fairly recent authored books, we were still left with a huge amount of material. It is no exaggeration to say that a book critiquing textual apologism could have been written in each of the areas discussed in Part II and it has not been easy to keep our discussion down to a chapter on each.

How the literature was reviewed

We want to provide some discussion of how we went about studying the texts examined here. This may be particularly helpful to students of education management but it also provides a model for the cautious way in which this literature should always be approached. First of all, because our thesis was that most of the literature tended to ignore the wider structural and political dimensions of education management problems, we often initially skimmed the books as much to see what was being left out as to see what was included. For, as Eagleton (1976: 34–5) has argued, 'a work is tied to ideology not so much by what it says as by what it does not say. It is in the significant silences of a text, in its gaps and absences, that the presence of ideology can be most positively felt.'

On the basis of whether or not there was any significant mention of structural and political issues it could be fairly quickly decided whether we were dealing with a 'primarily problem-solving' text or some other form of apologism or dissent. It was then a matter of reading the text more carefully, looking at the following:

- How arguments were introduced, the scene-setting often being particularly telling;
- How arguments were packaged and how the text was weighted overall, that is what was the substantive emphasis of the text and what got only a token mention;
- What language was being used. To what extent was it saturated with managerialist terms and notions or was there a concious effort to avoid this language?;
- How sensitive issues like the market and performativity were being handled. What were the limits of the arguments in these areas – what was being mentioned and what was not?;
- Who/what the writers seem to envisage that practitioners are actually working for. Whether or not any particular concern with poverty and marginalized social groups was evident;
- What recommendations and implications were being drawn. To what extent were they about working within the status quo or contesting it?, and
- The references – what literature was being cited and what was not.

In all of this reading, because of the risk of taking particular statements out of context or reading more than we should into ambiguous statements, we tested our emerging reading by looking for other points within the text which suggested the same emphasis. At the same time we were also conscious that texts might be read by practitioners in ways that the author did not intend and looked for whether or not the author had anticipated and guarded against damaging or inappropriate readings.

Finally, where possible, we have tried to raise a laugh from the education management literature. Some texts as a whole are very funny (like Robert

Ramsey's thoroughly oversold *Lead, Follow or Get Out of the Way* – see Chapter 8), whereas others amused us when their authors came out with particularly outrageous statements or contradictions (for instance Keith Morrison's (1998) argument that business management literature is affirming of humanity, see Chapter 9).

PART II
The textual apologists

5 Educational marketing

It is hardly surprising that accompanying and assisting the global shifts towards a market in education has been the speedy development of a considerable body of literature on marketing. As Kenway and colleagues note, this literature includes at one end of the spectrum simple users' guides, management manuals, tips and checklists of do's and don'ts. At the other end, it includes densely argued articles that draw on technical language: 'we read of environmental scanning, market audits and information processing schemes' (Kenway *et al.* 1995: 16). Yet this literature exists within the context of widely expressed doubts about the contribution of marketing to the social good of society. As Alvesson and Willmott (1996: 119) note, marketing is perhaps the most visible and controversial of the management specialisms; its academic status is also rather precarious. They refer to Brown (1993: 28), who talks about 'marketing's perennial search for academic respectability' and of 'the discipline's lowly standing in the scholarly caste system'. Perhaps because of this, a striking feature of the education marketing literature is that it sometimes suggests more ethically minded (or 'socially responsible') marketing techniques, practices or concepts.

Nevertheless, the same will not be offered here since, while we are acutely aware of the (uneven) pressures on educators to engage with the marketing literature (either simply to survive or to maintain 'competitive advantage'), we argue that any notion of socially responsible marketing is ultimately flawed; that we should not be marketing any social service at all, let alone education. Later, ways in which educators can – and should – resist the marketing of their 'products' to 'customers' will be suggested. The imperative for such resistance derives from the philosophical and empirical case against both managerialism and the extension of markets to education elaborated in Chapters 2 and 3. In essence, marketing is an 'adiaphoric' discipline – it renders people morally neutral or indifferent. All social relations are potential targets of the marketing discipline once market mechanisms become the preferred means of monitoring and evaluating social relations. As Glenn Morgan has observed, this involves

> a monetization and commodification of social relations. In this
> world, marketing can tell us the 'price of everything, but the value of
> nothing'! Anything can be marketed. It does not have to be the more
> obvious goods and services; it can be 'good causes', 'political parties',
> 'ideas'. The whole world is a market and we are consumers in a gigan-
> tic candy-store. Just sit back and enjoy it!
>
> (Morgan, cited in Alvesson and Willmott 1996: 124)

Since marketing is the quintessential handmaiden of the (new) managerialist restructuring of education, it, among all the management 'disciplines',
should have been the most resisted by educationists, particularly education
academics. However, what we encounter in the education management
literature is an opportunistic embrace of marketing, subject to varying
degrees of textual apology or outright championing. At the same time, such
opportunism is largely unreflective and contradictory. It demonstrates little
concern with the empirical research on the impact of educational quasi-
markets already discussed in Chapter 3. It also lacks any sense of the history
of marketing as a business discipline and critiques from within business and
management studies, both of which are a focus of the latter part of this
chapter.

The primarily problem-solving

Some educational marketing texts have a clear problem-solving emphasis.
Needle and Stone's (1997) *Marketing for Schools* consists of Part One, *Marketing
Theory and Schools* and Part Two, *Practical Examples of Marketing for Schools*. The
cover blurb advises readers that the two parts can be read independently but in
a one-paragraph length introduction to their book, Needle and Stone
(1997: vii) write that

> Many senior managers in schools are uncomfortable with the concept
> of marketing as applied to school life. Most see themselves as educa-
> tors and not as marketers of a product. Nevertheless, recent changes
> in the way schools are run make some understanding of marketing
> principles essential for a head.

Not only is there an apparent contradiction here between the advice that
readers can skip over marketing principles and the view that they are 'essential
for a head', the deeply problematic and contested nature of the application of
marketing to school life is given only two sentences.

Barnes's *Practical Marketing for Schools* does not even offer this much.
Instead, marketing is only problematic to the extent that it is not 'a panacea

for a school's inadequacies: no amount of marketing will disguise or prolong the existence of poor educational services' (Barnes 1993: xi).

The overt apologists

Davies and Ellison (1997b) raise some of the problems of marketing education but are nevertheless strong champions of the role of marketing in today's schools:

> Educationalists are often very suspicious of marketing because of the link with commercialism and selling. The very word seems to sum up high-powered salesmen, plastic packaging, insincerity and something slightly disreputable. Teachers often see marketing as an intrusion on educational values and feel that they should be left to their professional role of teaching children. It is important for schools to realise, however, that they do not exist on an educational desert island, determining what to do and how to do it, but are accountable to the people who fund them and to the communities which they serve. All schools should already be involved in marketing because *every school has a reputation and that reputation has to be managed.*
>
> (Davies and Ellison 1997b: 3–4, emphasis in original)

The stress on accountability and the putative need to manage school reputation is a sleight of hand that does not address the genuine concerns of educationalists. Accountability is not unpacked. Nor does it follow that a school's reputation has to be 'managed', whatever that means. Unsurprisingly, we are not told whether it is ethical that schools with a poor reputation attributable to low socio-economic status should spend money and time on, we assume, refashioning their reputation via marketing techniques. Unquestionably, schools should be accountable, but only to the local community in terms of achieving social justice and providing authentic learning opportunities for their pupils and students.

Davies and Ellison need to ask whether marketization and marketing actually provide the basis for *educating* children and young adults. As Elliott argues, 'our [UK] Government's current project of "driving up standards" in schools has little to do with improving the quality of education within them, since the acquisition of specific competencies are not in themselves *educational achievements*' (Elliott 2001b: 562, emphasis in original). Elliott suggests that the need for clarification of educational priorities is greater than ever at a time when educational policy is being driven by economic imperatives and teachers at all levels are being held to account in terms of standardized learning outputs that are believed to possess *commodity value* for the labour market.

James and Phillips (1997) are generally supportive of post-welfarist education reform and the increased priority given to the marketing of educational organizations over the 1990s. Despite acknowledgement of the 'problematic' nature of the business models that underpin much of the educational marketing literature, they maintain that they do provide a 'useful framework of ways in which school can respond in a competitive arena' (James and Phillips 1997: 131). They note that advertising 'is not consistent with the values of many educational managers' (p. 135), but we are not offered any reflective commentary upon this statement. Instead, we are told that

> An important and challenging aspect of the management of market-ing is engendering of a market orientation in the organisation. Those with this management responsibility in schools can draw on other management systems such as total quality management . . . and other management frameworks.
>
> (James and Phillips 1997: 137)

They conclude that those responsible for educational marketing in schools 'are faced with a daunting task. This task is complex and challenging because of the multiplicity of different clients, the wide and often conflicting needs of those clients . . . and because of the 'value conflicts that educational managers often have to face in marketing their schools' (James and Phillips 1997: 137). Of course, that 'engendering' a market orientation is a 'chal-lenging' aspect of school marketing management derives from their sub-sequent point about value conflicts. Instead of asking whether such value conflict is acceptable, we are told that the task is complex and challenging. Practitioners wishing to engage in this daunting task are offered no practical advice. Instead, they are told that they can draw on other technicist manage-ment systems such as total quality management.

Marland and Rogers' relatively early text is another which sees few prob-lems with marketing. The authors write:

> In many parts of the country, schools now compete for pupils. The Education Act 1981 was the main legislative expression of this, and it defined more widely than ever before the right of parents to *choose* a school for their children. This was seen as part of the then Conserva-tive government's political stance. However, it would also be true to observe that parents had long wanted this right . . . The obvious and major problem with competition is the harm it does to the less pub-licly attractive school . . . However, in many areas the 'standard num-ber' legislation of the Education Act (No. 2) 1986 combined with the 'school choice' legislation of 1981 has led to more openly direct com-

petition. *However, this has its advantages . . . what has to be accepted as an irreversible shift of parent/school relationships is that, when transport permits, parents will choose.* One part of marketing will be addressed to competition.

(Marland and Rogers 1991: 5–6, our emphasis)

What needs to be emphasized is the unabashed ideological work that such texts do: their writers gloss over the far-reaching contradictory implications for authentic learning and social justice and require that educational organizations simply 'shut up' and 'put up'. In our view this constitutes the textual legitimation of neo-liberalism. However, we will later discuss the educational marketing proponents' lack of discussion and ignorance about the history of marketing, which never had a unity of purpose, particularly with respect to morality. Equally, there is no attempt to reflect upon marketing's role both as the so-called discipline of exchange behaviour and as a generator of false human needs. Indeed, there is a reprehensible lack of serious, sustained engagement with ethics in the educational marketing literature. This is unavoidable, since marketing itself, like the market, ultimately functions indifferently *vis-à-vis* individual actors.

The subtle apologists

If academics like Davies and Ellison act as some of the boldest proponents of marketing, others are more subtle apologists but their arguments are by no means unproblematic. For instance, Gold and Evans (1998) note that schools are paying much more attention to their image and the ways in which they can attract pupils, which involves producing attractive publicity material, creating attractive grounds and reception areas, holding open days for prospective parents, getting positive publicity in the media and so on. Here arises the need for marketing. They also note that many schools are refashioning themselves to present an image that they feel will appeal to middle-class parents and thus schools are becoming more alike in their attempts to model themselves on the traditional grammar school.[1] Gold and Evans (1998: 77) then ask what should be the role of schools in ensuring that the substance of schooling is sound and that the image does not take precedence? Their reply involves fleeting reference to Kenway *et al.*'s (1993) call for 'socially responsible marketing', but we are not told what it is and what it might entail in practice. They conclude as follows:

> Schools and their management teams will have to decide whether their marketing activities are appropriate and whether the commercialisation of some aspects of education is justified. Is the role of

the school to try to ensure its survival and use all means to do this in competition with other schools in its area? Or do schools have a wider responsibility to their local communities, which will include: the acceptance of pupils with problems and learning difficulties; the maintenance of a balance between academic success and personal growth and development; and the cultivation of a critical awareness of the social and political environment in which they are operating?

(Gold and Evans 1998: 78)

Such rhetorical questioning may be intended to get school managers thinking for themselves but the lack of advice is not helpful given the moral indifference of market processes. We are told on the book's cover that 'The direct and interactive style of the book engages the reader in the current debates surrounding education – including the ethical and moral dimensions of school management – and examines ideas and pragmatic solutions informing good practice'. But if this is the case then where is the discussion of debates in the field of marketing? Is marketing ethical? Do the authors agree with 'socially responsible marketing'? Why do they leave ethical decisions to schools and their management teams? What 'solutions' are available to those schools deemed failing by Ofsted? Is there good practice concerning educational marketing? Moreover, why marketing and why now?

On the whole, marketing, particularly in its 'relationship' and/or 'societal' forms is welcomed by the subtle apologists. However, such welcome is ever prefaced by the (unavoidable) need to assuage the majority of educators who, the subtle apologists argue, would balk at the importation of business concepts and practices. Thus, to Evans:

The very mention of the word marketing sends chills down the backs of many educationalists. Preconceptions and myths abound about what marketing is. This book will expose those myths and demonstrate that marketing is not the evil that many believe it to be.

(Evans 1995: vii)

For Mike Sullivan, an earlier writer:

many teachers and administrators are suspicious or even hostile to the idea of marketing schools and the education service. They seem to equate marketing with the 'stack it high and sell it cheap' philosophy of the discount supermarket. It's glaringly obvious that schools are not commercial organisations and children, unlike bars of chocolate, are not commodities. There are marketing techniques that are totally inappropriate to education, these include: cut throat competition, volume discounts, aggressive advertising, free coupons, 'two for the price of one' and money back offers.

(Sullivan 1991: 1–2)

In fact, for Sullivan (1991: 3), 'Much as we might like to, we can't turn the clock back on these fundamental changes [Education Reform Act 1988], we have no choice but to proceed with all faith in the new and make it work'. However, 'proceeding with all faith in the new' is clearly equivocal. Indeed, Sullivan emphasizes that fact that education is not about some form of factory farming, predicated upon controlled diets of programmes of study and attainment targets. But this is to miss the point of the quasi-market philosophy that underpinned the Education Reform Act 1988 (and which, unbeknown to Sullivan, was to be extended and consolidated by the Conservatives and New Labour). Indeed, that academics *should* be fighting to 'turn back the clock' in this area, not accept the quasi-marketization of education as a *fait accompli*. Contradictorily, Sullivan decries aggressive advertising yet includes a chapter on aggressive marketing in his book. Furthermore, Sullivan does not eschew the language of customer and product, and this is common to all the academics and professionals appraised here. Evans, for example, suggests that 'marketing is a collection of activities that the institution performs to enable it to offer a better service for customers' (1995: viii).

For Foskett (1999: 34), 'The concept of marketing is for most educationists an imported, even alien, concept'. He has also written with Jacky Lumby that 'The importing of a marketing philosophy and practice has undoubtedly offered some useful ideas, but can also be dangerously misleading. Its translation to a sector which has social as well as financial aims requires caution' (Lumby and Foskett 1999: ix). They go on to echo Sullivan's argument that schools and colleges are not commercial organizations and that there are inappropriate marketing techniques:

> Many schools and colleges have interpreted the term [marketing] as meaning selling or promotion. This may lead to a focus on attracting potential students and presenting a consistent positive public relations front to all, a stance which can be detrimental to the development of teaching and learning, and has been captured in a number of metaphors such as Hargreaves' 'Kentucky Fried Schooling' or Brighouse's 'bewildering bazaars'. The pressures leading to such a response, the need to retain or increase student numbers, the frequent and public notice of successes and failures, are understandable, *but the premise of this book is that they must be resisted, and that the management of external relations is a strategic responsibility of educational leaders which cannot be relegated to 'bolt on' publicity and public relations activities.*
>
> (Lumby and Foskett 1999: x, our emphasis)

There is a palpable contradiction here: on the one hand, there are structurally induced pressures that encourage instrumental behaviour; on the other hand, they must be resisted. But not all schools and colleges are so positioned that they can resist. Furthermore, school leaders are enjoined not simply to engage in activities that 'bolt on' publicity – this hardly sits well with the professed need to resist the pressures that encourage manipulative activities that do indeed go beyond mere 'bolting on'. The point is that teaching and learning will ever be (unevenly) at risk while we have structural arrangements that encourage competition among schools and colleges precisely because such structures require winners and losers. As Davies and Ellison put it: 'Second place is first loser' (1997b: 57). Market competition undermines social justice, since it creates inequality and fails to provide all with the opportunity to develop autonomy and to realise their individual projects. As we discussed in Chapter 3, there is considerable research to underscore the fact that marketization of education is unfair and inimical to authentic learning and creativity. Yet in his most recent text, Foskett seems to be disregarding this evidence. Writing with Hemsley-Brown he has suggested that

> While the jury is still out on the depth and significance of the negative effects of choice on social segregation, it appears that the evidence of its existence is now fairly well established. What is still missing, though, is any attempt to measure the aggregate gains and losses of choice and marketisation, for without such an analysis it is not easy to make judgements about the benefits and disbenefits of marketisation which are based on anything other than a concern for issues of social equity.
>
> (Foskett and Hemsley-Brown 2001: 15)

Does this mean that the negative effects of marketization related to social equity are acceptable for Foskett and Hemsley-Brown? We should not even be thinking in terms of further measurement or empirical research, since markets inherently operate 'without regard for persons'. Instructively, they write:

> Much of the literature on education markets during the late 1980s and early 1990s (e.g. Hatcher, 1994) focused on such analysis [of the nature and impact processes], but pursued a rather sterile line of argument by seeking to damn the introduction of education markets by showing that they did not compare to the classical notion of the 'free market' or by caricaturing them in the light of common critical perceptions of the idea of 'selling'. Brighouse (1992), for example, complains of school markets as 'bewildering bazaars', while

Hargreaves (1991) has characterised marketisation as the introduction of 'Kentucky Fried Schooling'.

(Foskett and Hemsley-Brown 2001: 15–16)

Now the dismissive tone of this suggests a shift from the earlier (Lumby and Foskett) quotation, but the main problem here centres on not distinguishing between abstract and concrete discussions of the nature of 'the market', which provides spurious legitimation for the continuation of market practices. Characterizing Hatcher's critique as sterile disguises their approval of market mechanisms *per se* in education. Of course we cannot talk of perfect competition in classical economic terms and the characteristics of real markets will differ from the model presented by Bowe *et al*. What obfuscates matters is the assertion that 'hence the "market" is a highly generic one, which is operationalised in the real world by an almost infinite variety of forms' (Foskett and Hemsley-Brown 2001: 16). This is to conflate the abstract and the concrete, which accounts for the incorrect assertion of near-infinite variety.

Indeed, the problem with all of the marketing literature that defends market mechanisms is an inadequate philosophical discussion of the market.[2] As Sayer (1995: 116) notes, philosophers and economists tend to think of markets in abstract terms, sociologists and anthropologists more concretely. These are not incompatible, though they are easily confused. While, concretely, markets do not approximate the model of markets provided by classical economists, it does not follow that markets *per se* are justifiable in education: this is the implied *non sequitur* of Foskett and Hemsley-Brown's position. To reject market mechanisms in education derives from an abstract analysis of their essential properties. As Sayer argues, we can expect differences between the behaviours that markets encourage and the actual (concrete) behaviour of actors. The point here is that the logic of the market is that all that matters to actors is what they have to sell, what they want and can afford to buy, and costs and prices. Thus we must not lose sight of the indifference of market processes. Ethical issues naturally enter the debate here. As we will argue, marketing is unethical.

However, while behaviour in concrete markets may be influenced by other considerations (for example, Lumby and Foskett's concern about inappropriate marketing practices, presumably on ethical grounds), these are not essential market considerations: many things can happen in concrete markets, but not all those things are the products *of* markets (Sayer 1995: 125). Nevertheless, market incentives and pressures are powerful.[3] Indeed, the very reason that educators are suspicious of marketing (and marketization) is precisely because they encourage instrumental morality: the information, penalties and incentives provided in markets do not encourage people to act morally, except in so far as their actions serve market ends.[4] Yet, for Lumby and Foskett (1999), schools and colleges should now engage systematically with competitive positioning strategy, utilizing the marketing mix strategy.[5] Indeed, they talk of the need for 'sales communication'. While they note ethical concerns, they remain equivocal, talking in terms of probabilities rather than actualities. To be fair, however, implicitly they take the adoption of relationship marketing as a means of attenuating the amoral tendencies of the market (see also Foskett 1999). Yet, as discussed below, relationship marketing fails to save marketing from its mired history of unethical foundations.

The limitations of marketing

Educational marketing proponents seem largely unaware of the limitations of marketing as a field of academic enquiry *per se*. As Alvesson and Willmott (1996) point out, debates about the credibility and contribution of marketing have tended to take place outside of the marketing specialism. 'Indeed, it is probably fair to say that, of the management specialisms, marketing has been one of the least self-reflective and, seemingly, the most self-satisfied. As a discipline, marketing is generally at a low level of theory development' (Alvesson and Willmott 1996: 119).

However, Desmond (1998) argues that it is the case that the public perception of marketing does not square with the fact that morality has been a prime concern for marketing academics since its inception. It is worth quoting him at length here:

> Given the fact that the academic discipline of marketing set sail with high ethical hopes, it is scarcely surprising that marketers are concerned to see that ship founder on the rock of public opinion. What went wrong? [. . .] On occasion those who have sought to answer this question have come up with solutions which have had the unintended effect of creating further problems for the subject. Each 'solution' has led to a new strand of marketing theory and as a result the subject is fragmented into a number of quite different approaches: 'social' marketing, 'green' marketing, 'activist' marketing, 'relationship' marketing, 'postmodern' marketing, to name a few. Because of this diversity it is probably more accurate to talk of *marketings* than of a unified academic discipline.
>
> (Desmond 1998: 173, emphasis in original)

Foskett is one of those who has championed so-called 'relationship marketing'. Indeed, Foskett and Hemsley-Brown (2001: 73) argue that relationship marketing is 'clearly paramount to primary schools in influencing parental choice'. The contradictory and superficial championing of relationship marketing will be critically explored in our discussion of marketing's attempts to find 'solutions' to criticisms of immorality.

Now, as Alvesson and Willmott (1996: 120) note, marketing theory and research remains strongly positivistic in its disregard of the historical and political construction of its research 'objects'. The overriding concern has been the scientistic refinement and testing of instruments that are intended to measure the ever-increasing number of variables that ostensibly enhance the capacity to predict consumer behaviour. Despite some signs of disillusionment with the positivist paradigm, alternative methodologies have not yet seriously begun to reshape marketing theory and research. Moreover, in presenting itself as 'the discipline of exchange behaviour', marketing does not consider how asymmetrical power relations mediate exchanges. Thus to Alvesson and Willmott (1996: 120–1):

> Identifying exchange as its central concept, marketing provides a deceptively simple, easy-to-understand formulation of the complexities of human interaction and neglects to discuss how structures of domination and exploitation shape and mediate relationships [. . .] A practical outcome of conceptualising social interaction as exchange is to depersonalise and commodify relationships.

They argue that the concept of exchange is beguiling because it suggests that each individual is a sovereign consumer who is free to pick and choose in the marketplace. The discourse of exchange inflates the individual's sense of autonomy and aims to recognize and expand the individual's sense of freedom. Crucially, this does not acknowledge that social relations of inequality privilege or exclude participation in marketized transactions. Equally, as O'Neill (1998) argues, one of the great deficiencies of market society lies in the way in which it privileges the choices of 'consumers' over the skills of 'producers'. O'Neill does not suggest that producers should not answer to consumers. Answerability *per se* is not the issue; rather, the manner in which producers must answer that is the proper source of criticism. The problem is that in the market where consumer sovereignty reigns supreme, information is passed back without dialogue. Such lack of dialogue is held to be something that should be celebrated. That there is no *educative* dialogue is an informational *failure* of the market, not a virtue, argues O'Neill. He points out that the problem is not just one of education here but also of power. Mutual interdependence also throws up the issue of trust. 'Trust in the scientist, the nurse, the doctor, the builder, the farmer and so on are both part of life and inescapably a possible source of problems' (O'Neill 1998: 99).

O'Neill notes that there are two kinds of institutional response that can be made to the problems of trust: contractarian and deliberative. The contractarian response hedges individuals and association by contractual obligations and targets, which they are to meet, and to which they can be held to account for failing to do so. This (external) accountability underpins marketization of education and is readily accepted by the educational marketing literature, as we have seen. This approach has major failings. As he argues, the spread of contractual relationships itself undermines the conditions of trust. Contract presupposes trust. Furthermore, this response distorts the workings of the practices themselves, since contracts require explicitly stated conditions to be met, and thus the practice is directed towards objectives that can be explicitly stated.[6] The point is that 'a contractual framework of the kind exhibited in the increasingly audit culture of modern societies undermines the proper pursuit of those practices' (O'Neill 1998: 100). In contrast, the deliberative response places associations within the context of a framework in which the reliability of judgements is open to scrutiny of citizens through deliberative institutions. This model, however, has difficulties that derive from the necessary limits to the citizens' maturity in matters outside their competence. O'Neill recognizes that this might seem to point to an impasse. Nevertheless, he discusses an alternative (Aristotelian) model of the public use of reason that does provide a defensible account, which is the best we can hope for.

Equally, far from securing consumer sovereignty and satisfaction, it is the case that many of the marketing methods actually frustrate or undermine the realization of this ideal. It has been noted how students of marketing are presented with theories and methods that claim to weaken or skirt the will of consumers by inducing them to act habitually (for example, by encouraging brand loyalty)[7] or in an impulsive way, and so on. However, it should be queried whether increases in consumption bring about lasting happiness or increased satisfaction. Many investigations in wealthy countries suggest that this is not the case (Alvesson and Willmott 1996). Levels of satisfaction can actually decline when material living standards improve. We should question the so-called needs that marketers attempt to induce in us. Indeed, Leiss (1976) underscores the role played by mass consumption society's greatest advocates – the marketers – in creating psychological problems, namely, fragmentation and destabilization of 'needs' and a growing indifference to more basic needs and wants. Thus, for example, as Alvesson and Willmott note, when Coca-Cola or Levi's associate their products with youth – or with people's 'need' to appear young – an imaginary relationship between needs (for warm clothing) and goods (jeans) is produced and reinforced. The need for clothing or drink becomes closely associated with the image and value of glamour and youthfulness as opposed to proper use value as weather protection and relief of thirst.[8] Quite simply, such advertising feeds off the repressed fears of old age and death as they amplify the ideal of immortality (Alvesson and Willmott 1996: 123).

When we cast a critical eye at advertising, the deleterious effects here include the reinforcement of social stereotypes, the trivialization of language; the promotion of conformity, social competitiveness, envy, anxieties and insecurities (Alvesson and Willmott 1996: 123). Alvesson and Willmott argue that as desires are unremittingly aroused and exploited, people become more cynical, irrational, greedy and narcissistic: solidarity and individuality simply obstruct the fuelling of possessive individualism and the capital accumulation process. Advertising through the mass media

> plays a central role in the process of stimulating and legitimizing consumption . . . Through the use of sophisticated advertising and marketing techniques, the mass(ive) consumption of goods and services is routinely presented as *the* answer – perhaps the only answer – to widespread feelings of insecurity, frustration, disorientation and meaninglessness.
>
> (Alvesson and Willmott 1996: 124)

However, Alvesson and Willmott argue that the most important impact of marketing discourses and practices is not to make individuals buy a specific product or service. 'Rather, its more important and insidious effect resides in establishing the *generalized understanding* that consumption, which is increasingly customized and individualized, is entirely normal and unequivocally desirable' (Alvesson and Willmott 1996: 124, emphasis in original). Marketing techniques by and large promote the maximization of consumption that requires overcoming moral and rational reservations.

But for educational marketers this does not prove reprehensible or perturbing. On the contrary, as Kenway and Bullen (2001) argue, direct advertising is now considered a normal and uncontroversial practice through which schools seek to attract students and, consequently, finance and reputation. Indeed, contrary to Foskett and Lumby, Kenway and Bullen rightly note that as soon as schools enter market relationships it is inevitable that they advertise. One of the problems here, of course, is that money from school budgets is increasingly diverted to advertising and thus away from educational matters. Kenway and Bullen underscore advertising's inherent selectivity and persuading intent. It is about what they call *face value* and *best value*, following Young (1991). It follows that such advertising stands in diametric opposition to education

> in the sense that education encourages students to consider issues from many angles and to look beneath the surface, to examine assumptions [. . .] Through their advertisements, schools are constructing educational dreams which tap into a whole range of fantasies, some of which are only indirectly connected to education. A large number of schools now distribute professionally produced, multi-coloured, usually glossy brochures, booklets or folders complete with numerous colour photos. These usually depict attractive, happy, busy, often multi-cultural groups of children actively engaged

in learning, play, sport and cultural activities and almost invariably in school uniform.

(Kenway and Bullen 2001: 128)

As they note, schools are now constantly on the lookout to identify the best value to add: they are searching for the right commodity sign or market signal, which involves a key word, image or slogan that will mark them out as distinctive and attractive to parents. In Willmott's (2002a) research, for example, Westside primary school's troubleshooting headteacher quickly came up with the slogan 'Working for the Best' and arranged a variety of events that would involve local newspaper publicity. In due course, she changed the school's name in order to expunge past connotations of failure. The problem here is that such refashioning was undertaken for instrumental reasons. *But this is precisely what marketization encourages.*[9] Indeed, we now reach the heart of our critique and ultimate rejection of marketing in education: put simply, marketing is an adiaphoric subject. We underscore the contradictions and paucity of attempts to address ethics in the educational marketing literature and argue that relationship marketing cannot provide a more ethical basis for schools and colleges.

Marketing and moral indifference

On the whole, educational marketers gloss over the stringent criticisms of consumerism and the role of advertising and marketing techniques. However, a more educationally 'friendly' approach is alleged to derive from the new marketing paradigm of relationship marketing, as developed by Gronroos (1997). Thus, to Foskett and Hemsley-Brown (1999: 221):

> Paradoxically, just as schools and other public services were being urged to copy private sector marketing approaches, some of the basic concepts of marketing were being challenged. Gronroos (1997) maintains that establishing relationships with customers can be divided into two parts: attracting the customers and building relationships with customers, in both of which a key element is trust.

Oddly, there is no discussion of the background to the paradigm shift to relationship marketing and of past attempts to defend charges of amorality. Yet, one can trace a concern with morality to the very beginnings of modern marketing thought. While, as Desmond (1998) notes, most academic accounts of the developments of marketing thought are selective, focusing on the USA, the academic roots have been traced to the late nineteenth century to two economic schools of thought at the Universities of Wisconsin and Harvard.

The Wisconsin group headed a 'reformist' movement, which spearheaded the development of the American Economic Association as a protest against (British) laissez-faire economics. Of interest was agricultural marketing. Here, the economists worked closely with the state of Wisconsin to investigate claims that small farmers and customers were losing out to a cartel. In contrast, the economists at Harvard developed a more managerialist orientation in setting up the first business school in the USA. It was here that marketing as a 'discipline' was formed around the development of 'marketing science'.

By the 1960s, the Harvard view predominated. At the same time, the subject of marketing fragmented in response to growing protests about materialist values; a concern (elaborated above) that in practice marketing did not so much serve needs as frame and sustain them; and also in response to a range of environmental issues. Morally, the important attacks centred on marketing as acting primarily in the interests of production and as creating false needs, which we have discussed. Marketing academics reacted in a variety of ways to such trenchant criticisms. Some engaged in process of denial while others agreed that there was a problem and focused on the marketing concept. As Desmond notes, Philip Kotler made much of the theoretical running at this stage, arguing with Sidney Levy (Kotler and Levy 1969) that the marketing concept should be applied also to non-marketing business organizations. Kotler and Zaltman (1971) advocated social marketing *vis-à-vis* social issues such as drug abuse and healthcare. Kotler (1972a) developed the generic concept of marketing, namely the idea that marketing principles could be applied to any organization and to any of that organization's stakeholders.

> By reorienting the marketing concept to recognise societal needs it was argued that marketing could recover its worth to society. Kotler's (1972b) second paper of the year recognized the value of one such stakeholder; the consumer movement. In an attempt at *rapprochement* he argued that consumerism was good for marketing. He also advised companies which made 'pleasing' goods . . . that they should remodel their perspective away from the satisfaction of consumer desire and towards the satisfaction of long run consumer welfare.
>
> (Desmond 1998: 177)

However, while the fundamental marketing approach remained quintessentially business-oriented, the discourse of 'social marketing' has wormed its way into a multitude of social spheres, notably charity, religion and, of course, education. Desmond notes the prescience of Laczniak *et al.* (1979) who argued that the notion of social marketing could open up a Pandora's box, releasing ethical and social problems reflecting outside concerns.

In assessing the morality of the marketing process, Desmond draws upon the works of Zygmunt Bauman (1988, 1993, 1995), who looks at the processes of the creation of moral distance. Briefly, Bauman argues that the spontaneous recognition of the 'face' of the other enjoined by moral behaviour poses a threat to the structured monotony and predictability of the organization and its instrumental procedural evaluative criteria. Now without its resemblance to Marx's exposition of commodity fetishism, Desmond notes that actors rarely need to see the consequences of their actions, for example child labour in the production of textiles or the massive quantities of waste and pollution generated by the organization. As he puts it:

> These others are rendered as being adiaphoric, morally neutral or indifferent. Once the face of the other has been 'effaced', employees are freed from moral responsibility to focus on the technical (purpose centred or procedural) aspects of the 'job at hand'. The moral drive of the employee is redirected away from the other (which is now an object) towards others in the organization.
>
> (Desmond 1998: 178)

What needs to be recalled here is that the market itself renders its subjects adiaphoric. Commodified education permits people with sufficient money to buy the services without any justification to others who have equal, if not more, need for them.

Now, although there has been an explosion of 'voluntary' ethical regulatory activity within the past thirty years, authors report on the intransigence of marketing practitioners, who 'seem to be almost code-proof. This does not stop academics from continuing to exhort their flock to observe what codes there are and to recommend that new codes are devised to regulate the industry' (Desmond 1998: 180). However, many codes are simply not enforced, notwithstanding continuing calls for greater codification of moral behaviour. In quintessentially Taylorist (or managerialist) manner, the moral subject is subjected to means–end analysis, parcelled out as set of problems to be solved and viewed in relation to short-term goals of competitive advantage and consumer satisfaction. The effacement of the 'face' involves moral objectification, which in turn enables evaluation of human beings in terms of technical or instrumental value. As a surrogate for meaning, the literature on motivation in human resource management texts allows non-meaningful work to be interpreted through a technocratic lens so that the 'human resource' becomes a manipulable object of managerial control.

The 'removal of the face' in marketing takes place at a number of levels. In essence, this involves a denial of the moral capacity of 'the other'. It involves the veiling of the products' origins and the construction of the target market, the targeting of a particular group by means of mass marketing or segmentation. How-to-do tips and procedures are provided in the educational marketing literature. The point here is that the individual is no longer regarded as a moral agent, but as someone to whom something must be done, that is as a target for the marketing mix. We do not wish to detract overly from the intricacies of marketing techniques, such as SWOT analysis, environmental scanning and so on. However, it is important to delineate the marketing mix for our purposes. The marketing mix involves *product, price, place, people, promotion* and *positioning*. These elements form the link between the organization and the clients. The product, according to Davies and Ellison (1997b), is the education service. They write that: 'Using business terms such as "product" for education does seem rather harsh on the one hand, but on the other hand it provides a distinctive framework within which to analyse our activities' (Davies and Ellison 1997b: 20). No justification is provided. They go on to differentiate product range (like washing power, we suppose), product benefits, product life (presumably there's no sell-by date), and product quality.

Davies and Ellison assert that it is 'simplistic' to consider that price is applicable only to physical goods. Certainly price is a key factor in the private sector of education where parents pay different fee levels. However, while the introduction of formula funding (LMS) means that funding is dependent upon number of pupils, the very marketization of education (and its marketing) is about the reprehensible *commodification* of children. Place is the geographical and physical location of the school. Astonishingly, a 'significant factor in education is that a large proportion of the educational product is delivered through people in the school. Thus, a key determinant of the success of the educational marketing effort is the people in terms of their motivation and quality' (Davies and Ellison 1997b: 23). Promotion is about the techniques and approaches that can be employed to convey the intent of the school and the benefits of the 'product'. Positioning is about the way that 'clients' (presumably parents and children) view the organization in the marketplace. Here, a clear (and readily marketable) reputation is required. James and Phillips (1997) add another 'P', namely proof, that is evidence to confirm that customers have received service appropriate to their needs.

Crucially, the marketing mix process is *indifferent* to whether the target is someone who is identified as an object for the purposes of selling car insurance or promoting a 'no smoking' campaign. As Desmond argues, *someone else* decides that it is in the person's or society's best interests to sell them insurance or the no-smoking campaign; the person's own moral capacity is silenced, notwithstanding the fact that active participation may be sought. Desmond argues that even in the (rare) cases of academic invective against the marketing mix, specific groups of people ever remain fragmented 'variables', rendered adiaphoric and passive precisely because of the function of the marketing method. The target market is not usually known to the marketer as people. Instead, it consists of a group of variables, typically differentiated in terms of social class, demography, lifestyle, frequency of use or some other category.

> Once the marketer has obtained a database of marketing character-
> istics and 'cleaned' it (made sure that it is accurate), this may then be
> offered for sale to other interested parties, who no doubt will use the
> list as the basis for some form of 'personalized' approach to address
> the targeted individuals. For many companies this is what passes for
> 'relationship marketing'.
>
> (Desmond 1998: 184)

Thus, for example, Evans (1995) talks of cutting up the market, which is the
purpose of market segmentation, i.e. to enable the marketer to target marketing activities to specific groups more effectively and efficiently. He delineates
five generic categories into which individual consumers can be placed: demo-
graphic, geographic, psychographic, behaviouristic and cultural (Evans 1995:
24–6). Managerialist simplicity pervades the segmentation process, since,
among other things, it must fulfil the requirements of measurability, accessi-
bility and 'actionability'. For Pardey (1991: 74), the logic of market segmentation is that 'the individuals within a particular segment have behaviour
patterns in response to particular stimuli'. Furthermore, he highlights the
importance of the following variables: age, sex, ethnicity, religion, social class,
geography, employment and 'geodemographics'. In reifying human agency,
Pardey maintains that the Registrar-General's system for classification ('social
class') is reasonably effective in predicting social and economic behaviour.

Relationship marketing: bringing the (moral) face back in?

As we have seen, Foskett and Hemsley-Brown (1999) argue that relationship
marketing is acceptable, especially in primary schools, because of its emphasis
upon building and maintaining relationships and trust over time. Indeed,
within marketing itself many have replied that the discipline has moved on:
relationship marketing is vaunted not as another line of marketing theory but
as the basis of a new marketing paradigm. It is surprising that Foskett and
Hemsley-Brown do not address the development of relationship marketing.
Deeper analysis here may have prevented the authors contradictorily juxta-
posing the marketing mix and relationship marketing, since relationship marketing developed out of an attack on the marketing mix (the never-ending
'Ps'), which, Gronroos (1996) argued, is oversimplified and inherently pre-
disposed towards competition and production rather than meeting customers'
'needs'. Gronroos argued that rather than being in the customer's best interests, the implicit approach of the marketing mix is that it implies that the
customer is somebody to whom something is done. He argues that (a) marketing as a specialization has had the effect of alienating the rest of the organiza-

tion from marketing, in turn nullifying its integrative function; (b) the marketing specialists may become alienated from customers precisely because managing the marketing mix enjoins reliance upon mass marketing techniques.

The problem that Gronroos endeavoured to solve is the creation of distance by marketing processes. Gronroos 'suggests that these contradictions could be resolved by means of a "new paradigm", a dynamic and fluid relationship marketing approach, which alone can counter the strait-jacket of the clinical, transactions-based, mass market approach of the "4 Ps" ' (Desmond 1998: 186). In essence, the aim of relationship marketing is to establish and maintain relationships with customers and other partners, at a profit, which is to be achieved by the mutual exchange and fulfilment of promises. The establishment of a relationship can be divided into two parts, namely to attract the customer and to build the relationship with that customer so that the economic goals of that relationship can be achieved. *Internal* marketing is required to gain the support of the non-marketing specialists within the organization. Internally and externally, relationships are to be regulated by means of the exchange of promises, towards the establishment of trust, via the formation of relationships and dialogue with internal and external customers. Relationship marketing emphasizes qualities of dialogue and trust, and, as Desmond acknowledges, at first glance, it looks promising, morally speaking.

However, Desmond suggests that talk of internal marketing and the creation of win–win situations smacks of TQM (total quality management). He places a question mark over the extent to which we can argue that trust is predicated upon a system of rules. Following Bauman (1993), he notes that no business transaction would be possible without some form of trust in a partner's readiness to keep his or her word and act on his or her promise. Bauman then distinguishes this from a moral approach by noting that it assumes that calculation precedes morality: the connection between transaction and morality is questionable, since

> pernickety legal regulations and threats of stern penalties envelop the conduct of the parties to the extent of making their moral postures all but invisible and above all irrelevant, while making the breach of promise a 'bad business' in a quite tangible, calculable sense.
> (Bauman, cited in Desmond 1998: 189)

In essence, reciprocal relations stem from an explicitly selfish standpoint and attention is diverted from the person to the task in hand, namely the exchange of a service for a sum of money. Crucially, there is nothing personal in the putative relationship. 'The reciprocal duty of one partner to another is thus ultimately enforceable; "duty" has an extrinsic meaning but no intrinsic one; partners are seen as means to an end (my well-being) rather than as ends in themselves' (Desmond 1998: 189).

Furthermore, there are irremediable flaws that attend any attempt on the part of relationship marketing to dissolve the boundaries that obtain between strangers (customers) and organizations. He cites the example of Adelman *et al.*'s (1994) 'Beyond smiling', where the authors talk of the role of the marketer in providing social support that relates directly to the interpersonal context as a means of transcending previously defined acceptable limits for managing interactions with strangers. Adelman *et al.* cite the example of an estate agent who might find day care for the children of couples during their relocation. Moreover, they discuss the role that such service providers as hairdressers or bartenders play as quasi-therapeutic providers. However, Desmond cites Bauman here:

> The cult is no more than a psychological (illusory and anxiety generating) compensation for the loneliness that inevitably envelops the aesthetically oriented subjects of desire; and it is, moreover, self-defeating, as the consequence-proof impersonality reduced to 'pure relationships' can generate little intimacy and sustains no trustworthy bridges over the sandpit of estrangement.
>
> (Bauman, cited in Desmond 1998: 191)

The point is that the relationship must be *genuine*. Indeed, against educational marketers, the very rationale of quasi-marketization encourages non-genuine modes of human interaction: we want your children not because we value them as children but because we value them because of their monetary value and what they can offer us in terms of league table position. As emphasized throughout this book, *markets and marketization undermine the conditions for authentic trust and commitment*. How can parents and pupils genuinely trust schools that actively promote their schools without genuine (and, contradictorily, coexistent) educational and welfare aims? Producing glossy brochures is pretence; media publicity that does not engage with genuine educational achievement is equally pretence. To reiterate, we would not for one moment deny that most teachers and headteachers would want the very best educationally for their children and pupils: the point is that current education legislation – which is consolidated and legitimated by the education management industry – has set in train antithetical conditioning cycles that necessarily demote (to varying degrees) caring and educating.

Now, Desmond suggests that relationship marketing is about engineering culture through normative control; a set of reculturing process and practices that Hartley (1999) usefully dissects. Hartley (1999) has convincingly argued that as school management itself is becoming marketized, common to both internal and relationship marketing is the instrumentalization of the expressive or the rationalization of the emotions for performative purposes. In essence, we are witnessing attempts (as exemplified by Foskett and Hemsley-

Brown) to co-opt the consumer and employee at an emotional level for instrumental purposes. As Hartley notes, while businesses may know about our spending patterns, they also need, via marketers, to get us to trust them, for once the elusive holy grail of trust is attained, we, the customers, will be willing to form long-term relationships with them: enter Gronroos the 'new paradigm' of relationship marketing. As Hartley succinctly points out, this is not an easy task. In similar vein to Bauman, he writes that

> Have-a-nice-day smiles may seem sincere, but the script and the smile vary little, and therefore seems contrived. This is what Ritzer (1993) calls 'false fraternization'. Even allowing the workers a little leeway to vary the script may not do the trick. These front-line workers must instrumentalize their affects, for profit or pay, while appearing to be genuine in their quest to elicit 'customer delight'.
>
> (Hartley 1999: 313)

While it may be unavoidable for such contrivance in the business world of buying, selling and providing, do we really want teachers and headteachers engaging in McDonalds-type have-a-nice-day grinning? Do parents not want to be informed how children are faring educationally and maturationally, which may indeed not involve a have-a-nice-day smile? Again, there are social spheres that must be rendered immune from market values and market behaviour.

For Hartley, just as the restructuring of education turned on the mechanisms of relationship marketing, now the reculturing of schools and how they are managed appears to turn upon internal marketing, whereby the emotions are instrumentalized.

> The worker/teacher may now come to be regarded as an internal customer, a customer who is perhaps even to be 'delighted' by management, and who will in turn 'delight' the pupil. We may be on the verge of a new rhetoric of compliance in the management of education, especially of teachers.
>
> (Hartley 1999: 318)

He notes that school managers must literally perform or stage-manage their emotions, which gives the notion of performativity a new twist, whereby one of the important performance criteria (applied to headteachers) would be the effectiveness of their emotional performances. Unsurprisingly, then, he underscores the potential for emotional dissonance, whereby the emotions that teachers and heads are supposed to exhibit for instrumental (selling) purposes may run counter to their real feelings and emotions. Thus, primary heads in Bell's (1999) research engaged in media publicity for *authentic* (educational-ethical) reasons, that is to celebrate achievement and instil pride. In other words, heads and teachers should not be thinking instrumentally when they ring up their local newspaper or contact their local radio station.

Ethics and the educational marketers

It has been mentioned that there has been a paucity of (critical) analysis of ethics in the educational marketing literature. As we have argued, this is not surprising, since one of the essential properties of markets is that they operate (in the abstract) 'without regard for persons'. Equally, marketing practices must operate 'without regard for persons' since its essential properties enjoin de-agentification and the creation of 'moral distance' (notwithstanding relationship marketing's failed endeavours to close it). For Davies and Ellison, a slow-growth market means that most growth will come from taking pupils from the competitors' share.

> This poses ethical difficulties for schools who are unhappy about being seen as trying to attract away other schools' pupils. Many areas have local informal agreements about the distribution of publicity materials but each school needs to keep an eye on the situation.
>
> (Davies and Ellison 1997b: 60)

Rather, such a state of affairs *is* unethical. Davies and Ellison here are talking about concrete behaviour, whereby schools develop local agreements to attenuate the amoral action-tendencies that markets encourage. We do not understand why Davies and Ellison do not question the very rationale of marketization and their role as marketers given the unethical behaviour the latter encourages. They then note that another common problem in a slow-growth market is that 'schools concentrate a lot of energy on trying to locate a few new pupils, perhaps from outside the traditional catchment area, while neglecting the product and service which is being offered to the current pupils/clients, who may then go elsewhere' (Davies and Ellison 1997b: 60). Again, we have here another reason for reappraising the educational efficacy of markets.

David Pardey argues that the ethics of advertising and publicity cannot be ignored. He notes that, in general, people find the promotion of washing powder less problematic than the promotion of schools. Why is this, he asks?

> [The assumption] underlying our attitude towards the promotion of certain services stems from the strong ethical dimension of those services. Education, like medicine and law, is something to which people believe they have rights, and of which they expect certain ethical standards. Advertising is usually considered amoral, serving the pur-

poses of the organisation using it, whatever the ethics of that organisation or its products. Some would question this amorality; control of advertising by those who have economic power and influence over those who lack such power could be seen as serving a particular morality (or ideology). *It is beyond the scope of this book to debate this other than to assert that it is possible to use advertising and publicity to serve a range of purposes. In an educational system which is organised on market principles, it is necessary for schools not only to ensure that they are meeting the needs of the market, but that the market learns that fact and believes it to be true.*

(Pardey 1991: 174, our emphasis)

Merely asserting the propriety of what, in fact, Pardey has almost admitted is amoral really will not do. Maintaining that discussion of ideology and ethics is beyond the scope of his book (ironically) serves to aid the ideological nature of his project, which is to champion educational marketing precisely because we now have an educational system that is organized on market principles.

In contrast, however, Evans (1995) dedicates his final chapter to ethics. Indeed, he writes that marketers 'need to act with sound moral principles based on the ideas of fairness, trust and justice' (Evans 1995: 137). Yet, in essence, his account of ethics is characterized by a mixture of tautology and (relativist) subjectivism. The imperative here is to reject relativist subjectivism. In other words, ethics are grounded in an objective morality: without the latter – which presupposes an objective yardstick about human powers and potentialities (human flourishing) – then we would not be able to explain why, as Evans mentions, child labour and the caning of children are no longer accepted. For Evans, ethics, 'in the final analysis, are very much a matter of personal decisions . . . Activities regarded as unethical today may be acceptable tomorrow' (Evans 1995: 138). This is a classic statement of relativist subjectivism. Ethics are not grounded in standards independent of the knowing subject and are relative to specific space–time locations. In other words, while caning is deemed immoral (rather than unethical, *pace* Evans), there is no reason to assume that it will not be deemed moral. In other words, morality and ethics are reduced to personal say-so, which in turn enjoins that, since there are no objective grounds for our ethical standards, we can never be right that certain behaviour is unethical. Unavoidably, this begs the question of ethics.

Back to genuine educational celebration

As stated at the beginning of this chapter, we cannot pretend that the pressures to adopt marketing techniques (drawn uncritically and superficially from business models) do not exist. At the same time, while we accept the (anti-market) grounds on which Kenway and others reject business-style marketing and advertising practices, we do not advocate 'socially responsible' marketing in education, for the reasons elaborated above. However, it is painfully clear that those teachers and headteachers alike who accept our arguments against marketization and marketing nevertheless may work in schools deemed 'failing' by Ofsted or under financial pressure because of falling rolls, in turn feel under pressure to adopt aggressive marketing strategies. Indeed, it was precisely fiscal constraints (that were not attributable to mismanagement) in Willmott's (2002a) research that led to one teacher arguing that the school needed marketing. In contrast, Willmott found in another 'failing' school that marketing techniques were endorsed enthusiastically by the head, who stage-managed events in order to gain publicity.

We suggest that in cases such as Ofsted 'failure' or stringent financial constraints, teachers, managers, governing bodies and heads remain calm and simply be 'up-front' with parents about the fact that they are in the business (no pun intended) of providing children with an all-round education that involves caring, the nurturing of creativity, respect for fellow human beings and, of course, literacy and numeracy. It could be made clear *at the outset* in brochures (produced at the cheapest cost) that league tables militate against this; how marketization pits school against school; how league tables encourage a technicist, narrow focusing on certain subjects at the expense of others; how truancy figures and 'difficult' children encourage an increase in expulsion again because of league tables. All of this could be made clear at parents' evenings, that prior to marketization accentuated the positive, necessarily so, but did so for genuine educational reasons. In Willmott's research it was recognized by teachers and parents alike that SAT scores were relatively poor, yet the school provided a caring ethos, which was imperative in view of its particular intake of children.

We suggest that schools, as far as possible, open and maintain links with other schools – and not for instrumental purposes (that is, forging a 'strategic alliance'). Expertise, wherever possible, should be distributed and shared. Poaching should be avoided. We suggest here that heads of schools with declining rolls write to their local education authority, local government and parents. We do not suggest that this will be successful, but it will help to keep the spotlight on the damaging nature of current policy. In essence, we want schools to keep their eyes on genuine celebration. In schools that are not highly positioned in league tables, media publicity can centre on other achievements, for example sport or on the fact that specific children have battled against the odds – be it in mathematics or art.

6 School improvement

Although the school effectiveness and improvement literatures are often seen to go together, our focus in this chapter is primarily on the latter for two reasons. One is that it is clear that the school effectiveness movement has been losing ground to the more 'relevant' school improvement literature, especially in the UK where the two have traditionally been seen as more distinct than in the USA. The main reason for this is that while the school effectiveness literature is about identifying and indicating the characteristics of particularly effective schools, it is not able to show how effectiveness can be achieved, that is, the processes by which they can improve. For this reason, policy makers and practitioners have found the school effectiveness literature of limited practical use except to support the notion of schools being improveable and able to 'make a difference'. There has been much talk in both the school effectiveness and school improvement camps of the need for merging traditions (Gray *et al.* 1996), but Harris (2001: 8) has noted that 'while some form of synergy is clearly possible, it still remains somewhat elusive'. Meanwhile, school effectiveness proponents Charles Teddlie and David Reynolds have attempted to include school improvement as part of school effectiveness research (Teddlie and Reynolds 2000). We think this is best seen as an attempt to capture the high ground and prevent school effectiveness from fading out of the picture.[1]

Nevertheless, Teddlie and Reynolds (2001: 48) deny this is their intent, and this brings us to the second reason why we have not discussed effectiveness here, the fact that in the school effectiveness area there has already been much water under the bridge in terms of our critique of textual apologism and responses to it. Both of us have published previous critiques of school effectiveness research (Thrupp 1999; Willmott 1999) which have joined several other critical analyses of school effectiveness (Hatcher 1998b; Slee *et al.* 1998; Morley and Rassool 1999; Goldstein and Woodhouse 2000). More recently one of us has been engaged in an exchange published in the flagship journal *School Effectiveness and School Improvement* (Thrupp 2001a, 2002, see also Thrupp 2001d). From our point of view the involvement of school effectiveness proponents in this exchange has been useful in terms of clarifying their perspectives on matters such as social class and the instrumentality of their research but it has become increasingly clear that our critical concerns are not being heard, and in the latest attempt to cap the debate, Stringfield (2002) has protested too much. Indeed, it seems to us that his response is a highly defensive one and although this underlines the problematic position taken by the school effectiveness proponents in this exchange, the situation has now become one where continuing is pointless. We will not be responding further here.

The school improvement literature remains of interest, however, since (despite the school effectiveness attempt to colonize this territory) it has been much less at the centre of the previous debate. It is less easy to characterize from a critical perspective than school effectiveness because it is more diverse. For instance, the journal *Improving Schools* is quite wide-ranging and there is growing interest in alternative perspectives on school improvement (Harris and Bennett 2001). School improvement texts are beginning to become less generic – for instance, recent titles have included books focusing on teacher-led school improvement (Frost *et al.* 2000), governing bodies (Creese and Earley 1999) and improvement in relation to schools serving particular ethnic groups (Reyes *et al.* 1999). There is the further complication that some books with 'school improvement' in their titles turn out not to be school improvement texts *per se* but are looking at some element of official school improvement only loosely connected with school improvement, for instance inspection (Ferguson *et al.* 2000) or benchmarking (Kelly 2001).

Nevertheless, in recent times the school improvement literature, particularly in England, has mostly been marked by an extraordinarily close inter-relationship with government policy. Official school improvement builds on the school improvement literature, and the previous and present heads of the DfES's Standards and Effectiveness Unit (Michael Barber and David Hopkins, respectively) have both come to the role from professorial posts specializing in school improvement. Thrupp's earlier book *Schools Making a Difference: Let's be Realistic!* (Thrupp 1999) considered a spectrum of problem-solving and more critical work in the area of school improvement, and located both Barber and Hopkins at the most uncritical, unrealistic end of the 'improvement' authors considered (see pp. 160–81). In some ways it is therefore not surprising that Hopkins recently took over the leadership of the DfES's Standards and Effectiveness Unit from Barber, although, as discussed shortly, Hopkins position in his latest book is more searching than in his earlier work.

In many respects our discussion here follows on from the earlier *Let's be Realistic!* review so we want to say a little more about that review and what it was looking for. The review centred on two key issues. One was the extent to which improvement writers acknowledged any sociological limits to improvement related to the effects of an unequal social structure. For instance, was serious consideration being given to the impact of 'savage inequalities' (Kozol 1991) between schools, and, if so, in what way? Were any questions being raised about the 'school effect' in school effectiveness research or was this just taken at face value? Did improvement texts stress the potential for success against the odds in relentlessly upbeat or more cautious ways? The second issue revolved around the degree of support from writers for the neo-liberal politics of 'polarization' and 'blame'. What did they have to say about markets, managerialism and performative pressures such as those from league tables, target-setting and Ofsted?

The review found that while writers vary quite widely in their sensitivity to possible social class and market constraints on low SES schools (schools with a low socio-economic status), most of the work in this area was unclear about either the social limits of reform or the likely impact of market policies in education. To begin with, it found that issues of social class were often margin-alized because school improvement research tended to concentrate on organ-izational or instructional concerns and gave only limited weight to the social dimensions of schooling. This occurred partly by sampling. Research into schools undertaking improvement work has rarely included a diverse range of SES contexts. Improvement literature has also tended to favour generalized rather than context-specific discussion. This is seldom made explicit – it is more the case that the literature is vague about what sorts of students, class-rooms or schools are actually under discussion. The reader is therefore encour-aged to take the view that school problems and solutions are essentially the same regardless of their social setting. Another problem was the use of notions of school culture which neglect the culture of students and the community, for instance the idea of schools 'moving', 'cruising,' 'strolling', 'struggling' and 'sinking' (Stoll and Fink 1998). What was not discussed was the way these various models of school culture related to middle-class schools and working-class schools, white schools and minority/indigenous schools and so on.

School improvement studies were also found to be uncritical in their use of generic school effectiveness findings that take little account of school con-text. For example, Sammons' 11 school effectiveness factors (Sammons *et al.* 1995) were frequently cited in school improvement work. School improve-ment writers who criticized school effectiveness research tended to complain that it was too abstract or 'thin' to guide school improvement strategies rather than offering more fundamental critiques of its claims, its methods or its politics.

Finally, the review suggested that school improvement writers tended to be subtle apologists, more often not taking enough account of the difficulties inherent in post-welfarist reforms than overtly promoting them.

In as much as these remain key issues they will again be used to critically discuss the literature in this chapter, and indeed the *Let's be Realistic!* review will form our starting-point in places. Yet it does seem clear that there is increasing acknowledgement in the school improvement arena that insufficient attention has been given to the impact of the social context of schooling. For instance, Harris (2001) writes that

> Within the school improvement tradition there tends to be an undifferentiated approach to schools of varying socio-economic circumstances (Lauder et al., 1998). Little account is taken of culture, context, socio-economic status, catchment areas, the trajectory of improvement or indeed of all independent variables. It is only recently that the field has recognised the need to take into account contextual factors in selecting and applying school improvement strategies.
>
> (Harris 2001: 16)

Nevertheless, the extent to which social context is actually being bought into the picture in school improvement texts is another matter. Moreover, the extent to which the school improvement literature is becoming more politically self-critical is equally important. In the past few years numerous interventions designed to improve both 'failing' and 'successful' schools have come 'onstream'. Given that there are often very real concerns about the impact of these interventions, we should also ask what school improvers are writing about them (if anything). Do they think these official school improvement interventions are problematic or do they support them? If they support them, what reasons do they give for doing so?

One recent collection on alternative perspectives on school effectiveness and improvement (Harris and Bennett 2001) suggests that more of the recent concern about the context of school improvement has been about its social rather than policy context.[2] On the other hand, a shift in the political awareness of school improvement over the past few years is suggested by the difference between the 1996 and 2001 versions of *Success Against the Odds* (National Commission on Education 1996; Maden 2001). Both involve a series of UK school case studies, with the findings summed up in each case in a conclusion by Margaret Maden. (The 2001 version also has an introduction by John Gray which is discussed below.) Whereas there was relatively little emphasis on the social and political context in the 1996 version, Maden's (2001) conclusion begins with a section entitled 'Context is all'. This considers the social, organizational and political contexts within which the case study schools were operating since, 'of course, no school is an island unto itself' (p. 310). Here there is some discussion of community characteristics and histories particularly in terms of employment, parental aspirations and religious factors. In the same section there is also critique of the impact of policy: Ofsted, failing schools initiatives, the politics of 'blame', 'superheadism', and teacher recruitment problems. There is also a frankness to some of the writing stemming from the voices of those in schools. Take, for instance, the paragraph on 'Cries and whispers':

> It is surprising that some of these schools and their teachers do not feel entirely at ease with the changed policy context: 'bafflement and bitterness', 'accountability gone mad' and a sense of 'more work, less trust' at Columbia; anger and frustration at the bureaucracy overload at Blaengwrach and Crowcroft Park; dismay at the consequences of a short-term bidding culture at Sutton Centre. Reacting to some of the soundbites and rhetoric from government ministers and the Chief Inspector of Schools, Sutton Centre staff also express a general fed-up-ness with the heroes-and-villains drama unfolding around them, replete with 'superheads' and 'glitzy makeovers' for failing schools and teachers . . . [they] are not alone in feeling that their knowledge and convictions about the demanding nature of their educational task are neither comprehended nor appreciated by government or OfSTED. Such a context, with its atmosphere of teacherly scepticism and surprised disappointment is an unexpected drag-factor on a otherwise dynamic momentum towards further improvement.
>
> (Maden 2001: 314)

That schools and teachers 'do not feel entirely at ease with the changed policy context' is unsurprising to us, nor do we really think it 'unexpected' that it should create a drag on school improvement. Moreover, it has to be said that there is not a lot of analysis here. Nevertheless such discussion of the impact of policy is a big improvement on the 1996 version of this conclusion where the line taken was that successful schools should just make the most of post-welfarist reform:

> Government policy and ensuing statutory requirements are part of the larger context within which the school operates and moves forward. Exploiting and managing these, including those which might be viewed as irritants, is part of the successful school's improvement strategy.
>
> (National Commission on Education 1996: 354)

Maden maintains that the 2001 version emphasizes the costs of policy more because 'the importance of context is perhaps more strongly evident than when these narratives started in 1995' (p. 309) as that was a time when the 'odds' were 'mainly social and economic' rather than created by education policy (p. 336). While this will surely be partly true – for instance, by the time of the 1996 book only two schools had actually experienced an Ofsted inspection – it is also the case that the 2001 case study authors were *directed* to be much more attuned to both political and social contexts in their research. For instance, the 1996 version guidelines for case study authors were almost entirely school-centred (see pp. 364–9), whereas the 2001 guidelines asked authors to comment specifically on the 'impact of wider policies' and listed a range of initiatives the researchers should look into (p. 343). The guidelines also require more emphasis on social context than in 1996. For instance, in 2001, researchers were told to look at student turnover because 'this may not be a significant issue but recent research shows it to be important in some inner city schools' (p. 343). It seems to us, then, that the new emphasis on the impact of context may reflect not only the evolution of post-welfarist reform but also the fact that school improvement researchers are starting to ask different questions.

The issue remains, however, whether this apparent shift is reflected in other school improvement literature and whether it goes far enough to escape the problem of textual apologism. As in other chapters, most of our discussion is about subtle apologists but we begin by discussing some pure problem-solvers and overt apologists. Overall we are confident that social context and to a lesser extent political context *is* coming more to the fore in recent school improvement literature – but still not nearly enough. Some of the remaining tensions are highlighted by Mortimore and Whitty's (1997) booklet *Can School Improvement Overcome the Effects of Disadvantage?* which is often cited by school improvers at times when they want to stress the limits of school improvement. This is a particularly interesting account because, in an apparent attempt to head off New Labour's overheated school improvement agenda, it attempts to bridge problem-solving and critical perspectives on school improvement. Mortimore and Whitty (1997: 5) argue that

> Two possible avenues forward are often seen as mutually exclusive alternatives. One builds on the work in school improvement . . . The other is more fundamental and demands change not only to the nature of educational practice but also to the broader social and cultural contexts within which education takes place. We believe that an effective strategy for tackling disadvantage requires movement on both fronts.

Mortimore and Whitty's following discussion acknowledges some concessions: from a school improvement perspective that school improvement does have structural limits, from a sociological point of view that school improvement can make some difference. Nevertheless the two 'fronts' are still in tension in relation to how much they emphasize the ability of school improvement to deliver. For example, the school improvement section argues that 'committed and talented heads can improve schools even if such schools contain a proportion of disadvantaged pupils. In order to achieve improve-ment, however, such schools have to exceed what could be termed "normal" efforts' (p. 6). Making essentially the same point but with a less optimistic emphasis, the sociological section argues, 'Whilst some schools can succeed against the odds, the possibility of them all doing so, year in and year out, still appears remote given that the long-term patterning of educational inequality has been strikingly consistent throughout the history of public education in most countries' (p. 9). There is also the problem that the discussion of the school improvement literature in this booklet serves mostly to illustrate that it has done more to document cases of apparent 'success against the odds' than to explain them. This is hardly satisfactory from a sociological point of view where insights into the relationship between social structures and school prac-tice would be of more interest.

The primarily problem-solving

One might think that in the school improvement area it would be hard to overlook a critique of sociological and political issues because the schools which are usually seen to need most improvement are those in areas of social deprivation and because there is so much active policy concerned with improving schools on both sides of the Atlantic and elsewhere. Nevertheless, there are texts which would have to come into this category, for instance Horne and Brown (1997), Perez *et al.* (1999), Reyes *et al.* (1999) and Walsh (1999). *Building a Successful School* (Walsh 1999) is one of those 'popular' books which has no references to research or scholarship. The book is concerned with how to prevent 'failing' schools, and what is most disturbing about it is the way it seeks to simplistically hold school staff solely responsible for school 'failure'. The reasons for failure identified in chapter 1 are low standards, poor progress, poor teaching, a threatening environment and poor management, while chapter 2 seeks to explode what are regarded as the myths around failing schools including the myth that 'In inner city schools we can't get the staff', and the myth that 'Outsiders don't understand the problems we face'. This denies the problem that schools in socially deprived areas do not get the same shortlists of applicants as those in middle-class areas and the problem that the contextual constraints in low SES schools have been, and continue to be, widely underacknowledged by policy makers (Thrupp 1999). Nevertheless, Walsh is adamant that the answers lie in better teaching and management and it comes as no surprise to find that he is a 'senior LEA inspector and officer with significant Ofsted inspection experience' (back cover). Yet the book does not so much defend or 'sell' official school improvement as treat it as an obviously appropriate policy background to the problems represented by failing schools. In this respect the book is a good example of how problem-solving texts can act to textually apologize for post-welfarist reform even without overt promotion of it.

Another primarily problem-solving text is Horne and Brown (1997) which offers 500 tips for school improvement. This contains 48 sections generally providing 10 short tips, most of which are socially and politically decontextualized. This is unsurprising since the tips format required by books in this series undoubtedly precludes any more complex discussion of the problems and possibilities of school improvement. When the tips do raise features of post-welfarist education reform or refer to DfES and Ofsted sources and advice, this is usually done in an uncritical, taken-for-granted manner, which shades into overt apologism. This is true even when there is (rare) acknowledgement of debate:

> 8. Try the Competency approach [to appraisal]. This may be an emotive subject. But the Teacher Training Agency (TTA) has guidelines for training new teachers using competence-based appraisal. We assess pupils by giving clear criteria. So why not assess teachers in a similar way?
>
> (p. 111)

Lessons from High Performing Hispanic Schools: Creating Learning Communities (Reyes *et al.* 1999) is also a problem-solving analysis of sorts since it is sociologically blinkered despite seeming to hold out hope for a contextualized school improvement analysis involving a specific school population. After doing a good job of summarizing the 'educational vulnerability' of Hispanic students (pp. 1–3), this book goes too far in asserting that 'the current condition of education for Hispanic students need not exist':

> While most schools fail Hispanic students, some schools do not. The picture we show is far brighter and potentially far more optimistic than the tragic circumstances portrayed in the latest statistics on Hispanic youth. High performing Hispanic schools, in fact, do exist and they have a strong impact on the learning conditions for Hispanic students.
>
> (pp. 3–4)

Descriptions of the features of such 'exemplary' schools follow as well as discussion of how to emulate them, but the book fails to make a convincing case since there is only the thinnest discussion of actual student achievement levels. We are told the schools were 'outperforming most schools in the attainment of state academic standards (pp. 9–10) but there is no clear comparison of the relative attainment of Hispanic students in these schools compared with other schools or to white students in the same schools. Purkey and Smith (1983) pointed out in response to an earlier generation of exemplary schools studies that an 'unusually effective' school serving pre-dominantly low-income and minority students may in fact still have considerably lower levels of attainment than a white middle-class school because of the pervasive influences of social class on achievement. The same is also likely to be the case here, and without more information we remain unconvinced by Reyes *et al.*'s 'essential conclusion': 'that there are no excuses for anything other than high-impact schools and high-performing Hispanic students' (p. 208).

The overt apologists

The best example of overt apologism in the school improvement area would have to be the work of Michael Barber (Barber 1996b,c) which was discussed in the *Let's be Realistic!* review. As that illustrated, Barber's work both refutes the social limits of reform and uses school improvement arguments in support of managerial and performative policies (see Thrupp 1999: 162–5). However, as noted earlier, Barber left the academy and it is hard to think of anyone in the school improvement area who has subsequently taken such an obviously apologetic stance.

One more recent school improvement text which we think, on balance, has to be seen as 'overtly apologetic' is *How to Improve Your School* (Brighouse and Woods 1999) which draws on Birmingham's much-acclaimed approach to school improvement. Here the analysis is socially decontextualized – despite the introduction mentioning 'great deprivation' affecting some schools (p. 2), the 'rather smoother waters found elsewhere' (p. 3) and arguing that the book draws its conclusions from 'this range of contexts' (p. 3). There is also some critique of policy. This is strongest where there is a discussion of the management model of 'ensuring compliance':

1. Decide what is right.
2. Regulate that the single solution will be implemented by everyone.
3. Inspect to ensure that the solution is being followed.
4. Publicly punish deviants and inadequates.

We believe there is a danger that such a model will be the unintentional result of some national actions. This is clearly more likely to happen when, as is now the case, we have Secretaries of State who can exercise an enormous number of powers rather than at a time when the Secretary of State had only three powers to affect the system, as was the case some years ago. The danger of course with this model, even without its fourth step, is that should it be accompanied, as it is with a thorough model of external inspection, the likelihood is

that schools will find their lives dominated by a dangerous combination of 'ensuring compliance' and 'problem-solving'.

(p. 147)

On the other hand, there is too little of this for subtle apologism (and no
critical policy literature is cited) whereas the book makes many references to
official school improvement policies and documents in an essentially supportive manner. Consider, for instance, the discussion of target-setting which is
thoroughly uncritical (despite its mention of 'critically intervening'):

> National testing is now established at 7, 11 and 14, which, together
> with public examinations at 16 and 18 means that a range of perform-
> ance information is available at school, LEA and national level. Indeed,
> much of this information is now provided annually to schools through
> their LEAs and through PANDAs (Performance and Assessment)
> reports from QCA. It is now a requirement for schools to set targets for
> improvement based on this data at ages 11 and 16, although targets
> need not always be strictly related to national assessments and exam-
> inations. Schools could critically intervene by self-setting targets to
> take action at various fixed points to raise educational standards,
> whether for the school as a whole, certain groups within the school, or
> for individual pupils. The effective use of targets, especially quantita-
> tive targets, helps schools to articulate clearly what is expected of
> pupil, class or group – or indeed the school as a whole and this is clearly
> set out in the DfEE's publication, *From Targets to Action* (1998).
>
> (Brighouse and Woods 1999: 132–3)

What makes this book overtly apologist rather than just problem-solving,
then, is the way it more actively 'sells' recent policy, in this case target-setting.
Given Brighouse's reputation as a progressive educationalist, this may be considered surprising, but when he wrote this book Brighouse was Birmingham's
chief education officer while Woods was a senior education advisor for the
Department for Education and Employment. Such roles require being mostly
'on message' with government policy and the book can be seen to reflect this.

The subtle apologists

Subtle apologism continues to be the main problem with more serious school
improvement literature, even with the shift towards acknowledging context
noted earlier. Here we briefly sample a number of recent texts before focusing
on some of the work of two British school improvement writers, John Gray
and David Hopkins.

Improving School Effectiveness (MacBeath and Mortimore 2001a) is an edited collection that centres on a project in Scotland, which had both an ethnographic element concerned with 'identifying the brakes and accelerators of improvement' (p. ix) and a statistical school effectiveness element. What is particularly noteworthy about this book is the way the initial chapters provide a substantial and quite critical discussion of both socio-economic issues and the costs of post-welfarist reform. For instance, there is discussion in chapter 1 of the UK as an increasingly unequal society and one with substantial levels of child poverty (MacBeath and Mortimore 2001b: 3). There is also, along with discussion of more usual school effectiveness findings, a good discussion of context including the admission that 'as researchers we recognise that [the compositional effect] is a factor which we may have underestimated in the past or failed to examine with exploratory tools which were sensitive enough' (p. 14). Likewise, in chapter 2 (MacBeath and McCall 2001), there is a nicely critical view of English education policy, drawing especially on the arguments of Davies (2000), and against which Scottish education policy is seen to be generally more reasonable.

In terms of acknowledging wider social and political context this is an exceptionally good start for an education management text and while it is not kept up throughout the book, it does return in places, for instance the discussion of 'external contextual influences on internal capacity' of two case study schools (Stoll *et al.* 2001a: 185–8). And yet by the concluding chapter 'Beyond 2000 – where next for SESI?' (Stoll *et al.* 2001b), the analysis has become almost entirely school-centred and decontextualized. In this chapter Stoll and colleagues propose ten effectiveness and improvement imperatives for the next decade for 'practitioners, policy makers, researchers, parents and other educational partners'. These are:

- develop a wider range of skills and qualities for a fast changing world;
- emphasize learners and learning and consider implications for teaching;
- listen to the pupil's voice;
- facilitate deep learning of teachers;
- promote self-evaluation;
- emphasize leadership and management;
- ensure high-quality critical friendship;
- build communities, networks and partnerships;
- take a connected approach to improvement;
- strive for sustainability of improvement.

We could suggest obvious others, such as 'acknowledge and try to respond to social inequality' and 'contest managerial reform', but our concern is more that within these areas there is not enough discussion which follows on from the contextually much sounder way this book starts off. There is just one paragraph which notes,

> As we argued in the opening chapter of this book, individual schools make a difference to the amount of successful learning achieved by an individual, but it would be foolish to imagine that the school can – by itself – overcome the effects of sustained disadvantage. This is the conclusion reached in a review of the evidence by Mortimore and Whitty (1997). Schools exist within a wider system that has an enhancing and constraining role on the capacity of schools to be all things to all children. If we wish to raise standards, as Coleman and Jencks concluded thirty years ago, we have to work on what happens outside school too and make demands on members of that wider system to play their part.
>
> (Stoll *et al.* 2001b: 204)

This is quite right but it is not enough. On the other hand, there is a problematic emphasis on school change (see Chapter 9 in this volume) as well as the inappropriate importation of business models of leadership – see the discussion of Chowdhury (2000) on pp. 201–2 – and decontextualized models of schools being 'exuberantly effective', 'dutifully diligent', 'mechanistically moribund' and 'haphazardly hanging on' (Stoll *et al.* 2001b: 199). In short, we do not see the messages of this concluding chapter reflecting the balance of concerns in the introductory ones and so the overall effect of the book fails to challenge the social and political status quo.

There is a similar problem with Alma Harris's book *School Improvement: What's in it for Schools?* (Harris 2002). The introductory chapter, 'School improvement in context', has some useful discussion of the impact of wider social and political matters on school improvement, although not as much as MacBeath and Mortimore's book as discussed above. The introduction notes that 'successful school improvement can only occur when schools apply those strategies that best fit their own context and particular developmental needs' (p. 7), and the conclusion has a section on being 'realistic but optimistic' which points to the need for 'context-specific' improvement approaches (p. 115). Yet for the most part this book offers a conventionally decontextualized school improvement analysis complete with schools which are 'improving', 'failing' 'trapped' and 'dynamic' (pp. 15–16).

Both *Improving School Effectiveness* and *School Improvement: What's in it for Schools?* therefore exhibit the same tension of promoting the importance of context while presenting a largely decontextualized analysis. One way to interpret this tension is to say that the authors are only paying lip service to context. However, it is also likely that even leading school improvement writers have yet to find ways of breaking out of the generic discourses which have dominated school effectiveness and improvement for so long. The challenge is to bring context into the picture and yet provide an analysis which others see as similar enough to their own situation to be useful. This would require texts aimed at particular kinds of schools rather than those for all schools as is the case with nearly all the texts discussed here.

When it comes to the impact of reform on schools, Harris (2002: 114) writes:

> Many schools currently feel pressurised by the, often competing, demands of new government initiatives and strategies. This initiative overload in schools is, at worst, counter-productive to schools taking charge of their own change and development. It prevents many schools from concentrating on the issues and concerns of most importance in their school, in their particular context. It is unlikely that the constant stream of initiatives will subside in coming years; consequently the real challenge for schools is to harness the energy of external reform and use it for their own ends. The aligning of external change and internal priorities may not always be possible but it offers schools one way of reconciling the competing demands and tensions inherent in the current climate.

There are echoes here of Maden's argument in the 1996 version of *Success Against the Odds* noted earlier, and the argument is appealing because it suggests that practitioners can mostly have their cake and eat it too. Yet the most likely outcome of embracing post-welfarist reform is values drift towards managerial schooling being accelerated. We also think that if schools' internal priorities are genuinely educational, there would be very little chance of alignment with external change since it is so problematic, as pointed out in Chapters 2 and 3. This kind of argument is apologist in as much as it encourages those in schools to see their way forward through post-welfarist reform rather than passively or more actively contesting it. As will be clear from the 'implications for practitioners' sections of this and other chapters, it is advice about the latter which practitioners need in managerialist times.

The New Structure of School Improvement (Joyce *et al.* 1999) also indicates concern about managerialist politics, making the argument, for instance, that schools need help rather than admonition, and that 'high stakes' managerial accountability measures will not work.[3] However, Joyce and colleagues seriously underplay the impact of social inequality on schooling and school improvement. Few 'serious' school improvement books are as confident as this one that schools can turn around the effects of structural inequality. An upbeat discussion, 'Unlocking the shackles of demography', highlights the apparent success of large-scale school improvement programmes such as Success for All but ignores the weight of evidence against school improvement being able to overcome the effects of social disadvantage. It even offers the misleading advice that

> there are numerous examples of schools where [the socio-economic, ethnic and gender] characteristics of students do not predict perform-ance. Where the learning environment is working optimally for all students, these variables do not predict attainment or lack thereof . . . If there are large demographic differences in achievement, you know right away that some aspect of the school can be improved.
>
> (Joyce *et al.* 1990: 64)

This is completely overstating the case for school improvement. How many schools are there where students' social backgrounds do not (substantially) predict their achievement? Surely the pervasive impact of structural inequality means that even excellent schools could still have large differences between the achievement of different groups of students? Moreover, even if some teachers and principals *can* achieve extraordinary levels of achievement with low socio-economic and minority students, how sustainable is this, and how useful is it in policy terms? As Mortimore and Whitty (1997: 6) note: 'we must . . . be aware of the dangers of basing a national strategy for change on the efforts of outstanding individuals working in exceptional circumstances'. By implying that there are technical solutions to social inequality in education, this kind of insufficiently cautious discourse fosters the politics of blame surrounding so-called failing schools in a policy climate dominated by managerialism.

Gray

The *Let's be Realistic!* review discussed Gray's work and noted that his analyses tend to be more careful and more realistic than most. For instance, in *Good School, Bad School* (Gray and Wilcox 1995), Gray approached previous case studies of school improvement with a healthy scepticism:

> Most case studies of improving schools report that some improve-ment (eventually) occurred. In our view such studies, biased as they tend to be towards the change efforts that worked, probably give too rosy an impression of how much change can take place over relatively short periods of time.
>
> (Gray and Wilcox 1995: 244)

Nevertheless, the review suggested that Gray's preferred role was that of the 'neutral' researcher providing 'objective' findings for policy makers and that his work was insufficiently critical when it came to the nature and impact of policy. The same problem is apparent in an introduction that Gray wrote for the 2001 edition of *Success Against the Odds* discussed earlier (Gray 2001). This provides an excellent account of the limits and possibilities of school improvement and yet remains coy about the impact of national policy on schools.

Gray sets the scene as follows:

> It would be encouraging to think that policy-makers had somehow succeeded during the last three years [1997–2000, the first three years of New Labour's first term] in beginning to weaken the 'link between disadvantage and educational performance'. The history of educational reform efforts in this area however, underlines the extent of the challenges and counsels a degree of caution. Politicians meanwhile have learnt to drive harder bargains . . . '*Improving* against the odds is now the name of the game'
>
> (pp. 1–2, emphasis in original)

This is about right, although we would have said 'considerable caution' about the lessons of history and would have wanted to link the harder bargains of politicians to the managerialist trends in public policy more generally. Gray goes on to say that he does not know whether the *Success Against the Odds* schools would have improved or not over the past five years but because they were already at the peak one could not expect them to have improved much, indeed 'continuing to live with the fractures and stresses of social deprivation may be challenge enough' (p. 3). This seems realistic and fair.

Gray's next section (pp. 4–7) is about apparent national improvements in school performance and classroom teaching. Here Gray notes that part of what seems an improvement in classroom teaching is most likely due to Ofsted's decision to alter the scale employed to judge lessons. However, he does not mention that the improvement in primary and secondary test scores may also reflect not genuine improvement but issues such as teaching to the test and cheating. Related to this, his discussion about league tables (pp. 7–8) talks of schools 'vary[ing] in their understanding of the national changes and the speed with which they explore and exploit their implications but, within a relatively, short time, most seem to have caught on and caught up' (p. 8). 'Catching on and catching up' is not a critical enough description of the performative pressures schools are placed under, and while the word 'improve' is placed in quotes to indicate improvement may not really be occurring, a discussion of the likely costs of national initiatives is needed here.

The difficulties of defining improvement are the subject of the next section of Gray's introduction and one of the key issues discussed here is whether improvement should be measured in terms of outcomes or processes (pp. 9–11). Gray notes that Harris (2000: 6) has suggested that 'what distinguishes the school improvement movement from other school reform efforts is the under-standing that it is necessary to focus upon student outcomes in academic performance as the key success criteria, rather than teacher perceptions of the innovation'. Gray comments that 'as a description of an orientation amongst influential contributors this is probably *increasingly true*. However it does not, as yet, accurately reflect the criteria employed in most school improvement studies' (p. 11, our emphasis). Here Gray could have discussed *why* school improvement research is becoming increasingly outcomes-focused since it undoubtedly reflects the managerialist emphasis of policy.

The following section is entitled 'The dimensions of "improvement" ' and takes a suitably cautious approach to what has really been achieved in cases where improvement is said to have occurred. This section also discusses Special Measures, part of the regime of official school improvement in the UK. Here Gray comments that 'the case of so-called "failing" schools in England, however, presents a situation where questions about the speed and extent of improvement have become crucial to schools' survival. These schools have typically been given only a two year window to secure a turnaround' (p. 16). Although one senses that Gray thinks this is problematic, he provides no dis-cussion of the rights or wrongs of the policy. Similarly, he goes on to raise questions about the supposed success of Special Measures but only in the most gentle way. Instead of saying that firm evidence for the success of Special Measures just is not there, particularly given Ofsted's weak inspection meth-odology and highly politicized stance, he uses phrases such as

> Unfortunately, whilst inspectors have doubtlessly been able to con-vince themselves that changes have occurred in specific cases, more systematic evidence [on improvement in achievement] across large numbers of schools has yet to be published . . .
>
> (p. 17)

and

> evidence on what it is [about improved 'capacities'] which has actu-ally impressed inspectors is harder to come by.
>
> (p. 18)

Still, Gray next provides a frank summing up of the limitations of school improvement research

> First . . . [most] of the literature simply asserts that 'improvement' has taken place . . . Second, the extent to which improvement is reported to have taken place is heavily dependent on whose perceptions are given greatest weight . . . Third, . . . progress in one area may well be at

the expense of progress in others. Fourth, there is as yet little agreement about the timescales over which *major* improvements take place ... Fifth, changes to school management and organisation seem easier to secure than changes to classroom practice ... Sixth, ... most studies to date have been rather short on evidence of *measured* improvements over time ... Seventh, some researchers have argued that it is more difficult for schools serving disadvantaged areas to make progress on many of the traditional indicators ... [more] evidence on this issue is needed. Finally, there is a shortage of evidence about the extent to which schools manage to sustain improvement.

(Gray 2001: 18–19, emphasis in original)

Such acknowledgement of the extent to which school improvement is empirically 'up for grabs' is very refreshing compared with most school improvement texts. Gray goes on to elaborate a number of these points. For instance, he points to most schools adopting a quick-fix 'tactical' rather than longer-term capacity-building approach to school improvement and notes the links between this and performativity as schools play the 'improvement game' (p. 30). Gray also discusses the constraints of context at some length and notes that even teachers may undervalue what low SES schools are achieving with their own students (pp. 32–4).

Gray's final comments are also interesting because he returns to post-welfarist education reform by recounting the rather desperate measures being used in Texas to raise test scores – pep rallies, 'camps', 'lock-ins' to do test drills and the like. But rather than railing against the educational damage being done by such an 'unfortunate' approach to boosting test scores, Gray's main concern is that policy makers have a too restricted view of what school improvement involves. Although he suggests that such trends are potentially worrying for the UK, his assessment of New Labour's school improvement policies like Education Action Zones and Excellence in Cities is more favourable because of the way they deliver resources to schools and allow some autonomy to schools to respond to their local context.

Overall it will be clear that we have mixed feelings about this account. On the one hand, we support much of what Gray has to say, especially his careful, no-nonsense approach to how much improvement is really likely to be occurring. On the other hand, Gray's criticisms of current education policy are too restrained to avoid the problem of textual apologism. In our view the reader does not get a sufficiently critical perspective on post-welfarist reform and the net effect will be to encourage readers to go along with policy, rather than contest it.

The jointly authored book *Improving Schools: Performance and Potential* (Gray *et al.* 1999) borders on overt apologism in places. In this book Gray and colleagues comment that 'There is much in the school effectiveness research that resonates with . . . the apparently increasing concern of government to intervene with a view to improvement' (p. 29). Yet Hatcher and Hirtt question this, suggesting that this comment, and the various examples Gray and his colleagues provide to support it, is very much a case of wishful thinking:

> Let us put a blunt question to the school improvement movement: how do they see the body of theory and practice which they are developing relate to the neo-liberal agenda which is driving government policy? . . . Does the Tory marketisation of the school really represent what school improvers mean by the school as a unit of change? How closely does Michael Fullan's conception of pressure and support correspond to the pressure exerted by Chris Woodhead's regime? Is their notion of the role of the Head the same as that envisaged in the Green Paper, controlling teachers through performance-related pay? The answers are: of course not, there is a gulf between them, which the school improvement movement typically (with some exceptions) prefers to gloss over . . . Gray and his co-authors scarcely mention key elements of the official agenda such as increased selection and differentiation, and make no mention at all of the drive towards commercialisation and privatisation.
>
> (Hatcher and Hirtt 1999: 20–1)

On the other hand, there is a section on school contexts in Gray *et al.* which involves at least some muted criticism of educational quasi-markets:

> Within a value-added framework for analysing school's performances the 'disadvantaged' natures of the school's catchment areas should not, of course, explain their levels of effectiveness, or should do so only marginally. But, in fact, the problems associated with social disadvantage and creamed intakes clearly figured prominently in the legacy with which each school had to deal. Such concerns also formed part of the backdrop against which efforts to improve had to be formulated. A good deal of the energy (and especially that of the senior management) that might otherwise have been devoted to developing and sustaining change efforts *within* the schools was actually spent shoring up relationships with local communities to make sure the school survived.
>
> (Gray *et al.* 1999: 63)

Although not as acute as in his introduction to *Success Against the Odds*, the book also has Gray's trademark carefulness stamped on it in places: 'In the areas of school effectiveness and improvement it seems unwise to assert too forcibly what works' (p. 31).

Hopkins

Hopkins has been a prolific writer in the area of school improvement for many years (see, for example, Hopkins 1987, 1996, 2001; Hopkins *et al.* 1994). The *Let's be Realistic!* review focused on *School Improvement in an Era of Change* (Hopkins *et al.* 1994) and argued that this demonstrated an extremely decontextualized approach to improvement issues and a rather diffident stance to the politics of reform. To begin with, this text employed only generalized models and concepts, which rarely acknowledged any impact of social class or socio-economic status (SES) on school processes. For instance, although Hopkins (Hopkins *et al.* 1994: 20) argued that the school improvement agenda was about changing the culture of schools, his discussion concentrated on organizational notions of culture rather than making any mention of social class culture and its impact on schools. Even his discussion of the importance of pupil and parent involvement in schools made no mention of the impact of social class. When 'context' was discussed, it was never SES context (or gender or ethnic context for that matter), but other, more general contexts such as the classroom (p. 118) or the 'size, shape and location' of schools (p. 151). Meanwhile, Hopkins sometimes discussed the politics of reform but his position was vague. For instance, in Hopkins *et al.* (1994: 12) he argued: 'We have no evidence to suggest that accountability and increased competition, as strategies for improving the quality of education for all, actually work'. He also commented that 'we appear to be living in an Alice in Wonderland world of educational reform where the sole rationale for many policies is the public support for them by a small group of ideologically committed politicians' (p. 18). On the other hand, he did not cite any of the critics of British education policy and he spoke of working with schools 'within the framework of the national reform agenda' (p. 2). Mostly, however, he seemed to prefer to hedge his bets as to the outcomes of reform. We were told, 'Whatever one thinks of our national reforms . . . The jury is still out', and 'Whatever one's position . . . there are lessons to be learned' (pp. 5–6).

By 1998, however, Hopkins was indicating a growing concern with the social and political context of schooling. He noted 'a failure to embed school improvement initiatives within a contextual and diagnostic analysis', and went on to indicate the importance of SES and market contexts, among others (Hopkins 1998: 1048). On the other hand, he seemed to hold the view that school improvement could hold out in the face of neo-liberal ideologies and reform programmes. In 1996 he argued:

> schools which are developing [as a result of school improvement] are those which are able to 'survive with integrity' in times of change . . . In other words the schools that are developing continue to keep abreast with innovation within the context of a pervasive political

> reform agenda, whilst remaining true to the educational futures they desire for their students.
>
> (Hopkins 1996: 32–3)

Yet, as Hatcher (1998b) points out, the research evidence on the impact of reform simply does not bear out this claim, rather he suggests that 'it is not so much that "school improvement" has enabled schools to resist the Conservative offensive, rather that "school improvement" itself has tended to accommodate to it' (Hatcher 1998b: 270).

In view of the above we wondered whether Hopkins' most definitive book *School Improvement for Real* (Hopkins 2001) would demonstrate a shift towards a more socially and politically critical stance. The answer is not straightforward. It is certainly a much broader and more contextualized book than the kind Hopkins used to write. Nevertheless, from a critical perspective it contains numerous contradictions, tensions and silences.

A key problem stems from Hopkins' view of policy. This book says much more about policy than his previous ones (which is good), but it is clear that, following Milbrey McLaughlin, Hopkins primarily sees national policy in managerialist times as ineffectual rather than damaging: 'policy cannot mandate what matters' (McLaughlin 1990: 12, cited in Hopkins 2001: 5). This is variously because reform is not proximal enough to the classroom, because there is not enough attention to the way school organization supports learning and because most reforms do not adopt a systemic perspective which has depth as well as width (p. 5). Hopkins therefore stresses the need for school improvement to 'drive down to the "learning level" ', in other words to concentrate on teaching and learning in schools rather than assuming that changes at other levels will bring changes in the classroom. He is also keen to differentiate his approach of 'real' or 'authentic' improvement which supports teaching and learning from what he describes as the 'quick fix and short term responses which characterise many current school improvement efforts' (p. xi). He says that 'Governments whose policies emphasise accountability and managerial change fail to realise that if teachers knew how to teach more effectively they would themselves have done so decades ago' (p. 1).

This is important but only goes part of the way because what is not here is a recognition that policy may often reach its goal but in a negative sense, that is be damaging rather than just ineffectual. (Examples of the damaging nature of post-welfarist educational reform were discussed in Chapter 3, for instance the way Ofsted inspections and target-setting lead to fabrication, teaching to the test and loss of creativity or the negative impact of the market on children's self-concepts.) This helps to explain why Hopkins can appear critical of reform on the one hand but is able to lead the DfES's school improvement programme on the other. It is because fundamentally he agrees with the direction of New Labour's reforms[4] but just does not think they will work without the more proximal and sophisticated approach to school reform taken by school improvement. Indeed, his framework for school improvement actually builds in Ofsted, Local Management of Schools (LMS), the National Literacy strategy and the National Curriculum on the assumption that these could be a force for good, that is that the 'national reform agenda' could pull in the same direction and be reciprocal with other elements of authentic school improvement and this would allow it more chance of success (see pp. 68–9).

This perception of policy is developed in Hopkins' final chapter, 'The policy context for school improvement'. This begins with a critique of 'performance based' approaches to large-scale reform as being ineffective because they do not focus on teaching, learning and capacity-building at the school level. However, there is no discussion of such policies being inequitable as well. The chapter continues with lessons for policy from the research on authentic school improvement, discussion of local infrastructures and networks, a policy framework for authentic school improvement and ways that governments can move this agenda forward (Hopkins 2001: 184). This is all interesting and there are many points on which we could agree, at least in part. But most of Hopkins' recommendations (pp. 182–200) are also problematic or raise difficult questions. Here are the recommendations with our comments and reflections in brackets:

- Keep an unrelenting focus on student achievement and learning. (This is intended to be wider than test scores but agreeing the focus of schooling is not simple – there is a whole politics of curriculum 'basics' and frills to contend with.)
- Develop curriculum and teaching programmes that are based on what is known about learning. (It is all very well developing curriculum and teaching programmes as a menu for teachers but this is a top down model and may not lead to the best classroom practices.)
- Pay attention to context – one size does not fit all – develop knowledge about what works and where. (It is good to see attention given to social as well as to performance contexts and we shall come back to this. Hopkins also indicates the need for a range of curriculum and instructional programmes suited to the contexts of different schools. But how far would he take this? Taken to its logical end this is a call for curricular justice, a fundamental shift in curriculum, pedagogy and assessment to suit groups other than just the white middle class (Connell 1994). However, this goes against the historical trend of school curricula being determined by dominant social groups. It would face enormous political resistance but there is nothing to indicate that Hopkins realizes the profound implications of what he is proposing.)
- Build capacity and strengthen known capacity-creating components. (Hopkins indicates that teacher and leadership training and schemes

for inspection would be part of capacity-building. Yet these activities are themselves currently infected by reductionist managerial and prescriptive approaches to education so that exposure to such courses is often likely to compound poor teaching and management rather than improve it.)

- Nurture professional learning communities and provide incentives for teacher and school enquiry. (It is all very well nurturing professional learning communities through workshops and through reorganizing schools as Hopkins suggests, but managerialism is working against this because of the intensification of work and the divisive effects of performance-related pay which result in the declining sociability of teaching.)
- Improve research and dissemination and make it practitioner-relevant. (The notion of evidence-based policy has become fashionable. But governments have a knack of discounting evidence they find unpalatable; it is a real, if unfortunate, part of the political process – see Elliott 2001b.)
- Create a commitment to, and allow time for, effective implementation. ('Implementation' is a term we have a problem with because policies are rarely simply implemented: they are changed, struggled with, modified, subverted and so on. What is clear, however, is that this process is rarely of interest to politicians because of its lengthy timeline. As Levin (2001) points out, announcing new policies has much more political mileage.)
- Link pressure and support at all levels of the system. (Here, we would simply point out that 'pressure' has important costs and is in tension with nurturing professional learning communities. It reflects a low-trust view of teachers and fails to tap into virtue ethics – making sure people are well trained then leaving them to get on with the job.)
- Establish local infrastructures and networks, supported by quality external facilitation. (We have no problem with local infrastructures and networks. But Hopkins also argues of LEAs or school districts that, apart from their school improvement role, 'it may well be that many – if not all – of these organisations have reached their "sell-by date" '. This chimes with the neo-liberal attack on bureaucracy but, as discussed in Chapter 9, the strengths of bureaucracy are often bypassed or played down.)
- Ensure policy coherence. (This sounds great but, as discussed below, there are many reasons why policy is not nicely coherent.)

Hopkins' policy framework for authentic school improvement involves the following:

- Clear targets. (The problem with targets is that they encourage more concern with outcomes than process and this leads to fabrication and a hollowing out of authenticity.)
- The development and piloting of curriculum and instructional programmes that directly address the government and school targets. (We agree with the point about schools not having to reinvent the wheel but, as above, have concerns about creating top-down models and working towards highly specified targets.)
- A menu of programme options of different kinds for schools. (The problem here is that the contextual specificity of schools will always severely limit the usefulness of 'off the shelf' programmes.)
- Funding targeting to those in greatest need. (We agree with a redistributive approach to policy but a good level of universal provision also needs to be maintained.)

This would require a 'fundamentally new and radical way of thinking about education reform'. Governments can move this agenda forward by the following means:

- By regarding the principles Hopkins outlines as an integrated approach to school improvement policy. (As indicated, the principles also present many difficulties – to regard them as 'an integrated set of research-based criteria against which policies can be formulated and evaluated' would be to discount research that raises different patterns and trends.)
- By having a clear link between resources and outcomes and avoiding having schools manage multiple bids and getting involved in a set of programmes which are not coherent. (One of the problems with educational processes is that often there is no very clear link between resources and outcomes. We agree that the bidding process encouraged by the managerial funder/provider split is burdensome and counter-productive.)
- By having policies which are aligned both horizontally and vertically. (This sounds great, but again, as discussed below, there are many reasons why policy is not nicely aligned.)
- By regarding the building of local capacity as being as important as a coherent national policy. (We have no problem with this as a genuine project but not where local arrangements are simply used to relay problematic national policy. We would also be uneasy about the use of initial teacher training to disseminate teach 'key improvement strategies and skills' (p. 199). The focus of Initial Teacher Training (ITT) has to remain on good teaching in the first instance.)

- By insisting that schools be thoughtful in their approach to change and improvement but not require everyone to do the same thing at the same time. (If schools are to be thoughtful in their approach to change and improvement, their staffs need to be exposed to critical perspectives but this is typically not the case in government-sponsored courses and materials. Also, in this section Hopkins says that 'governments could continue to focus, if they wish, on matters of achievement, standards and accountability, but they would now do so with more confidence that their policies are likely to bring about the conditions they say they desire' (p. 200). This hardly suggests a clear critique of the market, managerialism or performativity.)

Most of these issues relate to the general problem with Hopkins' approach to policy – the fact that it comes out of a 'policy science' rather than 'policy scholarship' approach to policy. Grace (1995: 2–3) describes policy science as

> a form of social and educational analysis which attempts to extract a social phenomena from its relational context in order to subject it to close analysis. Following the models of natural science from which it is derived, it is relatively uninterested in the history or cultural antecedents of the phenomena under investigation. The concern of a policy science approach is to understand present phenomena (especially present crisis phenomena) in order to formulate a rational and scientific prescription for action and future policy.

Grace goes on to note that what tends to be excluded from the policy science perspective is the relation of surface social phenomenon to the deep structure of historical, cultural, political, ideological, and value issues and the analysis of power relations within which policy questions are located (p. 3). This is exemplified in the way Hopkins' approach to policy is not linked back to its neo-liberal and managerialist roots (indeed Hopkins hardly uses such terms), and in the way history and social structure have such a thin presence in his writing. Nor is there any substantial critique or reference to critical literature on the national or international policy context. The result of Hopkins' policy science approach is that, just as Ball (1994: 68) has described his account of development planning as a case of 'management in the best of all possible schools', his is a vision of policy-making at its unrealistic best. To Hopkins it is only the 'cynic' who thinks devolution along with accountability at the local level is a case of governments trying to have their cake and eat it too (p. 3).

In contrast to policy science, policy scholarship (or critical policy analysis, policy sociology) resists the tendency of policy science to abstract problems from their relational setting by insisting that the problem can only be understood in the complexity of those relations (Grace 1995). As Ben Levin (2001) well illustrates, the problem with policy-making is that party politics, civil service politics, economic and electoral considerations all probably get more influence in the policy process than educational considerations *per se*. Indeed, Levin (2001: 23) suggests that 'an adequate account' of policy-making should take account of the following:

- Political decisions are shaped by many considerations, including the requirements of staying in office and the vicissitudes of the moment as well as the beliefs and commitments of policy makers and their advisors.
- Politics is substantially shaped by symbolic considerations that may have little to do with the real effects of policies.
- Human abilities to understand problems and generate appropriate solutions are limited and often inadequate to the complexity of the problems. The entire process of policy development and implementation takes place in a context that is constantly changing, multifaceted and very difficult to read.
- Strategies for reform may focus on elements that are politically salient but that cannot produce the kinds of changes we really want, or, to put it another way, the focus may be on what can be done instead of on what might really make a difference (this is Hopkins' major point too).
- Institutions such as schools or governments posses considerable ability to resist or alter policies to fit their own dynamics.
- History and culture are very powerful influences on policy and practice.

Ball (1998a: 126) goes further:

> National policy making is inevitably a process of bricolage: a matter of borrowing and copying bits and pieces of idea from elsewhere, drawing upon and amending locally tried and tested approaches, cannibalising theories, research, trends and fashions and not infrequently flailing around for anything at all that looks as though it might work.

Against such views of policy, Hopkins' view of what is feasible is far too technical and rational. Many of his proposals simply would not work as intended and could be expected to have all kinds of unintended effects. Nevertheless, it is his view of policy which colours his stance on the role of school improvement:

> Strategies for authentic school improvement are needed because externally imposed changes are not capable of directly enhancing the

> learning and achievement of students. If, as McLaughlin argues (1990) policy does not mandate what matters and local implementation determines outcomes, then some form of linkage to mediate between policy and outcome is required.
>
> (Hopkins 2001: 58)

Here it can be seen that school improvement is intended to fill the void left by ineffectual policy. In this respect there are echoes of the 1996 stance noted earlier, that schools can do well despite policy. As Hopkins points out, the Improving the Quality of Education for All (IQEA) project – an example of authentic school improvement – encouraged schools to see the potential in adapting external change to internal purpose. However, because Hopkins has no particular problem with recent post-welfarist policy (except that he sees it having too little impact), there is no sense in this book that school improvement might actually mean *resisting* damaging reforms. Nor is there any searching discussion of school improvement's political and ideological use in the current political environment.[5] Instead, practitioners are being asked to embrace change:

> school improvement strategies [need] to evolve and become more authentic, in order to meet the challenge of external change. At the start of a new century it is not sufficient for school improvement to develop on its own terms, it also needs to be responsive to the changing demands of the external educational environment.
>
> (Hopkins 2001: 57)

This signals another problem with Hopkins' account: the uncritical way it views other education management literatures. There is a chapter on school change and school effectiveness and we are told 'the field of school improvement . . . lags behind both of these areas of research and practice, and has much to learn from them' (pp. 34–5). But in fact these are both deeply problematic literatures (see Morley and Rassool 1999; Willmott 1999, 2002a; Thrupp 2001a for the school effectiveness literature, Chapter 9 of this book for the school change literature). We are told (Hopkins 2001: 18) that authentic school improvement is interventionist and strategic, influenced by the contemporary emphasis on development planning. But again, both strategic human resource management and the school development planning literatures are deeply problematic (see Chapter 7 of this book).

Hopkins sees value in critical theory and is keen to locate school improvement within that philosophical tradition (Hopkins 2001: 18). Nevertheless, this is a long reach since his book indicates little concern with fundamental social and political critique. The references in this book also suggest that critical writing about education in relation to social structure or politics is mostly off the radar. And is school improvement really emancipatory in any fundamental sense? We are told (p. 18) that authentic school improvement is empowering in aspiration in the tradition of Dewey, Freire and Stenhouse. But if this were true we would expect much more discussion in school improvement of the curriculum and of matching the curriculum to student interest.

The final issue we want to signal has to do with context. There is a great deal of discussion of context in Hopkins' book and it is seen as a feature of authentic school improvement programmes – 'Context-specific – they pay attention to the unique features of the school situation and build strategies on the basis of an analysis of that particular context' (Hopkins 2001: 17). This seems a welcome shift from Hopkins' earlier book, and in the policy chapter late in the book the impact of poverty does get serious, if qualified, mention:

> Much also depends, of course, on what we mean by 'lower-performing' and 'higher-performing' schools. The social context of the school has a powerful effect both on achievement levels and on strategies to improve achievement. Problems of poverty, especially, are unlikely to be managed using a strategy that focuses only on curriculum and instruction (Levin 1995, Mortimore and Whitty 1997). The policy implications are two-fold. First make provision for contextual differences in policy prescriptions. Do not, however, allow this to be used as an excuse by underperforming schools. Poverty may explain a certain level of under-achievement, and this may provide an argument for additional support. It is not however a reason to accept failure on a continuing basis.
>
> (Hopkins 2001: 186)

What is interesting here is the clear distinction made between schools affected by poverty and those 'underperforming', whereas we would argue that poverty is related to 'underperformance' through compositional effects on school processes (Thrupp 1999). Surely, too, if poverty has an impact on achievement, it is going to have a continuing impact until the poverty itself is addressed. But in any case, when Hopkins considers context he more often means differential capacity for improvement and this is generally discussed in a way which is not linked back to wider social context. So, for instance, his chapter on differential improvement talks about the strategies which can be employed to improve the 'failing or ineffective' school, the 'low achieving' school, the 'good or effective' school. But the reader gets very little sense of these different contexts being linked back to social structure which is generally missing from most of the book.[6] Instead, Hopkins continues to put much weight on teacher expectations:

My own experience of school improvement interventions in a wide range of settings suggests that all too often there is a powerful and insidious collusion at work in many social, urban and educational settings that create a hegemony which fundamentally depresses learning: 'the kids around here just can't learn' or 'that is a nice caring school, what a pity about the results.' The challenge therefore is to discover how an ethos of high expectations can be created in a context where many believe there is little cause for optimism.

(p. xii)

Some recommendations for practitioners

We have argued that while there have been some significant contextual shifts in the school improvement area over the past few years, important problems continue. In particular, school improvement writers remain mostly caught up in problem-solving discourses that do not tap into critical research on social inequality or the impact of post-welfarist educational reform such as that highlighted in Chapter 3. Consequently their protests about current government policy are muted.

We think practitioners in schools need to be aware of these problems in the literature but it does not mean that improved schools are not worth working towards. Instead improvement needs to be radically recast as part of a much wider social and educational project. Yet while there are case studies of schools which have taken alternative paths to improvement (see, for example, Apple and Beane 1999), we recognize that the ethical and educational pitfalls of official school improvement are becoming increasingly difficult to avoid.

Most immediately, then, the challenge is to 'do no harm' in pursuit of official school improvement. This will often mean different things in advantaged and less advantaged school settings. To give a few examples, staff in popular, high SES schools could be modest about the relative popularity of their schools, accepting that a school deemed to be of poor quality or failing may, in real terms, have teachers and senior staff who are working harder and smarter than themselves. They could also be honest in their public statements about the way in which their schools gain advantage from their high SES intakes and support any moves to provide additional resources to disadvantaged schools which need them most. On the other hand, staff in low SES schools could take heart from knowing that what they are doing is of genuine importance, and that they are probably doing it as well as can reasonably be expected given the circumstances. They could also commit themselves to improving the learning of the students currently at their school rather than targeting middle-class families as a means of bringing about a change in the status of their schools. In all schools, practitioners could refuse to engage in unfair practices such as 'educational triage' and ensure that their own school's practices are the least selective or exclusionary possible. Heads and teachers should also make good use of the potential gulf between official policy and classroom practice in the service of their students. For instance, when schools are often being asked to impose inappropriate or damaging curriculum or assessment innovations, paying only lip service to what is required or fabricating performance may be entirely justifiable.

A further challenge involves all those important things that good schools should do but often do not do because of performative pressures. These include teaching about social inequalities and political processes, teaching a culturally appropriate curriculum, and teaching a wider and richer curriculum than that encouraged by official school improvement. Stealing time and energy to do this is, we accept, a major challenge and, again, fabrication will often be required. Nevertheless, the key goal is not only to be more searching about what constitutes good schooling beyond the reductionist targets encouraged by official school improvement, but also to put that perspective at the centre of school life rather than having it crowded out by managerialist concerns.

7 School development planning and strategic human resource management

Initially, we intended to devote separate chapters to school development planning (SDPing) and (strategic) human resource management (HRM); then, as we decided to focus on ascendant literatures, to write only about strategic HRM. However, we have looked at both since SDPing and strategic HRM are now inseparable in the burgeoning education management literature, even if strategic HRM, it will be argued, must incorporate, and ultimately overshadow, SDPing. Indeed, *Performance Management in Schools* (DfEE 2000: 6) maintains that the School Development Plan (SDP) 'will provide an important background'. As Fidler (1997) puts it, 'Development planning is a useful precursor to strategic planning' (p. 87). Further, he holds that 'it should be clear that since strategy is such a fundamental part of a school's operations its creation must be integrated' (p. 92). And for Valerie Hall (1997), 'Strategic management and planning increasingly become everybody's responsibility' (p. 160). She maintains that while strategic HRM can be both liberating and constraining, it allows managers to combine accountability and freedom.

However, the above claims are not based on any evidence; indeed, despite a few notable exceptions, the education management literature on development planning, strategy and human resource management is unreflective and tends towards uncritical acceptance and legitimation of the status quo. In fact, there is an active elevation of 'strategy', incorporating relatively recent management fads such as business process reengineering (BPR), all of which complement and extend the managerialist restructuring of education. As argued throughout this book, the very premises on which such textbooks are based are flawed. Again, the reason for writing this book stems from the need to expose the silences and omissions of such literature and to suggest ways in which we can avoid – or at least be aware of – its anti-educational nature. This chapter addresses SDPing in the first instance then moves on to (strategic) HRM. Until recently, HRM was commonly known as personnel management. The change to HRM need not detain us. Within HRM techniques of recruitment, selection and motivation have been developed and refined in order to identify and harness the energies of employees. Instructively, the HRM orientation has been adopted by the apologists, since the

> HRM orientation appears particularly pertinent . . . as to the ways in which it is anticipated that the management of autonomous educational organizations will develop in a market environment. The HRM perspective articulated here is fully consistent with the notion of flexible, responsive schools and colleges.
>
> (O'Neill 1994: 201)

School development planning: textual apologism and contradiction

We want to make clear at the outset that we are not against planning *per se*. Yet planning should be an educational aid rather than a managerial tool of (external) accountability. In other words, the implementation and evaluation of any plan(s) should take into account contextual features such as 'school mix' (Thrupp 1999), prior funding arrangements (that may not be the responsibility of the school), and teachers' skills and experiences. The problem arises immediately when one places planning in an outcomes-based managerialist framework. In his critique of the aims-and-objectives approach in education, Bottery argues that if aims and objectives are interpreted too rigidly (or, we would add, plans executed too rigidly), necessarily they

> exclude the interests, experiences and understanding of those being taught. They prevent the true educational experience from taking place, and ultimately must alienate those taught, for it becomes very clear very quickly that theirs is a voice which will not be heard . . . A too-rigid adherence to the notion of aims and objectives is only a modern instance of the kind of bad teaching that has been going on in some schools and some classrooms for an awfully long time: only now it seems to be given official blessing.
>
> (Bottery 1992: 27–8)

Logan *et al.* (1994), while noting the potential of SDPing for 'organisational learning', nevertheless suggest that it denies the moral aspects of management: 'The central dilemma raised in SDP revolves around the issue of whose interests is the school now serving – the state, system, teachers, community or pupils?' (cited in Ball 1997c: 329). It is precisely the lack of direct engagement with such dilemmas that results in contradictory discussion of the utility of planning in some of 'more apologetic' literature. Smith's (2001) research, for example, indicates that teachers have responded to the government training agenda by emphasizing those short-term examinable characteristics that can be most easily evidenced and assessed. In turn, this may not engage pupils or facilitate professional engagement. Smith (2001: 323) quotes a headteacher, who said he had asked a job applicant how he knew he had taught a good lesson and received the answer 'because I planned it'. The headteacher considered this underscored the unfortunate reality that 'some breadth may have been lost in the training process'.

Just as the educational value of planning is recognized, equally we accept the potential of target-setting. At the same time, however, we have found that even relatively critical texts on school development planning and strategy are not as explicit as they should be in terms of providing the cigarette manufacturer's equivalent of an educational health warning. In other words, as Fielding (2001: 145) argues,

> the broader, more profound point is that there are real dangers that distorting the importance of clarity within a strongly instrumental process like target setting runs the risk of severely weakening its essential links with the larger undertaking which it is designed to serve. Target setting is a means to a wider educational end, not an end in itself.

Crucially, then, as he notes, while the pragmatic virtues of target-setting may include an apparent capacity to raise test scores, we need to ask questions about *how* those tests scores are raised (for example through an increasing incidence of 'teaching to the test', greater competition and substantial individual and group pressure), and *whose* test scores are raised. In turn, this raises concern about the moral integrity of the application of target-setting under conditions of external pressure. Thus, we are against the managerialist usurpation of target-setting that promotes efficiency over ethics and the concomitant virtual abandonment of real educational experiences for children and students.

Like Fielding, we have no objections to measurability *per se*, but object to what Fielding calls the 'idolatry of measurement', which, he rightly notes, is both more likely and more necessary within a context that sets its standards and rests its future on the attainment of publicly accessible, readily understandable outcomes. Those teachers who harbour deep-seated worries about the managerialist imposition of target-setting that underpins SDPing should, as far as possible, voice their worries, since any strength of conviction about the necessity of measurement 'blinds its proponents to the limitations of current instruments and we all end up not only mismeasuring the measurable but misrepresenting the immeasurable or elusive aspects of education which so often turn out to be *central to our deeper purposes and more profound aspirations*' (Fielding 2001: 146, our emphasis). As Fielding also asks:

> How many teachers, particularly those of younger children, are now able to listen openly, attentively and in a non-instrumental, exploratory way to their children/students without feeling guilty, stressed or vaguely uncomfortable about the absence of criteria or the insistence of a target tugging at their sleeve?
>
> (p. 146)

Willmott (2002a) found that even (primary) schools deemed successful by Ofsted are now narrowing the curriculum in order to meet government literacy and numeracy targets. This is not an aberration and the trend is now towards homogeneity in terms of school organization. For instance, we have met primary heads who have felt guilty about devoting a whole week to arts-based activities. As Woods *et al.* (2001) note, despite less paperwork, less stark confrontation, more collegiality and trust on the part of Ofsted, in practice there is still a narrowness and exclusiveness of vision and homogeneity of practices based upon performativity. Indeed, teachers are still not trusted and are seen in a managerial rather than developmental context. Moreover, in their case study of Coombes primary school, Woods *et al.* found that while teachers there have appropriated the literacy hour to some degree, they remain perturbed by its prescriptive nature, unlike the looser-framed National Curriculum. In sum, Coombes teachers are finding their child-centred principles increasingly squeezed, 'and there seems little likelihood of this easing in the foreseeable future – rather the reverse, as the numeracy hour fills more of the day' (Woods *et al.* 2001: 88).

This chapter spells out the problems and dangers of the policies that middle or senior managers in schools are currently required to follow, implement and create. Although many are statutory requirements, there are good reasons to be deeply concerned and we will return to possible responses at the end of the chapter.

SDPing's overt apologists

For Leask and Terrell:

> Increased accountability through the publication of league tables of examination results, greater publicity about what goes on in individual schools and parental choice of schools has led to increased collective responsibility for the performance of the whole school.
>
> (Leask and Terrell 1997: 3)

This is an implicit acceptance of the accountability regime. Indeed, a few pages further, they write that

> As a middle manager you *will* need to accept that change is inevitable, systemic and essential . . . The introduction of the National Curriculum and its revisions is a case in point. Some may believe that after such a period of rapid change, a period of stability and consolidation is called for, however, they will be disappointed. *There will not be a period of 'no change' because there are too many interest groups attempting to perfect different aspects of the system.*
>
> (Leask and Terrell 1997: 10, our emphasis)[1]

The latter complements the *dirigiste* tone of, for example, the 1997 DfEE White Paper *Modernizing the Comprehensive Principle* (see Ozga 2000b: 100–7). At best, the authors are resigned to the incessant change that characterizes education reform at the moment. At worst, they are, by default or otherwise, legitimating the status quo. They write that 'the notion of continuously searching for better ways of achieving better results is not new to most teachers, although it has been popularised in much of the literature on change (Peters and Waterman, 1982, Hopkins *et al.*, 1994)' (Leask and Terrell 1997: 10). However, there are sound arguments against such unremitting change (or 'continuous improvement' in TQM-speak) and the change literature, which we address in Chapter 9 on school change. The point here is that while teachers are ever searching for better ways of achieving better results, such results may not be higher SATs scores. That is to say, we need to be crystal clear about the ways and the means: Leask and Terrell are conveniently forgetting to make explicit that development planning has been co-opted by managerialism. Indeed, the crude factor approach of school effectiveness, which readily lends itself to managerialist co-option (Willmott 2002a), is embraced. It is worth quoting the authors at length here:

> After constructing a model of best classroom practice, according to the research, [Creemers] goes on to describe the school conditions that support this practice in the classroom. Creemers' work identifies a number of factors which ensure effective learning in the classroom. He considers student level factors such as student aptitude, motivation and time spent on task, and he accepts the socio-ethnic variance in these factors. Nevertheless, he minimises this influence and argues for attention to be given to *an equally important, but more controllable, factor of teacher and organisational behaviour. He emphasises that what the teacher does in the classroom is important.* He then goes on to describe classroom and school level determinants of effectiveness including quality in policies about classroom instruction and its evaluation . . . These make a great deal of sense to any practitioner. Following this work, we suggest that the key school managers in leading and developing effective classroom practice are middle managers.
>
> (Leask and Terrell 1997: 7, our emphasis)[1]

As previously argued (Thrupp 1999; Willmott 1999), the generic tendency of school effectiveness research has been to play down (or deny) the reality of 'school mix', which Leask and Terrell, following Creemers, are quite content to do. The point is neither to minimize nor to inflate the reality of 'socio-ethnic variance': instead, SDPing should explicitly cater for such 'variance'. Yet, of course, such planning is now geared towards managerialist ends (competitive target-setting), which immediately precludes any serious consideration of educational outcome inequalities that derive from socio-economic and ethnic backgrounds. Indeed, the inequitable nature of the market educational reforms is taken as given. Equally, however, we are frustrated by the contradictory nod in the direction of such educational psychologists as Piaget, Bruner and Vygotsky. Yet there is no more than a nod: the nuts and bolts of such theorists are not discussed. We would prefer it if textual apologists like Leask and Terrell consistently follow the logic of the education reforms, that is, eschew Piaget *et al.* For, as Ball (2001b) argues, the contradictory nature of New Labour's reforms derives in part from an inherited and ultimately self-defeating, impoverished view of 'learning'.

Ironically, characteristic of this text is its inability to offer management solutions with regard to the implementation of education policy reforms. Thus, Leask and Terrell (1997: 35) write that, 'How you deal with difficult staff depends on circumstances'. Here, we arrive at one of the depressing ironies of much of both the educational and business management literature: their inability to provide neat solutions. Such solutions are chimerical: precisely because all managing is inherently value-laden, people-centred and ever operative in the open system that is society, ineluctably simple solutions can never be found.

The DfEE's *Performance Management in Schools* (April 2000) argues that

> Performance management works best when it is an integral part of a school's culture; is seen to be fair and open; understood by everyone and based on shared commitment to supporting continuous improvement and recognising success.
>
> (p. 4)

Apparently, 'there is strong evidence that where schools and individual teachers are clear about what they expect pupils to achieve, standards rise' (DfEE 2000: 3). How school managers actually deal with the 'challenge' of raising standards and daily exigencies we are not told. However, Paul McCallion, author of *The Competent School Manager* (part of the government's Achieving Excellence in Schools series), writes in respect of management style that

> The process by which effective leaders motivate others to achieve . . . can be variable. This aspect could be referred to as the 'approach' to

> leadership. *There is no absolute right or wrong leadership approach. These are defined in many different ways.*
>
> (McCallion 1998: 83, our emphasis)

So, there is no 'absolute' right or wrong way to manage or lead and, indeed, there are many different ways to lead in a non-absolute right or wrong way. McCallion immediately discusses the autocratic, or what he calls 'directive', style, thereby denuding it of its insidious practical import. This is held to be the most effective approach in a crisis, but may also be counter-productive, he informs us. McCallion remains unperturbed, since it is 'also true, however, that many people are happy to work for what is called a "benign autocrat". That is a leader who expects full obedience but in return will look after her people' (McCallion 1998: 83). Disappointingly, we are offered no evidence of the many people who are happy to work for a benign autocrat. Moreover the case studies that McCallion depicts are, he tells us, not seen to be prescriptive. In fact, in most of the case studies, 'there is no immediate solution as such, and analysis given, therefore, seeks to highlight the issues' (p. 129).

Hargreaves and Hopkins (1994)[2] echo the view of other overt apologists and government documentation that SDPing 'properly managed', will result in higher standards:

> There is no magic formula for bringing about school improvement; nor is it easily achieved, particularly by schools in socially deprived areas. Nevertheless ... even schools suffering from high levels of deprivation can achieve genuine improvements through careful rational planning and the commitment of teachers, heads, pupils and governors. That development planning can be effective is thus no longer in question.
>
> (Hargreaves and Hopkins 1994: ix)

It seems to us that we *are* being offered a magic formula, namely rational planning plus commitment. However, again, because schools are peopled and because schools operate in an open educational system, rational planning is not the best starting place for school improvement however it is defined. Hargreaves and Hopkins also promote HRM, and we will address their approach in the latter section of this chapter.

SDPing's subtle apologists

Quasi-marketization of education necessarily results in greater uncertainty for schools in terms of survival. Immediately, we can query the educational utility of planning: why bother if schools cannot predict pupil numbers, examination success and the non-flight of staff? Again, the problem is not that planning *per se* is anti- or non-educational; rather, it is the disregard for the wider (externally accountable) context that makes much of the literature a frustrating, and often contradictory, read. For example, Skelton *et al.* (1991) rightly note at the outset of *Development Planning for Primary Schools* that the creation of a plan does not guarantee success. But, in the next breath, we are told that 'in a time of increasing complexity, the usefulness of development plans in helping schools define a workable, reasonable and practical plan of action seems to us beyond doubt' (1991: 5). So, while a plan is useful, it may not issue in success: the logic is far from impeccable here. In order to be useful, some modicum of success is surely needed.

We are also told about increased accountability, which is uncritically accepted as given by Skelton and colleagues. Contradictorily, however, the authors maintain that 'we have to find ways of restoring the relatively low morale among many of our colleagues' (1991: 9). Moreover, they write that SDPing is 'as much about saying "No" as well as "Yes" – "No" for professional reasons' (1991: 10). This suggests movement to critique of the reforms, where professionalism dictates that certain (managerialist) aspects of the (imposed) planning process be rejected. It is a pity that the authors do not delve further, providing concrete examples of resistance and the limits of this. As well as arguing that school development planning and Ofsted inspections work as sophisticated 'disciplinary technologies', Ball (1997c) adds that procedures and techniques that are intended to make schools more visible and accountable paradoxically encourage opacity and the manipulation of representations (see also Chapter 5).

Skelton and colleagues argue that while target-setting is a planning mechanism with a number of benefits, we must avoid the temptation – and the pressure – to adopt success criteria or performance indicators, that is instructional targets, for everything. As they argue, the danger is of attempting to measure the immeasurable. To them, SDPing 'isn't an answer to all of the difficulties of a school. What it does is to establish, through appropriate and co-operative involvement, a series of targets, action steps and review procedures . . . Within the process things will still go wrong' (Skelton *et al.* 1991: 101). Furthermore, they argue that 'development planning cannot, by itself, create an effective school in which children and young people receive a focused and appropriate education which helps them to develop intellectually, spiritually, physically and emotionally' (p. 189). Overall their account remains a case of subtle apology but one that almost promises textual dissent.

MacGilchrist *et al.* (1995) have also written about SDPing. They recognize that at its worst, development planning may distract heads and teachers from other tasks and, 'if there is no pay off in terms of increased learning opportunities, it [planning] dissipates their time and energy' (1995: xii). They also underscore the fact that schools are being made more accountable and discuss the way that school effectiveness does not address adequately the issue of causality. However, we are not proffered alternatives. There is mention of the fact that targets should be expressive (as opposed to instrumental) but, again, only a superficial gloss is provided. Equally, the authors are critical of narrow management paradigms and the imposition or recommendation of unrealistic targets. In contrast, we have looked more closely at the nature of targets (above) and the need to contextualize them: while MacGilchrist *et al.* are right to highlight their concerns, they do not go far enough in scrutinizing the 'whole picture'.

Indeed, while we have noted their concerns about school effectiveness, later they write that SDPing is the means by which school effectiveness criteria can be integrated with school improvement strategies. As we have argued, school effectiveness criteria include a (shifting) number of 'factors' that are deemed, in positivist fashion, to constitute an 'effective school'. One of the so-called effectiveness correlates includes ethos or culture. MacGilchrist *et al.* maintain the importance of the latter, stating that development planning transforms the culture of the school by, among other things, 'creating management arrangements that empower' (p. 42). For us, along with other critical commentators, bringing the 'whole picture' back in necessarily means querying the notion of empowerment precisely because of the managerialist accountability measures in place. Interestingly, none of the headteachers in their research identified improving the pupils' achievement and the quality of their learning as the central purpose of development planning (p. 79). While we could speculate on why this should be, what we want to emphasize is the inherently contradictory nature of SDPing, which derives from its managerialist usurpation. In other words, it is not being suggested that SDPing on its own is contradictory; rather, it is the managerialist purposes to which it is being put. Of course, teachers and heads should plan, but planning in a context of unremitting pressures (specifically competition and target-setting) means that real learning needs will be eclipsed, the extent of which will depend on the school mix (intake) and extent of collegiality and positive educational leadership. Indeed, the oft-noted reality of teaching to the test is part of a deliberative planning process.

In fact, MacGilchrist *et al.* move away from their implicit critique and ultimately tread the managerialist path by emphasizing (a) measurable outcomes; (b) the need for a 'corporate plan', linked to resources; (c) the need for a clear 'mission'; (d) a focus on data collection. The business connotations are palpable here. The authors need to consider the contradictory manner in which they mix the need for both educational and accountability practices linked to planning. Such contradictory mixing is a recipe for disaster if education is the genuine priority.

(Strategic) human resource management

One of the most informative books on HRM in schools is Seifert's (1996) book *Human Resource Management in Schools*. His text is the exception that proves the rule, namely that textual apologism and outright championing of managerialist HRM reigns supreme in the education management literature. As the back cover blurb explains, Seifert provides a practical guide to the main issues of HRM facing school managers 'at a time when recent educational reforms have given rise to many problems in this area'. The book deals with a whole range of HRM topics including: the role of employers and managers; recruitment and selection; trade unions; performance, training and pay; conditions of service; employee relations and disputes; redundancy. Seifert emphazises the downward pressure on unit labour costs as a direct result of Local Management of Schools (LMS) and the 'serious problems and opportunities' that derive from the latter. Seifert, in his preface, does not 'shy away' from the 'bad news and difficult options'. Indeed, in chapter 1 he writes that 'not everyone will like this'. For us, this evinces a sense of guilt and frustration at the education reforms. He writes of the ugliness of such notions as productivity[3] and is critical of the drive towards developing 'mission statements' for all and so-called excellence: 'Excellence may become a burden if achieved, but too often it is a chimera which enchants school managers away from the realistic purposes of school life' (Seifert 1996: 19). He also writes that the top-down nature of the reforms causes immense difficulties; children may be neglected; work intensifies – particularly the intensive use of expensive staff.

Indeed, Seifert rejects the managerialist co-option of the appraisal mechanism and alleged educational effectiveness of performance-related pay. He notes that once any school has acquired new staff, the performance of those individuals becomes increasingly important to their employer. The main mechanism used, at present, to determine the job activities of teachers is appraisal. Seifert cites Fletcher (1993), who writes that 'appraisal does harm because managers cannot effectively differentiate between individual staff and organisational systems as the cause in performance variation and that the latter rather than the former are the major factor' (Seifert 1996: 98). Moreover, Seifert argues that what started out as a mechanism designed to improve professional development has been turned into a political weapon to control school staff and to satisfy political considerations of dismissing poor performers within schools.

Again, we are not opposed to appraisal *per se*. The point is that it needs to be part of a wider scheme of *professional* development. It is worth quoting Seifert at length here:

> The pressures on managers, however, to lower unit labour costs have meant a shift in the use made of appraisal. It can now be used as a tool

of control in which poor-performing teachers are blamed for the school's failures, and in which the outcome of the appraisal interview determines both pay and job security. This process of hijacking appraisal is part of the wider debate on control over definitions of what constitutes professional attitudes and behaviour among teachers . . . The Education (School Teacher Appraisal) Regulations 1991 came into effect in 1991 . . . [The] *purposes are entirely managerial, having no explicit reference to education other than being directed towards the appraisal of school teachers.*

(Seifert 1996: 101, our emphasis)

Given the competitive underpinning of education reforms, it is hardly surprising that government officials and education academics concur with some HRM specialists who argue that payment systems must be competitive and linked explicitly to contribution and performance. However, in the many detailed case studies of extant schemes, a strong pattern of discontent and failure emerges. For example, Seifert refers to the study of performance-related pay in the Inland Revenue, where the motivational effects have been very modest. Consequently, Seifert finds it difficult to square the research evidence with the claims of educational writers such as Tomlinson, who writes that 'performance-related pay is part of a necessary change to school and college culture, if standards are to be raised significantly without a massive and possibly wasteful input of new resources' (Tomlinson 1992: 2). As Armstrong and Murlis (1988: 177), succinctly put it: 'there are, however, special problems in introducing performance-related pay into the public sector'. As Seifert argues, the link between effort and reward is very complex.

Moreover, increased effort is not the same as high motivation. The direction of effort towards hitting performance targets, to gain higher pay or to avoid dismissal, does not result necessarily in better teaching . . . where performance-related pay acts against teachers' strong attachment to felt-fair earnings comparability, the outcome can only be division, demotivation and demoralisation, contrary to the claims of its proponents.

(Seifert 1996: 103)

In a balanced assessment of performance-related pay, Evans writes:

Although it is not an enduring motivator, pay may serve to spark off an initial interest in treading a path that leads to professional development on a grand scale. Without the right environment, though, the path could easily trail off to a dead end . . . Although they certainly deserve it, paying teachers more will not, in the long run, ensure their continued high performance. That will be secured at the institutional, not national, level by school cultures that provide teachers with opportunities to achieve.

(Evans 2001: 115)

Furthermore, on the issue of appraisal, Seifert asks the following questions: How would one teacher's appraisal be compared with another's? Will all teachers have the same opportunities to win bonuses? What action will be taken by teachers who believe that they deserve the bonus that was given to another? Finally, Seifert concludes that, in terms of HRM, 'the new freedom from LEA controls contains *too many dangers to be welcomed by school managers and governors'* (Seifert 1996: 161, our emphasis).

HRM's overt apologists

However, the dangers highlighted by Seifert (1996) have – and continue to be – dismissed out of hand by the rest of the education management literature on HRM, as we will see. Caldwell and Spinks, whose work was discussed in Chapter 3, have recently completed their trilogy, about which they write:

> The local management of schools was one of the four major initiatives of the Conservative Government that drew fierce criticism from across the political and academic spectrum, invariably labelled by its critics as a market-oriented, ideologically driven thrust of the New Right. Our third book *Beyond the Self-Managing School* is published in 1998, coinciding with a range of initiatives of the Labour Government, one of which is the extension of local management, known as devolved funding, that significantly increases the level of financial delegation. Such was the acceptance of local management that each of the major political parties in Britain vowed to retain it in the campaign lead-up to the 1997 election.
>
> (Caldwell and Spinks 1998: vii)

Already we would want to query the implicit *non sequitur*, namely that because each of the main political parties accepted devolved funding that it is the right policy initiative. It would be useful to dissect their response to critics and address the contradictions, but this would detract from our generic theme. In fact, as we shall see in our discussion of strategy, parts of their book are, frankly, hilarious. However, notwithstanding the lip service paid to critics, Caldwell and Spinks, in their attempt to exonerate themselves, write that

> Events have subsequently demonstrated that, while some elements of
> a market orientation unrelated to our work have their pitfalls, the
> broad features of the 1988 Education Reform Act, especially local
> management of schools, are eminently sensible and have drawn wide
> support.
>
> (Caldwell and Spinks 1998: 25)

They go on to write that: 'We demonstrated how concepts that appeared
initially foreign to those in school education, such as marketing, can be
adapted' (Caldwell and Spinks 1998: 28). We have already argued for the
inappropriateness of marketing. Essentially, as far as the authors are concerned, 'we were not writing a book about education policy in Britain' (Caldwell and Spinks 1998: 31). Yet they were actively creating and buttressing the
neo-liberal project that was – and remains – about the imposition of a market
orientation. Given such denial we fear that it would be pointless here to
recapitulate our argument for the transcendental need to avoid a market orientation and to reiterate the need for Caldwell and Spinks to pay sufficient attention to the research findings that document the deleterious, anti-educational
impact of the reforms.

Yet, for Colin Riches, 'If schools or colleges do not perform in the sense of
achieving results which satisfy their customers they eventually close like bank-
rupt businesses!' (Riches 1997: 15). Again, the case against the conflation of
business values and educational values has already been made. Contrary to
both Caldwell and Spinks and Riches, we are not against devolution *as long as
there are sufficient financial resources at the outset. But the reality of competition and
the threat of 'bankruptcy' palpably undermine this.*

Valerie Hall has also actively championed the use of (strategic) HRM.
For her,

> The shift towards school-based management has been accompanied
> by a shift in the language used, both inside and outside education, to
> describe the processes involved. The term . . . HRM has been accepted
> more readily in non-educational settings *but is daily gaining currency in
> education.*
>
> (Hall 1997: 140, our emphasis)

Evidence for the latter claim is not provided. Furthermore, she notes that
'describing people as "human resources" continues to be controversial for
those commentators like Bottery (1992), who prefer to see people as "resourceful humans" ' (Hall 1997: 140). Contrary to Hall, it is not simply a matter of
preference how we choose to 'see' people.[4] Indeed, the process of preferring must
make reference to the ways things are – in this case people. We will return to
the palpable lack of reflection and engagement with critiques from within

business and management studies shortly. Hall is quite content to admit that there are 'pressures on school managers to make hard executive decisions about people'. For Hall, these are 'choices open to school managers'. For us, the very rationale underpinning such 'choices' is dangerously flawed. However, Hall's, like most HRM management texts, distinguishes between so-called hard and soft normative models of HRM. As she puts it: 'The "hard" model is associated with utilitarian instrumentalism: ends are more important than means. The "soft" reflects developmental humanism: means are as important as ends' (Hall 1997: 144).

> Yet, in the context of managing schools, both the means and the ends are people . . . I would argue that how managers in education go about selecting, motivating and developing staff will be influenced by the beliefs they have about people as people and people as employees.
>
> (p. 144)

This is precisely what we have said above in relation to human resources and resourceful humans. The whole point of Bottery's criticism derives from its Taylorist heritage, namely that people are viewed in the same way as machines: that is, as a resource to be manipulated, exploited and discarded. This is the quintessential contradiction that underpins the education reforms: (Taylorist) dehumanization that is impossible in theory and in practice (Willmott 2002a). Hall then adds that 'favouring contracts that make staff easily expendable demonstrates sharply drawn boundaries in perceptions of people's personal and professional identities, i.e. taking a "hard" line' (Hall 1997: 144). But the point is that we should never be in the position of being able to adopt a 'hard' line in education. Even the so-called soft approach needs to be analysed at the concrete level: any competitive economic system will, to varying degrees, negate it. To her credit, Hall recognizes that it is not always that case that 'soft' approaches are less controlling: 'People-centred programmes like Investors in People (which many schools are becoming involved in) can seem as manipulative in their attempts to gain staff commitment as "hard" approaches' (Hall 1997: 145).

Surely, then, we should not even consider the alleged humanistic nature of the soft approach? However, Hall, contradictorily, remains unperturbed:

> The new managerialism, in which people are seen mainly as resources, fails to challenge the values informing the reforms. Yet my own study of women heads at work (Hall, 1996) showed how they aimed to transform the constraints of new responsibilities into a form of entrepreneurialism that was ethically based. Their strategies for 'bringing out the best in staff', a key function of HRM, reflected other research evidence about what effective school managers do . . . They

> demonstrated a resistance to the government's economic and polit-
> ical imperative to get more for less (Seifert, 1996) and *its implicit*
> *attempts to transform their consciousness.*
>
> (Hall 1997: 146, our emphasis)

First, Hall is quite right that the new managerialism sees people mainly as
resources – hence Bottery's criticism – yet at the outset Hall 'prefers' such HRM-
speak and concomitant managerialist practices. Second, the fact that Hall welcomes resistance to the economistic nature of the education reforms begs the
question of why she 'prefers' the adoption of HRM. Third, instead of just
acknowledging Seifert's critique, she should explicitly adopt its implications
and reject the trend towards HRM. Frankly, Hall's discussion is deeply contradictory. Hall wants resistance (though we would certainly want to place a large
question mark over the extent to which all can resist) precisely because the
reforms are managerialist and thereby attempt to transform teachers' consciousness, yet she plays an active role in such consciousness transformation
by advocating (strategic) HRM. Hall even goes on to suggest that 'one way
around the dilemma of prioritising individual and school needs may be in
refusing to see them as dichotomous' (Hall 1997: 152).

We could easily continue with pinpointing the contradictions that
characterize Hall's work. However, the point to make is that texts like
Hall's ignore the critiques of HRM from within business and management
studies (from which education management academics selectively borrow).
In essence, HRM elaborates a battery of 'objective' techniques for managing
the selection, motivation and promotion of employees. Crucially, HRM
specialists

> do not go to the root of the problem by advocating the removal of
> constraints that impede employees discovering for themselves what is
> meaningful for them. Instead, they contrive to design and reward
> work in ways that are intended to increase employee motivation . . .
> Within HRM discourse, employees are understood to be 'motivated'
> so long as they are productive – regardless of whether their work is
> experienced as personally meaningful.
>
> (Alvesson and Willmott 1996: 99)

Following Sievers (1986), Alvesson and Willmott argue that the idea of motivation here is a 'surrogate for meaning', in a world where experts dominate
decisions about how organizations and jobs should be designed, and thus the
work almost invariably lacks any deeply valued meaning. Indeed, as a surrogate for meaning, 'the literature on motivation allows non-meaningful work
[for example, competitive SATs-based league tabling] to be interpreted through
a technocratic lens so that the "human resource" becomes a manipulable

object of management control' (Alvesson and Willmott 1996: 99). Further-more, they point out that so-called soft versions of total quality management (TQM), in particular, incorporate HRM thinking as they proclaim that 'liberating people at work to become more truly themselves and more creative' (Bank 1992, cited in Alvesson and Willmott 1996: 100). Thus, rhetorically, to Hargreaves and Hopkins (1991: 15), 'Management is about people: management arrangements are what empower people. Empowerment, in short, is the purpose of management'. However, the basic problem with the latter claim is that it is assumed that emancipation and creativity are gifts that can be bestowed upon employees by managers, whereas, arguably, 'they are necessarily the outcome of individual and collective struggles to overcome forms of dependency. In the absence of such struggles, it is others – e.g. managers – who decide how and when people are "truly themselves" and what counts as being more creative' (Alvesson and Willmott 1997: 100).

Beyond school development planning: what you need is strategy!

As we mentioned earlier, SDPing has been eclipsed by the exhortation that school managers now adopt a *strategic* approach to HRM in order to maintain, or to achieve, competitive advantage in the educational marketplace. In fact, as Legge (1989, 1995) points out, the battery of techniques employed by HR specialists is, in principle, yoked to the strategic objectives of the organization. For David Middlewood (1998: 5), developing strategic thinking is 'of critical importance'. Instead of the school development plan, we are now enjoined to develop the *strategic* school plan. Indeed, for Davies and Ellison, development planning was misnamed: instead, it should be renamed operational target setting: 'schools need to build "operational targets", especially as a result of government pressure and legislation' (Davies and Ellison 1999: 3). Davies and Ellison go on to consider 'in depth the limits of strategic planning for anything other than the most predictable activities and develop a concept called strategic intent' (Davies and Ellison 1999: 3). Humbly, they recognize the limitations of their previous approaches to planning, at the same time refusing to engage with concurrent criticisms. The specifics of their response need not detain us. For Davies and Ellison:

> These five Ps [Mintzberg's 5 Ps for strategy] can be seen to be coming from a competitive environment, drawn from both the military and business roots of strategy . . . Some of these concepts are more directly transferable to an educational setting than others. The problem in education is that there is a feeling of being unable to control what is happening because of externally imposed changes *but this is, perhaps,*

> *an over-used excuse for not developing appropriate strategies for the circumstances.*
>
> (Davies and Ellison 1999: 47, our emphasis)

So, no excuses! Some of the debate centres on whether schools should be planning strategically for the short or long term. For example, a longer-term approach is advocated by Knight (1997). He adopts the language of strategy and the customer, uses business examples, yet argues that the customer should not be interpreted literally, again despite talk of 'collapse of customer confidence'. Finally, his book ends with the idealist fallacy (or fantasy?) that the 'sky is the limit' (Knight 1997: 119). We find such idealism particularly unhelpful given that any competitive system enjoins that there will be winners and losers. Furthermore, again in idealist fashion (like Valerie Hall), he wishes away the material constraints on real learning:

> I do not believe that it is in any way satisfactory, in educational organisations, simply to reiterate platitudes such as 'we live in a competitive world' or 'education has to exist in a free market'. Such assertions in themselves deny much of the value-driven basis of education which is essential for the delivery of effective learning opportunities to young people.
>
> (Knight 1997: 23)

Simply avoiding the reiteration of such 'platitudes' does not alter the fact that education policy is underpinned by them. In contrast, Davies and Ellison (1999: 144) candidly admit that 'there are no easy, ready-made panaceas which can be transposed onto a school to provide instant and outstanding success in every area'.[5] However, while it is difficult to plan in the long term precisely because schools operate in a now-volatile open system, the crucial point is that schools should not be thinking, worrying, fretting or stressing 'strategically' since this, quite simply, threatens to undermine their competitive position in the global marketplace. Ultimately, the issue of whether strategic planning can ever be rational or short term is not the point: schools should get on with educating instead of scrambling for woefully inadequate slices of the funding cake.

Strategic intent

Despite talk of strategy's elusive nature (Knight 1997) and the apparent need for strategy to prefix decision-making, planning and thinking, Caldwell and Spinks (1998) offer no less than 100 'strategic intentions for schools'. We have many concerns about the list, especially the time it would involve, although particularly instructive is strategic intention number 10: 'Without sacrificing any source, schools will seek to reduce their dependence on funding from the public purse by seeking other substantial support, avoiding approaches that yield minimal resources from effort that diverts time and energy from the support of learning'. This smacks of support for the neo-liberal project – but of course, Caldwell and Spinks are not writing about education policy. Why should state schools wish to reduce their dependence on state funding? If anything, research shows incontrovertibly that LMS creates stress, work intensification and a narrowing of the curriculum for schools whose numbers decrease yet whose 'management' is found to be sound (see, for example, Willmott 2002a). For instance, as a school governor of an infants' school, Willmott is helping a head to find ways of maintaining educational excellence in the face of a decrease in pupil numbers and hence money. The head is in the process of having to make redundant one of her staff and combining two infant classes. Who will help her financially? Equally, how can time and energy not be diverted in the search for extra money and ways of saving money?

For Davies and Ellison (1999: 15–16):

> Strategic intent is an approach which seems to have a lot to offer to those in schools, as an alternative to strategic planning . . . With strategic intent the school needs to establish a process of coping with and using the rapid change and turbulence. It does this not by detailed planning but by 'binding' the staff together in the furtherance of key priorities.

We are not told exactly how to put the flesh on the strategic intent bones nor are we told quite how to bind staff apart from the need to create the 'right' culture. However, the real import of Davies and Ellison's book is the acceptability of schools behaving like flexible firms, hiring and firing when necessary.[6] Indeed, Davies and Ellison (1999: 11) are content to stress that there 'will be changes in staffing patterns and arrangements, more para-professionals, core and periphery staff, fixed-term performance-led contract'. Such hard HRM discourse, however, is couched in the language of imagination and invention (Davies and Ellison 1999: 54). As Davies and Ellison (1999: 57) encapsulate: 'Achieving a specific strategic intent involves significant creativity with respect to means' and the 'leveraging of resources to reach seemingly unattainable goals'. Instructively, following Boisot (1995), they argue that any organization operating in a regime of strategic intent can use a common vision to keep the behaviour of its employees aligned: back to the good old battery of HRM techniques to be deployed in typical manipulative fashion. As they put it:

> If we have flexible budgets that adjust with the number of pupils, then staffing flexibility on the supply side is an organisational

necessity. The challenge is to find ways to empower teachers to be
responsible for their career and salary management.

(Davies and Ellison 1999: 35)

Empowerment here means blaming teachers when there is insufficient
money. Moreover, what of the HRM specialists in schools if teachers are now
responsible for their career and salary management? As well as being a governor,
Willmott returns regularly to 'Southside' primary school (see Willmott 2002a).
Here, complaints about the 'cost' of older staff are commonplace. Equally,
as already mentioned, there are plans to make redundant one of the staff at an
infants' school, which is attributable to factors beyond the school's control.
Contrary to Davies and Ellison, there should be no such challenge: the challenge in a managerialist climate is how to sustain professional integrity,
in other words to enact the moral obligation to be honest and open about
structures and processes that are fundamentally not in the interests of children
and staff.

However, Davies and Ellison and Bush and Coleman proffer re-engineering
as part of the strategic way forward. Bush and Coleman are more cautious:

It *may* be appropriate for strategic thinking and planning to
encompass the possibility of radical change. Here, the concept of reengineering outpaces the approaches described above. As with TQM,
re-engineering is a concept, derived from business, that *may* have
applications for education.

(Bush and Coleman 2000: 66, our emphasis)

Davies and Ellison (1999) are less cautious and cite the work of business process reengineering (BPR) gurus Hammer and Champy (1993), who define
reengineering as 'the fundamental rethinking and radical redesign of business
processes to achieve dramatic improvement in critical contemporary measures
of performance' (cited in Davies and Ellison 1999: 26). But, as Alvesson and
Willmott (1996) point out, common to all recent major ideologies and techniques for improving corporate performance ('Excellence', TQM and BPR) has
been the contradictory championing of empowered employees and strong
leadership. They ask readers to consider BPR, the latest of recent managerial
techniques, which is distinguished by its identification and promotion of new
information and communication technologies as means of radically trans-
forming work. In essence, all activities are speeded up and unproductive dupli-
cation is eliminated. However, Alvesson and Willmott argue that

[notwithstanding] the lip-service paid to concepts like 'empowerment' and 'team work', there can be little doubt that the intent of BPR
is to *impose* and sustain a *totalizing* solution. Hammer and Champy

(1993), the leading advocates of BRP contend that . . . *If radical change threatens to bubble up from below, they may resist it and throttle it. Only strong leadership from above will induce these people to accept the transformations that reengineering brings* . . . [Indeed] Hammer and Champy brazenly identify the need for 'Czars' (not champions) who will ruthlessly push through reengineering programmes without regard for the personal, social or even the economic costs involved in such a coercive approach to organizational change.

(Alvesson and Willmott 1996: 98–9, emphasis in original)

They go on to argue that such developments represent a nascent technocratic totalitarianism: 'Whatever is deemed by experts to be effective in terms of gaining a competitive advantage or maximizing output, however insidious or demeaning, is regarded as legitimate because . . . leaders committed to change "have no choice in how they deal with those attempting to impede their efforts" (Hammer, 1994: 37)' (Alvesson and Willmott 1996: 99). This echoes the generic education management literature on both culture and reengineering, that strong (non-collaborative) leadership is needed to expedite managerialist policy. Thus, to Lumby, 'whichever approach to achieving strategic change is chosen, it is clear that there is a role for leadership' (Lumby 1998: 201). Now, what is particularly disturbing is the tendency to leave the ethical decisions to the reader, whose decision-making is not helped by the equivocal nature of the literature, that swings in schizophrenic like fashion from 'yes, do adopt a democratic or collaborative approach' to 'well, it isn't always possible or desirable to adopt a democratic approach'.[7]

Just talk?

Finally, Alvesson and Willmott (ironically) describe the colonizing tendency of strategy in business texts, which is apposite here. Indeed, they write that such a colonizing tendency is

> Productive of some peculiar effects – such as people saying 'strategically important' when by 'strategically' they simply mean important . . . The term 'strategic' is bandied about to add rhetorical weight, misleadingly one might say, to managerial activity and academic research projects.
>
> (Alvesson and Willmott 1996: 133)

Thus Fidler (1996), for example, prefixes thinking, planning and decision-making with 'strategic'. Indeed, we have seen that Fidler asserts that strategy is a fundamental part of a school's operation. But even if this were to be taken seriously, how would a 'strategy' help the head in Willmott's infants' school? Nevertheless, Alvesson and Willmott argue that while such name-calling is innocent and trivial, the expansion of 'strategy talk' from the military to all sectors of organizational life has political effects: such talk frames issues in a manner that privileges instrumental reason and gives the initiative to those who successfully claim to be strategists. As they neatly put it: 'In effect, the adoption of strategy talk has self-disciplining effects as employees contrive to gain credibility and influence by demonstrating and promoting the relevance of their work for attaining objectives that are deemed to be "strategic" ' (Alvesson and Willmott 1996: 134). Moreover, the successful dissemination of 'strategy talk' serves 'to construct the perceived common-sense understanding that organizations are strategy-driven and that employees outside the strategic core should realize their limited overview and understanding' (Alvesson and Willmott 1996: 134). In turn, this facilitates the introduction and development of 'new' forms of management control (BPR, TQM), for those outside the core must subordinate themselves to the implications of strategy.

What can we do, strategically speaking?

As argued in all our chapters, there are, at present, stringent constraints that prevent non-managerialist heads and staffs from circumventing the education reforms. However, this is not to say that we should subject ourselves to the kinds of insidious forms of self- and collective surveillance in order to achieve strategic objectives imposed by central government, via local education authorities or other conduits. If anything, we should recognize the validity of planning, but planning for real learning. Next, it needs to be accepted that, by law, we have to come up with plans, be they 'strategic' or otherwise, in order to satisfy Ofsted and like-minded bodies. Then, we must laugh at the bizarre way in which official documents, education spokespeople and academics have jumped on the 'strategy bandwagon'. Other useful responses could be as follows:

- Spend the minimum time necessary to provide the ('strategic') paper work required at present;
- Recognize and make clear among all staff that current funding arrangements mean that for some schools some of the time teachers will be made redundant for reasons beyond their control. Therefore, there should be no secrecy or behind-the-scenes machinations when it comes to deciding who should be made redundant;
- Plan for real learning outcomes, but do not berate yourselves if students and pupils do not achieve them: teaching is a two-way relational process;

- Wherever possible, plan for creativity and spontaneity: be resolute and make time for 'art weeks' and such like;
- When paying lip service to 'strategy talk', always remind yourselves of its anti-educational import and ever keep an eye on the dangers of repeating managerialist mantras;
- Finally, keep sane and remember that this sorry state of affairs cannot persist.

In essence, we are suggesting that teachers channel (differential) potential opportunities for dissent by recognizing the paradoxical dangers and ensure as far as possible that such 'disciplinary technologies' do not take hold and stymie plans of educational value.

8 School leadership

Leadership is regarded as something more than and different from management by many writers, including those holding critical perspectives (for example, Grace 1995). As a result they might dispute the place for a chapter on school leadership within a book on education management. Yet Bush and Coleman (2000: 4) argue that 'the distinction between leadership and management is often overdrawn'. One reason they give for this is that 'many leaders in education actually spend a large proportion of their time on tasks that could best be termed administrative or even clerical' (p. 21). They also cite Glatter (1997: 189), who comments:

> Methods . . . [are] as important as knowledge, understanding and value orientations . . . Erecting this kind of dichotomy between something pure called 'leadership' and something 'dirty' called 'management', or between values and purposes on the one hand and methods and skills on the other, would be disastrous.

We tend to agree, but we also think the dichotomy is even more problematic for political reasons. As Grace (1995: 27) has put it, 'the concept of management can be more easily commodified than can the less tangible but nevertheless "real" concept of leadership [but] . . . leadership has been recontextualised as a form or part of management'. Grace seeks to reconstitute educational leadership as a phenomenon distinct from management, and while we agree that leadership should ideally be something more than management, the leadership literature is generally so unquestioning of problem-solving and managerialist assumptions that attempting to extract leadership as a conceptual category of higher calling is a lost cause. For instance, many leadership texts advocate transformational leadership, which is supposedly all about empowering staff and sharing leadership functions.[1] We shall see, however, that as typically used by school leadership writers, transformational leadership is not a critical concept because it rarely involves much critique of either post-welfarist education reform or the role of schooling in reproducing social inequality. If it is 'radical', it is only so within the frame of post-welfarist education reform. As Gunter and colleagues also note, transform-ational leadership is central to textual apologism in the area of educational leadership:

> We are told, and told repeatedly, that headteachers should have a vision of where the school is moving towards . . . Engagement with 'followers' is through neutral processes which either transmit the vision or ensure a triumph over competing visions. It is not really clear what the status is of competing or alternative visions, their existence is recognised (and encouraged) by some writers, but ultim-ately the headteacher needs to use a combination of personal cha-risma and/or organisational levers to ensure compliance.
>
> (Gunter *et al.* 1999: xxi)

Also problematic are 'post-transformational' leadership (see, for example, Day *et al.* 2000) 'instructional leadership' (Hallinger and Murphy 1985) or 'educative' leadership (Duigan and MacPherson 1992), because while they link leadership to teaching and learning, they again leave out the sociology and politics of education.

Because the leadership literature has become so linked to managerialism, it would be unhelpful to allow it any recourse to the conceptual high ground as Grace and others allow. Rather, the distinction we think should be drawn is between critical and uncritical leadership studies seen in turn as part of a wider debate around critical and uncritical education management. Yet if the (uncritical) school leadership literature is best seen as another problematic education management literature, it is clearly also more complex and messy than most because of its reach – in order to make good schools, school leaders are supposed to be able to see the big picture and the literature may be drawing on any or all of the education management literatures already mentioned as well as many other sources. In an often-cited quote, Christopher Hodgkinson complains that the resulting mix has little intel-lectual coherence:

> I set out to explore the swamp of literature on leadership. It goes on and on and ranges from the sublime to the ridiculous with little in between. Taken as a whole it is a shambles, a mess full of philo-sophical confusion . . . It is full of word magic of the worst kind.
>
> (Hodgkinson, cited in Ribbins 1993: 21)

It is not surprising, then, that leadership is an area where the writer's perspec-tive on reform can be easily overlooked – lost amidst the 'vision' thing for instance. However, school leadership also strays into areas where education management reaches some of its most thorough working through including historical, sociological and philosophical analyses. Indeed, there are important elements of textual dissent in the leadership literature, including a raft of what Grace (1997, 2000) calls critical leadership studies.

All of this means that school leadership is a site of considerable academic struggle, aiding the managerial colonization of education, and also, to a significant degree, contesting it as well. One way in which managerial colonization occurs is when leadership texts are overtly framed within managerial government policy. An example is provided by the collection *Principles of School Leadership* (Brundrett 1999), which draws on contributions from both academics and Teacher Training Agency (TTA) programme staff. Noting this, Brundrett ignores tensions between academic 'higher ed' and practically relevant TTA courses and argues for their complementary nature:

> The underpinning rationale for the Government's headship programmes owes much to the work of a generation of researchers who have told us much about school effectiveness and improvement strategies. Much of this research has also begun to inform the content of the higher degree programmes offered by higher education institutions. For this reason the NPQH [National Professional Qualification for Headship] allows candidates to take account of their previous learning and experience, including work on recent and relevant higher degree programmes. It is also good to see that a number of higher education institutions are allowing reciprocal remission from the requirements of their courses for those who complete the NPQH.
>
> (Brundrett 1999: viii)

More generally, managerial colonization occurs as school leaders are asked to take on the sorts of generic hints for effective business leaders found in airport bookshops. We have already noted that Jossey Bass intersperses general leadership and management offerings among its education titles. Here, along with the more usual education-oriented titles you will find *The Passion Plan* (Chang 2001), *Leadership A to Z* (O'Toole 1999), and *The Five Practices of Exemplary Leadership* (Kouzes and Posner 2000). The *Jossey Bass Reader on Educational Leadership* (Jossey Bass 2000) is also instructive. This book comprises five parts with an introduction by Michael Fullan. The most surprising thing about the book is the way part one unashamedly starts off with an assortment of writers on business leadership, including abstracts from Peter Senge and TQM writers such as Deming and Glasser. An unidentified editor rationalizes this as follows:

In part one, the reader will notice a strong representation of works written by experts in management or business. Why are these authors, many of whom have never worked in a K-12 environment, included so prominently? They are responsible for theories and practices that were successful in business and were then applied to schools. As many survivors of top-down reform can attest, not all of these movements were embraced or worked the miracles on school systems that their champions touted. However when talking about leadership in schools, they must be included. Total Quality Management (TQM) which surged from business to the schools in the 1980s, would now be called a fad by many educators. However the roots and vocabulary of today's pressing reforms – accountability, shared decision-making, and the focus on leadership as an invaluable part of school change – can all be traced back to TQM. Therefore W. Edward Deming's writing is represented here, as is that of William Glasser.

(p. 1)

Fullan's introduction to this collection is no more critical:

The Jossey Bass Reader on Educational Leadership provides a much needed anthology that organizes in one place the best of the literature on leadership. Part One contains six groundbreaking articles from leading thinkers in organizational leadership. These are deliberately selected to demonstrate that leadership has a strong conceptual base which is basic in all human situations. John Garner's classic article on *The Nature of Leadership* introduces the section followed by several featured pieces on theories of quality leadership.

(Fullan 2000: xix–xx)

On the other hand, less tied to specific managerial 'technologies' and raising many questions of power and social relationships, school leadership is an area where those taking more critical stances have shown interest and taken a strong foothold, not just critiquing the textual apologists but also providing critically informed alternative accounts. This can be seen, for instance, in texts by Blackmore (1999), Gunter (2001), Grace (1995, 2002) and Smyth (1989), and in the way the 31 chapter *International Handbook of Educational Leadership and Administration* (Leithwood *et al.* 1996) has a section of six chapters devoted to critical perspectives.

Here we again work through a spectrum of leadership perspectives, ranging from the most unapologetic to the textual dissenters. We focus mostly on the subtle apologists, especially Leithwood, Sergiovanni and Southworth, and also on the textual dissenters, particularly Blackmore and Grace.

The primarily problem-solving

It is not surprising that school leadership should have its share of primarily problem-solving texts since ready solutions may have strong appeal when school leaders are appointed, often without much training but with the public responsibility for improving schools. The demand for problem-solving texts is also probably reinforced by the powerful influence of common-sense ideologies around the ability of good leadership to conquer all and by related policy developments like the UK phenomenon of 'superheadism'.[2] School leaders are also relatively powerful practitioners, used to having a public voice and being respected for their many years of practical experience and their know-how. These factors can form a potent mix and leave school leaders turned academics or consultants ideally placed to write problem-solving leadership texts which involve little consideration of educational research, theory or politics.

One good example is Robert Ramsey's *Lead, Follow or Get Out of the Way: How to be a More Effective Leader in Today's Schools* (1999). The preface does an unashamed sales job:

> ... the first ever comprehensive leadership guide exclusively for school administrators. This unprecedented handbook ... is the only available resource ... that pinpoints all of the specific know-how, skills, attitudes, and habits that separate effective leaders from run of the mill school managers ... [In] this unusual manual ... each chapter is packed with school tested advice and real world examples of what readers need to know to become effective leaders in today's schools, every section contains dozens of samples, figures, ready to use forms and timesaving checklists to help apply the guide's practical lessons in leadership ... a practical and complete guide ... may be the best bet yet for releasing the real leader inside of you. There's nothing quite like it on the market today. Are you interested?
>
> (p. x)

The book itself is basically made up of checklists of tips. Ramsey provides 30 qualities of an effective twenty-first century school leader, 20 school-tested strategies for upgrading morale, 25 methods for getting performance from staff, 10 tips for successfully selling a new idea, 10 tips for making new ideas work, 7 habits of highly effective school leaders and even 101 ways to be a better school leader tomorrow. In short, one gets the impression that Ramsay could run an entertaining day seminar but the book is full of truisms and platitudes. There is no discussion of research findings or of the political and social context of education and its implications for school leadership. Ramsay has no problem recommending that school leaders read and learn from business leadership texts and even provides a chapter on Machiavellian methods of leadership on the grounds that heads need to know them even if they do not intend to practise them. Leadership here, then, is a state of mind: think it and you can do it:

> Leadership isn't a title or an entitlement. It's not a right or a gift. It's a decision. You can become an effective school leader if you make up your mind to be . . . Don't spend your time pining or whining. Either lead, follow or get out of the way. It's your choice.
>
> (p. 211)

At one level this kind of thing is quite amusing. However, it distracts from more complex analyses of school leadership and its problems.

The overt apologists

Davies and Ellison's (1997a) book *School Leadership for the 21st Century* is a leadership text that provides considerable overt support for post-welfarist educational reform. Here we concentrate on the initial chapters by Davies and begin by quoting at length from his opening paragraph. Consider both the language and the substantive argument:

> It is our contention that there are two waves of reform that occur in education systems. The first is the changes to the structure and framework of the system. In the case of the UK, the National Curriculum, national testing and examination frameworks and school-based financial management allied to parental choice and new inspection and reporting systems can be seen to have been a radical reform and restructuring of the education system. The effectiveness of such reforms is of course partly determined by the nature of the reforms themselves and their implementation strategy but also in our view by the effectiveness of the second wave of the reform movement. This consists of the changes in the leadership and management behaviour of the individuals who are leading and managing the individual schools themselves. Just as the old saying 'you can take a horse to water but you cannot make it drink' is true, so giving individual leaders and managers in schools new responsibilities and accountability relationships does not, in itself, make them innovative and educationally entrepreneurial when their previous experience was in directive risk-adverse bureaucratic structures. The key to full realisation of effective schooling in a reformed and restructured education system depends on the capability of the leaders and the staff at the

school level. We contend that having a clear understanding of the changing context in which education is now operating and of the constantly changing nature of selfmanaging schools, allied to a clear understanding by the educational leader of her/his own leadership and management skills to operate effectively in that environment, are prerequisites to undertaking successfully the key task in leading and managing a school. *These understandings and skills enable the second round of reform at school level, that of creating effective schools in this new environment, to take place. These leadership and management perspectives form the central thrust of this book.*

(Davies and Ellison 1997a: 1–2, our emphasis)

Davies' argument here may be summarized along the following lines. 'The main problem with the neo-liberal reform of educational structures is that they do not necessarily lead to changes in the hearts and minds of school leaders who cling to outdated ideas. As supporters of these reforms, we are trying to deal with this unfinished business of market and managerial colonization and this book is part of the process.' If left in any doubt, the reader is told that the book is 'of particular value to those on the Teacher Training Agency's programmes for headteacher development as it combines a similar competency and content approach' (p. 2). Ironically, there is much critical empirical research which has explored in great detail the extent to which the reforms after 1988 have colonized the perspectives and practices of heads (see Chapter 3). But this literature is not mentioned, presumably because it is much less convinced that turning out 'educationally entrepreneurial' school leaders is a good thing.

However, this is just the introduction. Chapter 2 is about the global context of school leadership and draws on business process reengineering (discussed in our previous chapter). In defence of this, Davies comments:

While critics of much modern management writing decry it as 'pop management', we believe that it is irrelevant where the ideas come from as long as they help us to develop our own frameworks for making sense of schools and their contexts and to develop strategies for effective leadership. Using a reengineering approach, [the next two chapters] examine the radical changes about to impact on the education world and set out basic questions to ask about the nature and development of selfmanaging schools ... we consider it equally important to reengineer mindsets as well as processes within schools.

(Davies and Ellison 1997a: 4–5)

By now it will be clear that we have a serious difficulty with the pragmatism implicit in the view that it does not matter where ideas come from so long as they work. As for the notion of 'reengineering mindsets', this is at least a refreshingly frank acknowledgement of what textual apologism is all about. Nevertheless, we need to consider these context-setting chapters in more detail to see how Davies conceptualizes post-welfarist educational reform. The starting-point of his argument is that incremental improvement 'while beneficial, will not be enough to cope with the changes facing schools in the future' (p. 13). Rather, what is needed is a 'much more radical and fundamental rethink of the nature of society, education and the role of the school'. Drawing on Hammer and Champy's *Reengineering the Corporation* (1993), Davies argues that reengineering is needed because schools are having to respond to 'customers', 'competition' and 'change'.

The discussion of 'customers' notes that while people are increasingly used to getting good quality and service in relation to consumer goods, this is less the case in the public sector, including education. The comparison leads to friction between the 'consumers and producers of education services' (p.15). Yet this is where using business reengineering to frame the problem already falls down, because schools can often not satisfy what parents are looking for, i.e. not just high quality schooling but positional advantage. Because of this, 'the customer' in education cannot be understood through a business reengineering lens: it requires a sociological understanding of the role of education in an unequal society.

Davies' account of 'competition' is similarly inadequate. He talks about intensified competition in the global economy and then asks, 'Does any of this apply to education? Is education not somehow different from the business world? While it may be different, education is not isolated from the pressures and trends that are making themselves increasingly evident' (pp. 15–16). Yet each of the examples he gives is problematic. The first that unless 'our children ... develop high quality thinking, problem-solving and technological skills to compete with the best in the world, they will be competing for the low wage/low skill jobs' (p. 16). The fundamental problem here is that just as 'our children' cannot all attend the best schools, they cannot all get the best jobs. 'Schools can't make jobs'. Thus there is not just an educational problem of upskilling but a political problem of occupational hierarchies and unequal income distribution. Second, Davies suggests that schools face competition from non-traditional technological sources as the prime means of education. But because education is fundamentally a social process, it is most unlikely that technology will lead to the demise of face-to-face education, at least at the school level. Hence technology is not so much a competitor as a tool. Third, Davies notes 'the changes that schools are having to make by adopting marketing strategies to respond to competition' (p. 16). We have already made the point in Chapter 5, that schools do not *have* to make such changes, other kinds of non-marketing response are preferable.

When it comes to 'change', Davies argues that constant change and increasingly rapid change is the norm, and that 'the expectations of customers, the nature of competition and the ongoing rate of change itself are unlikely to leave education in a backwater' (Davies and Ellison 1997a: 16). The implication he draws is that 'education should be at the forefront of society's attempts to come to terms with this new reality. It is difficult to imagine that education, and the nature of schooling, will not itself have to change radically' (pp. 16–17). But we do not like the inevitability of all this – there is nothing here about critically exploring the nature of change and responding appropriately, in other words avoiding change for change's sake or indeed resisting change if that is the mostly educationally sound thing to do. Moreover, there is the real risk that educational change as conceived by Davies could end up racheting up damaging reform through unexamined response and indeed advocacy.

What follows the discussion of consumers, competition and change is a section called 'Fundamental rethinking and radical redesign'. Here we see more worrying advocacy of accepting and supporting the political status quo and working within it, albeit dressed up as 'breakthrough' thinking:

> We have all been told many times: I should like to do that but we don't have the resources. The speaker is either waiting for a fairy godmother (or should it be godperson?) to wave a wand in order to get more resources, and will do nothing until that happens or s/he is incapable of rethinking how to tackle a particular challenge. One reality of public finance in the UK, the USA and Australia is that funds from public sources are not going to increase significantly . . . in this environment a reengineering approach *within existing resources* would suggest that some basic questions are asked . . . We have to work smarter not harder and the smarter course involves not slicker ways of doing the same things but fundamentally different ways of doing those things. A useful saying to remember is that 'sacred cows make the best burgers' . . . In education for a considerable period of time, reports from both HMI and OFSTED have indicated a significant proportion of unsatisfactory lessons. We need a dramatic improvement in educational standards to achieve quality in present situations, let alone the standards which we will need to achieve in order to meet the educational demands of the next millennium.
>
> (Davies and Ellison 1997a: 18–19, our emphasis)

Various problems here include skipping over the reality that a lack of resources really is a serious issue for schools nowadays, that Davies is telling school leaders to just work within the status quo rather than work towards a properly funded state education system, the unrealistic idea that large gains can be made through working smarter not harder within existing constraints, the

willingness to take Ofsted reports at face value when they are evidently problematic, the concern with quality rather than equality, and the willingness of
Davies to join those fostering an uncritical sense of crisis around standards in
education.

The final part of chapter 2 is called 'Reengineering: cross national educational insights'. Here a set of bullet points about international educational
trends summarizes many of the features of post-welfarist educational reform
including increased testing, the development of specialist schools, quasi-
markets, performance pay, privatization and contracting out (see pp. 20–1). It
is clear Davies approves of these trends. In some cases this is because a favourable gloss is being provided through the language used: 'significantly
enhanced levels of parental choice', 'redefinition of leadership and management'. But if we are left in any doubt, he goes on to ask, 'how do we get this
sort of thinking down to the level of the day to day operation of the school?'
The answer is seen to be different patterns of education and resource use,
which leads into the following chapter on 'reconceptualising the nature of
self-managing schools'.

For space reasons we will have to leave our critique of this book, but the
two chapters just discussed set the scene for the rest of the book which is all
about how to be a smart school leader within a managerialist framework.
Indeed, it comes as no surprise to find the book dedicated to Brian Caldwell
who also has a couple of chapters which conclude this book (Caldwell 1997a,
b). Caldwell's (1997b) suggested 'seminal reading' for the school leader reader
is instructive: Peter Drucker's (1995) *Managing in a Time of Great Change*, Bill
Gates (1995) *The Road Ahead*, Kenichi Ohmae's (1995) *The End of the Nation
State* and John Naisbitt's (1995) *Megatrends: Asia*. Are these really the best bed-
time reading for school leaders? We would want to recommend books which
are far more educationally focused.

Nevertheless, there is no doubt that Davies and Ellison's overt apologism
would be well received by some practitioners. This is illustrated by Frank
Green's (2000) *The Headteacher in the 21st Century: Being a Successful School
Leader*. At the time of writing, Green was a headteacher ('principal *and* Chief
Executive') who had been involved in the senior management of schools for
19 years. His discussion favourably cites Davies and Ellison's work (both the
above book and their 1999 book discussed in the previous chapter), the Hay
McBer consultancy advice about effective heads and teachers promoted by the
DfES, Barber (1996b), Caldwell and Spinks (1998), and various business
management gurus like Drucker, Gates, Peters and Covey. It also repeatedly
links into the NPQH, a managerialist training programme for headteachers in
England discussed later in this chapter. There is even a short chapter on 'updating comprehensive schools' which, although it does not bother to explain
what is wrong with the comprehensive model, nevertheless intends that the
reader should 'become aware that the specialist schools programmes is making

a significant difference to the lives of thousands of our citizens' and should have 'decided that your school should seek to emulate or join one of the [specialist schools, Action Zones, Excellence in Cities, Beacon Schools and City Academy] programmes' (p. 167). Such uncritical promotion of post-welfarist policy is itself overt apologism and yet the point of this book is not to criticize school practitioners like Green. Rather we see Green's text as an example of how readily some in schools will pick up managerialist models of education management and hardly need encouragement by way of academic texts.

The subtle apologists

Although we have shown examples of school leadership texts which are primarily problem-solving or overtly apologist, most recent school leadership texts are characterized by a more subtle form of apologism. That is, they indicate some concern about school leadership within the context of post-welfarist education reform but they either fail to emphasize their concerns or are insufficiently critical to really challenge managerial models of leadership. Some recent leadership texts that we would see providing subtle apology for post-welfarist education reform and for the social status quo include those by MacBeath (1998a), Law and Glover (1999), Bush and Coleman (2000), Day *et al.* (2000) and Donaldson (2001). All of these texts raise concerns about post-welfarist educational reform but too often leave them hanging:

Leadership and Strategic Management in Education by Bush and Coleman (2000) does include a section which notes the moral and ethical dimensions of leadership and which briefly notes the work of Grace (1995) on the conflict felt by headteachers over competition and teacher redundancies (p. 26). However, for the most part it does not mention any problems with post-welfarist education reform; indeed, a section entitled 'Leadership of the autonomous school or college' promotes the marketing of schools, citing Caldwell and Spinks (1992) (p. 27).

Leading Schools in Times of Change (Day *et al.* 2000) is a book based on a study of 12 English headteachers which does better than most to highlight the problems of post-welfarist education reform and the inherent tensions for English school leaders. It argues that headteachers get offered the choice of being either 'subcontractors' or 'subversives':

> As subcontractors they become one more link in a chain leading down from those who have developed a policy through its various stages of implementation until it impacts on teachers and pupils. The limit that this role places on their autonomy and decisionmaking, combined with the visibility and public nature of their loss of control, is likely to undermine their moral authority as leaders as they seek to

> justify the unjustifiable. The role of the subversive, on the other hand, may raise issues of duplicity and intrigue, which may tarnish their moral lead within the school.
>
> (Day *et al.* 2000: 156)

But having identified this important tension, Day and colleagues give too much value to school leadership which manages to accommodate it: 'The heads in the study were neither subcontractors nor subversives, but, with integrity they skilfully mediated external changes so that they integrated with the vision and values which existed in the schools' (p. 156). To put it bluntly, we do not think managerialist pressures can be 'mediated'; rather, in a policy setting such as England's, a 'subversive' approach is needed for school leadership centred on social justice, as we outline later. Nor is the model of 'values-led contingency leadership' developed by Day *et al.* critical enough as it remains too centred on within-school issues and practices.

While *Educational Leadership and Learning* (Law and Glover 1999) appears on first glance to be a more standard 'how-to' text, complete with activities for readers, its first chapter on 'the context for educational leadership' demonstrates concerns about post-welfarist education reform, and this reappears in places throughout the book. Nevertheless, Law and Glover try to marry this concern with what is for the most part a conventionally uncritical discussion of education management and leadership. They claim that

> While this book acknowledges the complexities and difficulties inherent in combining both leading professional and chief executive roles, its argument is that effective educational leaders are capable of (and frequently do) combine *both* aspects. Rather than being mutually exclusive, they can be mutually reinforcing and complementary – helping to create a vital professional synergy.
>
> (Law and Glover 1999: 5)

Yet, like the work of Day and colleagues, this is a stance that does not take the tensions between managerialism and good education seriously enough. We would not object if Law and Glover were arguing that school leaders are forced to find a way through the tensions (which school leaders are), but it is wrong to argue that they can be creatively combined. Any 'combination' could occur only if one's notion of professionalism was defined by an insufficiently critical concern with social justice and genuine education.

Indeed, Law and Glover's approach provides only limited critique of post-welfarist education reform before moving into more traditional education management/leadership territory even if concerns are left unresolved. For instance, chapter 12 on managing resources and finance raises some important equity concerns about local financial management (LFM). One question they ask is: 'If income is linked to student numbers, how do schools/colleges provide for special needs students who require a much higher staff/student ratio?'(p. 212). In an activities text box, the reader is then asked to reflect on 'How far and in what ways are the advantages and disadvantages of LFM apparent in your own organisation?' This is a good question, but before long we are looking at cost–benefit analysis, budgeting and entrepreneurialism in a way which has all but forgotten the equity concerns just raised. Similarly, the chapter 13 discussion of parental choice and marketing includes some discussion of the problems implicit in the market as well as the ethical problems involved in marketing: 'it . . . remains dubious whether any level of expenditure would attract a potential educational consumer with offspring at Eton to attend an estate school in a socially deprived area' (p. 232). Yet the very next page moves on to 'schools' conciousness of the need to market themselves effectively, albeit at a low level', and provides some discussion of marketing approaches presumably intended to assist this, including, after Gray (1991), the five Ps of marketing – price, place, product, promotion and people.

Cultivating Leadership in Schools (Donaldson 2001) is described in a foreword by Michael Fullan as 'captur[ing] the depth of issues in clear, practical and comprehensive terms' more than any other book on educational leadership. Its praises are also sung on the book's cover by Sergiovanni (discussed shortly): 'Few books will teach you more about leadership, how it works and how it can slip into the nooks and crannies of a school'. In terms of how to build relationships within a school, this is probably true, and another strength of the book is its clear rejection of business models of leadership in favour of 'public school leadership'. But we searched in vain for more than a passing reference to educational reform or social inequality – this is a text with much discussion of 'mobilising people for moral purpose' but not of where that moral purpose should be directed.

Effective School Leadership (MacBeath 1998a) is much more cognizant of post-welfarist education reform, but offers strangely mixed messages and not just because it is an edited collection. This edited collection, based on an international study of school leaders in England, Denmark, Scotland and Australia, begins by noting that all were experiencing devolution, accountability, performativity and marketization. The book is positioned by discussing a series of questions which guided the study but there is an ambiguity here about whether it was intended to provide a critique of post-welfarist education reform or a guide to 'boxing clever' within it:

> These [reforms] brought new pressures and with them, changing expectations of schools and school leadership. For people in positions of leadership it posed the question 'whose expectations count and how should differing or conflicting expectations be resolved?' We wondered how headteachers, faced with the growing tensions of

management and leadership, were able to reconcile the conflicting demands on them. Were some better than others? If so what was their secret and where had they learned it?

(Kruchov *et al.* 1998: xii)

Further into the collection there seems to be some clear support for post-welfarist reform:

Principals must address their attitudes to change and futures orientation. Principals have no way of making their schools immune from the influences of governments, educational policymakers and members of the wider world of business, industry and commerce . . . Principals' learning must embrace the vision and values inherent in innovation and the requirements of mandated change.

(Dempster and Logan 1998: 96)

However, there is also some constrained but clear critique of the direction of reform, especially in a chapter on 'ethical challenges in school leadership':

On the one hand there are those who are pushing schools to operate like businesses and to pursue the educational equivalent of profit maximisation. On the other hand schools are ultimately concerned with the development of students who are not only employable, but also autonomous, responsible, moral individuals who are effective members of society . . . Heads who are able to model moral leadership in the way they run their schools are more likely, in our view, to concentrate on the ultimate goal of schooling, even though they are constantly under pressure to do otherwise.

(Dempster and Mahony 1998: 137–8)

But most of the time the discussion is more ambiguous than either of these. For instance, this chapter ending:

We can also see how reforms may begin to modify behaviour by accentuating certain aspects of the job and downgrading others and where some of the resultant discomfort for school leaders may arise as they feel themselves pulled away from what they regard as effective practice towards new models dictated from the centre.

(Reeves *et al.* 1998: 58)

Further confusing matters are contributions which do not relate clearly to the aim of the study, for instance MacBeath's opening chapter entitled 'Seven selected heresies of leadership' (MacBeath 1998b). Our problem with this book is not that it does not offer a critical perspective but rather that other readings are more likely because of the way the book is written.

These descriptions will have started to give a flavour of what we consider to be subtle apologism in the area of school leadership. We now consider in more detail the work of three well-known leadership writers – Leithwood, Southworth and Sergiovanni – who all take quite different angles on leadership but who all act as subtle apologists as well.

Leithwood

Kenneth Leithwood (see, for example, Leithwood *et al.* 1996, 1998; Leithwood 2000) has been described as 'one of the world's leading and most longstanding researchers on educational leadership'.[3] Certainly he is well known, prolific and, in a technical sense, very searching about what constitutes good leadership and how it can be fostered. In fact, Leithwood's writing is so jam-packed and relentless in pursuit of new ideas of various kinds that one can easily forget what he is not saying. From a critical perspective, his work does not offer school leaders any fundamental critique of post-welfarist educational reform or any sense of the possibility of contesting managerialism. It is challenging – but only within the frame. Leithwood, who favours a cognitive science approach to leadership, also undertheorizes the social.

These problems are apparent in his book (with Jantzi and Steinbach) *Changing Leadership for Changing Times* (1998) where we looked in vain for a seriously critical angle. The book begins by examining various models of school leadership and makes a case for a transformational and indeed 'post transformational' approach to leadership. Transformational leadership is seen as a place to begin because of its comprehensiveness and fit with context. Leithwood notes 'outstanding leadership is exquisitely sensitive to context' (Leithwood *et al.* 1998: 4) and that 'school restructuring undoubtedly frames the context for school leadership in the 1990s . . . widespread school restructuring has arisen from a combination of such trends as economic retention, neo-conservative ideologies and globalisation of the marketplace' (p. 23). So far so good, perhaps. However, the way Leithwood approaches school leadership is hardly critical. This is especially apparent when Leithwood *et al.* discuss the key case study of transformational leadership leading to improvement at Central Ontario Secondary School and also when they talk about the current restructuring context and likely future trends in education.

Leithwood notes that at the time of the research Central Ontario Secondary School (COSS) was not much affected by either quasi-market or funding problems. In this respect alone it seems like a case study which is not going to highlight the problems of leadership in an era of political restructuring. COSS does have important social problems which are seen to stem from declining 'social capital' rather than in terms of an structural analysis of the impact of social inequality on the school or community (pp. 45–6). As a result, the COSS solutions – a series of school-based measures and programmes to deal with student problems – do not extend to any of the critical solutions outlined at the beginning of Chapter 3 and could have only a limited impact at best. It sends domesticating rather than radicalizing messages to school leaders.

Leithwood describes four central features of the 'restructuring' context for leadership as follows: (a) the means and ends of school restructuring are uncertain; (b) school restructuring requires both first- and second-order changes; (c) school restructuring is increasingly focused on secondary schools, and (d) the professionalization of teaching is a centrepiece of the school restructuring agenda (pp. 24–7). Here is an obvious point for a critique of markets and managerialism but Leithwood's analysis is more about leadership which can anticipate and respond to the demands of the 'restructured' context. For instance:

> There is nothing clear about the purposes for school restructuring – higher order thinking or creating schools that are more responsive to the demands of the 21st century for example. Nor are the initiatives required to accomplish these purposes, such as site based management, teacher empowerment and teaching for understanding . . . at all clear. Under these circumstances commitment rather than control strategies are called for. These are strategies that help front-line school staffs to appreciate the reasons for change and that foster their commitment to developing, trying out and refining new practices until those purposes are accomplished (or until they change). Virtually all treatments of transformational leadership claim that amongst its more direct effects are employee motivation and commitment.
>
> (pp. 24–5)

> School restructuring is certainly about second order change. It . . . requires a form of leadership that is sensitive to organisation building; developing shared vision, creating productive work cultures, distributing leadership to others, and the like.
>
> (p. 25)

Critique, where it exists, is only in passing:

> Professionalisation of teaching is a centrepiece of the school restructuring agenda (not uniformly the case – recent changes appear to deprofessionalise the teacher . . . in England, Wales and New Zealand). In the USA and parts of Canada however, teacher professionalisation is part of the goal.
>
> (p. 26)

Why Leithwood does not contest post-welfarist education reform becomes a little more apparent at the end of the book when he considers a number of 'broad trends stimulating the evolution of schools', including the 'end of the "borrow now, pay later" school of public finance'. The problem is

> that in the 1990s developed countries around the world found themselves seriously challenged by debt, that there is enough public concern for the long-term consequences of ignoring debt to make debt reduction politically attractive goals, also that there is an ageing population who are less disposed towards willingly allocating their taxes to school. Thus the resources are significantly eroding and this is creating centralising pressures on schools in order to make more efficient use of available resources through so-called economies of scale.
>
> (p. 206)

This is one interpretation, but what is not here is an account of shifting political ideologies, the rise of the Right and neo-liberalism, shifts towards privatization and greater inequalities. There is more of a sense that Leithwood accepts the rationale for reform provided by neo-liberals, 'we can't afford to carry on as we are', 'there is no alternative', and so on. Similarly, another perceived trend is the 'end of society's willingness to assign major decision-making authority to professional expertise'. Here it is suggested that professionals of all kinds have been experiencing a rapid decline in the public's willingness to continue ceding autonomy and status because of higher levels of public education, greater access to information and concern that many professionals have betrayed the public trust. Leithwood and colleagues argue that this has also led to growth in advisory or decision-making roles for parents in schools. But what is not mentioned is the growth of individualism and a consumer culture under neo-liberalism, or the 'manufacturing' of parental involvement by governments seeking to develop market relations in education.

Overall, Leithwood and his colleagues nearly always tend to go with the neo-liberal justification for policy rather than critiquing it. Their image of future schools as 'high reliability learning communities' is revealing too. First, they argue that good schools will be communities which can foster 'social capital' (discussion of the school leader as 'transformative intellectual' sits rather oddly here). Second, drawing on Stringfield (for example, Stringfield 1995), schools should be regarded as high reliability organizations (HROs) which have to accomplish their goals more or less all the time. But this discussion seems to be buying into the 'standards' crisis and there are many problems in an HRO approach, not least the notion of failure free schooling.[4] Finally, schools will need to be learning organizations: 'so that changing is considered an ordinary activity rather than an extraordinary event'. Here the argument is linked to business literature on the learning organization – organizations behaving with brains (bureaucracies) or as brains (learning organizations). However, as we argue in the next chapter, bureaucracies are not as problematic as assumed here whereas continuous change is more so.

The problem is that, however interesting and complex, none of this seriously challenges the status quo, and Leithwood's other books are no more critical. However, it is unlikely Leithwood sees this as a problem; he would probably just see the critical view of leadership as a different perspective on leadership rather than having more fundamental implications for his own work. For instance, Leithwood seems pleased that critical perspectives receive 'substantial attention' in the *International Handbook of Educational Leadership and Administration* (Leithwood *et al.* 1996, see p. 6 of the introduction), but his own contribution is not among the critical chapters.

Southworth

Southworth's writing about English primary school leadership provides a good illustration of subtle apologism in as much as it has a veneer of criticality and yet remains framed by New Labour's agenda of official school improvement. His trilogy on 'improving primary schools' (Southworth 1998; Southworth and Conner 1999; Southworth and Lincoln 1999) provides good examples. Southworth begins *Leading Improving Primary Schools* (1998) by talking about his belief in the value of shared leadership and outlining various studies of primary headship. From this we get a sense that Southworth's work is very much grounded in empirical research on headteachers. However, there is nothing in the introduction about the political context of being a headteacher. Chapter 1 is about the importance of leadership in schools, and here he notes that schools are social institutions so 'leadership is thus both a social medium and involves social messages' (p. 8). Southworth then goes on to discusses various perspectives on effective and ineffective leadership. In some places this is a qualified discussion. For instance, on page 10 he cites the work of Mortimore *et al.* (1988) but notes that it has become dated because of policy changes – this is his first (passing) mention of the policy context. There is also some critique of the value of school effectiveness research:

> While the effective schools research has proved influential with policymakers, it is less illuminative for practitioners because it is limited in scope. The studies are also rather shallow because there has not been much follow up research exploring what effective school leaders actually do in their schools.
>
> (p. 10)

Southworth is also critical of list logic (Barth 1990), that is the assumption that if you create lists of desirable attributes they will happen: 'I do not view these lists in this way rather as things to work towards' (Southworth 1998: 19–20). He suggests we need to be cautious about offering a view of effective leadership which is untenable and that the identified characteristics are not a good guide to what distinguishes a good and bad head; indeed,

> *we may never discover* all there is to know about effectiveness. School leadership may be just too complex, too organic, too unpredictable, and too contingent that we can never be sure of very much ... I suspect we may never be clear about causal connections.
>
> (pp. 20–1, emphasis in original)

Despite this, Southworth (1998) offers more than ten pages of discussion about effective and ineffective leadership from the various perspectives of UK school effectiveness research, US literature on instructional leadership, UK literature on headship and from the point of view of staff in his own research. Against this background, his critique of effectiveness characteristics is easily lost. Why is there this emphasis on characteristics of effectiveness when he is critical of their limitations? Perhaps it reflects the fact that, as he notes, '[the lists] do seem to have currency with primary heads' (p. 18).

The book then moves on to a discussion of official views on school leadership. Here politics might be expected to come to the fore but there is only a brief discussion of the rise of managerialism:

> By the mid 1980s a stronger sense of advice and technical prescription is evident ... Leadership ... was being expanded by particular professional tasks and activities each aiming to enhance the efficiency and effectiveness of the school. This movement was no doubt associated with the increased emphasis upon school management throughout the 1980s and, indeed, the increased fascination with the importance of management in other sectors.
>
> (p. 25)

Southworth also notes a

> convergence of thinking about leadership between the effective schools research and the ideas of OfSTED and HMI. In the late 1990s this outlook has been refined further with the TTA intervention in the field of management training.
>
> (p. 26)

Nevertheless, his discussion of the Teacher Training Agency (TTA) and Ofsted are hardly searching. There is some concern about the simplistic and general nature of school effectiveness research (SER) but not of SER's connection to managerialism. It is also clear that school improvement is regarded as much more useful than SER ('While there has in the last few years been some convergence with SER, there has also been a growing appreciation that leadership is associated with school improvement' (p. 29)). Southworth's (1998) discussion of school improvement draws on Fullan (1991) whose work, along with Southworth's own, is seen to point to a more sophisticated appreciation of school leadership where the politics and cultural aspects of change come to the fore. But this is change within the school rather than concern with the wider political context. School leadership is seen as intensely intellectual (but not intensely political) and Southworth's key summary points about leadership include the idea that 'leaders are analysts of what is happening "in" the school' but not without and that 'leadership is differentiated. There are many ways of being successful' (p. 34) but not fundamental differences by school context.

Chapter 2 looks at five theories of leadership: situational, instrumental and expressive, cultural, transactional, and transformational. The first and last are of most interest here. The discussion of situational leadership concludes that 'sensitivity to the situation and the setting is vital' but leaves out the political context entirely and mentions the market context of schools only obliquely. Southworth sees transformational leadership as the best and most inclusive model in the sense that it recognizes transactional, cultural and situational dimensions of leadership and incorporates them into a more holistic conceptualization. Transformational leadership is thought to be popular because of its emphasis on change 'in our postindustrial age, organisations have had to learn to cope with the turbulence caused by new technology and ever faster communications (pp. 45–6). It is also timely 'because it fits with the quest for higher standards in teaching and learning, the search for more effective schools and the drive for continuous improvement in schooling [. . .] it chimes with the school improvement enterprise and it is congruent with the communitarian ideals which are also gaining currency' (pp. 46–7).

Nevertheless, Southworth's (1998) account of transformational leadership is disconnected from critiques of post-welfarist educational reform. Although a brief discussion of Grace (1995) raises tensions between the historical approach to English headship and transformational leadership (see pp. 46–7), the discussion is about empowerment, team leadership, development, learning, vision. Although Southworth concludes that 'these two chapters sustain the romance of leadership, something which has become a strong feature of organisational theorising throughout the greater part of the 20th century but especially the last two decades' (p. 55), this is only a critique of the idealized (rather than empirically based) nature of the literature. What is not highlighted is the lack of discussion in the literature of leadership's relationship to the wider social and political context within which it does its work.

Against the background of leadership theory, chapter 3 of the book is about 'what we know' about 'real life' leadership in primary schools.

Southworth notes that he is offering a general picture but acknowledges that headteachers are differentiated by the type and age level of the schools they lead, by gender and experience (Southworth 1998: 59–60). Curiously 'race' and class are not mentioned as factors differentiating leadership. Southworth goes on to discuss: (a) that headteachers are powerful people; (b) that headship is changing; (c) Ofsted, and (d) school improvement. It is in this section that educational reform gets the most discussion. Some points are particularly noteworthy:

- When Southworth talks about the changing nature of headship, he looks at the National Curriculum, Local Management of Schools (LMS), marketing, appraisal, governance, rational management and intensification. This is certainly getting into many of the key issues in 'real-life' schools but here his sources are those like Mortimore and Mortimore (1991) and Barber (1996b), rather than authors who are more critical of reform. Indeed, he argues (p. 85) that the 'transition to LMS has been successfully accomplished';
- Southworth argues that loss of control over the National Curriculum is compensated for by control over schools' finances and resources. In other words, he seems to take the rhetoric of devolution seriously;
- Southworth suggest heads have become accustomed to managing imposed reforms – now discontinuous – and have to 'anticipate and respond to new initiatives, challenges and opportunities' (p. 68). But there is no mention of resisting or contesting inappropriate reforms;
- Southworth regards the introduction of Ofsted in a positive light because he argues that it has served to put a brake on managerial ('CEO') work and refocus attention on professional leadership. The drift to management has been 'slowed if not halted' by the Ofsted school inspection programme as heads have had to start monitoring what was happening in classrooms, rethink their role priorities and as inspections are seen as a judgement on the head (pp. 71–2). But what is not mentioned here are the costs of Ofsted in terms of inappropriate performative pressures and the time-wasting actions which follow from them, and
- In relation to school improvement, Southworth argues that tracking pupil progress, action planning and the like leads to heads who are 'inclusive, data driven and improvement oriented'. But at this point he appears to forget that he is reporting the reality of being a head and begins to 'sell' a particular school improvement perspective. He moves into the advocacy of a particular kind of head, one leading a 'learning school' where staff development and pupil learning are given high priority because transformational leadership will create them, because schools have to be continuously improving, and

because leadership in the area of school improvement 'is not an option it is an obligation'. Moreover, we are told (p. 87) that heads need to be concerned with both the internal development of the school and with the external image of the school and with drawing upon external support and 'sponsorship' of the school.

The key point about all of this is that it is fundamentally about accepting the political status quo and working within it. There is no sustained analysis of education policy and its impact that might lead to different implications for good leadership. Related to this perspective, Southworth's (1998) view of heads is always respectful, with any criticisms muted. In the final chapter of the book, Southworth makes the telling point that, 'the real danger for me is in becoming detached from reality and setting out a personal manifesto which is unrealistic and unworkable [this kind of comment goes down well with real-world heads] . . . The best way forward is in learning from leading practitioners and disseminating their approaches' (p. 119). The difficulty here is that since the views and attitudes of heads themselves have been influenced by the generally managerial context of the past decade or more, they may now be very much part of the problem and have to be approached more critically than this.

Southworth's concluding chapter argues that leading improving primary schools involves: (a) evidence-based management and leadership; (b) leadership at all levels; (c) improving through professional learning, and (d) improving the quality of teaching. It also involves reflective leadership. There are undoubtedly some useful points made here, for instance the notion of shared leadership has considerable democratic potential if carried far enough. But the discussion involves cases of best practice in schools, with the wider context of school leadership now almost entirely out of view. Consequently, it fails to challenge Official School Improvement (OSI), rather it often supports it, for instance evidence-based management and leadership is about a 'data-driven approach', with much emphasis on target-setting and testing.

Two points made in Southworth's conclusion particularly highlight the limitations of his account. One is a strangely 'apolitical' understanding of critical leadership:

> Critical leaders are aware of traditions and ritualised practices and question them, whether they are their own or those of others. They also examine and reflect on how colleagues are feeling, their expectations, attitudes and commitment. In other words, leaders consider values, beliefs, norms and the moral import of the school and their own actions. Reflective, critical leadership implies there is a philosophical dimension to leadership as well as a practical one [but see for instance the uncritical 'philosophical' approach of Sergiovanni below]. Philosophy here means the 'examined life' and philosophical

leaders examine their leadership and that of others . . . Such examination is especially important in the context of school improvement.
When we embark on initiatives we need to check and evaluate during
the process not only how the change is going but whether it is bringing about improvements.

(Southworth 1998: 144)

The other revealing point is when Southworth raises the issue of schools
having improved examination results by narrowing the curriculum or paying
less attention to those who are unlikely to succeed. Here he asks, 'What are the
implications of these measures over time and for all pupils in the school? Is
this school improvement? What are those who take a lead in these schools
doing and is this what they should be doing? (p. 144). He notes that these are
moral questions for school leaders but there is no critique of the performative
forces which lead schools to take such damaging actions.

The other two books in the same series are similarly problematic. *Managing Improving Primary Schools* (Southworth and Conner 1999) notes that 'now
that self-managing schools have become established in England and Wales,
the next phase of development involves encouraging all schools to be self-
improving organisations and to achieve this staff in schools need to conduct
school self-evaluation' (p. xi). This is only the second sentence in the book – it
is hardly a critical start. Most of the book is devoted to how to collect and
analyse evidence for school development. All the issues it considers are
internal to the school and the references reflect its problem-solving approach.
Supporting Improving Primary Schools (Southworth and Lincoln 1999) is about
the EPSI programme, a school improvement project involving researchers
working with Essex primary schools, the local education authority and central
government. A chapter by Paul Lincoln, senior manager in Essex LEA, notes
that he initiated the EPSI partly because he was critical of government policy,
mostly in terms of how LEAs could be unjustly held responsible for failing
schools. But it is still necessary to fit within the OSI framework ('The EPSI
programme enabled us to grapple with some of the issues around how, as an
LEA, we could work most effectively with schools on their improvement strategies within the national context described above' (Lincoln 1999: 175). This
kind of discussion suggests that academics involved in such networks will
occupy positions from which it will not be possible to be very critical because if
their work did not fit with government policy they would soon be pushed out
of the loop. Yet, even here, there were enough critical insights to make this
book a case of subtle rather than overt apologism:

The EPSI schools could not be described as places that needed a 'save
and rescue' approach to their improvement. They were not schools
that necessarily needed an injection of strong leadership. Nor did the

schools fall neatly into the 'stuck' or 'moving' categories (Rozenholtz 1989), or Stoll and Finks (1998) classification of moving, cruising, strolling, struggling and sinking schools. These classifications are too simplistic and fail to demonstrate the differentiated nature of primary school improvement. The EPSI programme schools were differentiated by their improvement focuses, their starting points, school contexts, professional cultures and pace of progress. These differences should be recognised so that their improvement efforts and strategies can be examined to see if they are suitable for their needs and plans.

(Lincoln 1999: 194)

Sergiovanni

Sergiovanni's books provide a good example of a more 'visionary' or motivational strand within the school leadership literature (Sergiovanni 1992, 1996, 1999, 2000, 2001a,b). To Sergiovanni, leadership is a moral craft and his work has an important democratic emphasis in notions of leadership as 'stewardship' or the leader as 'servant' (Sergiovanni 1992) as well as a clear recognition that much of what is important in schools is not measurable and a critique of faddism and 'pop' management. In this sense, Sergiovanni's books do indeed provide a 'counterpoint to the various textbooks, commonly used in university courses, on principalship, leadership and organizational behaviour' (1992: xvii) and we have found much of what he writes about refreshingly different. Yet, from a critical perspective, Sergiovanni's approach is frustratingly free-floating. He employs an almost entirely school-centred discussion which aims to offer what he calls a 'concept boutique' and 'metaphor repository' to inform reflective practice (Sergiovanni 2001a: 344), but there is little discussion of the broader social context and Sergiovanni's texts rarely explicitly critique post-welfarist educational reform or provide direct advice on how to engage with it.[5] Rather, a great many readings are possible and because of this Sergiovanni does not avoid the problem of textual apologism even though we think his work has considerable critical potential.

The introduction to *Leadership: What's in it for Schools?* (Sergiovanni 2001b) provides a good flavour of Sergiovanni's approach. He begins by noting that 'today's leadership theories are too rational and too scripted to fit the messy world in which schooling actually takes place' (p. x) and he seems to be wanting to avoid a problem-solving approach:

> Perhaps most perplexing is the understanding of leadership that emerges from the belief that every problem has a solution. This is a belief prominent in the cultures of many Western societies. The US and UK are good examples. Leadership is identified with solving

problems and the purpose of leadership is finding solutions. A better understanding, I argue in this book, is that leadership is about helping people to understand the problems they face, with helping people to get a handle on how to manage those problems and even with learning how to live with problems.

(p. ix)

Leadership that counts is far more cognitive than it is personality-based or rules-based. Cognitive leadership has more to do with purposes, values, and frameworks that oblige us morally than it does with needs that touch us psychologically or with bureaucratic things that push us organizationally.

(p. ix)

He also talks just a little about the political context of schooling:

In this age of top-down school reform, the number of constraints that administrators and teachers and their schools face from distant authorities is increasing . . . Leadership becomes more and more like trying to run in soft sand. Yet things need to be done in schools. Problems need to be solved and improvements need to be invented and implemented.

(pp. 1–2)

This seems to be opening up a critique of managerial policy, but Sergiovanni goes on to define the problem as 'how one satisf[ies] pressures to comply with central requirements when one knows that rarely is there one best way'. He then quotes Schön (1987: 3) 'the practitioner must choose. Shall he remain on the high ground where he can solve relatively unimportant problems according to prevailing standards of rigour, or shall he descend to the swamp of important problems and non-rigorous inquiry?' (p. 2). Sergiovanni also adds that what school leaders cannot be is rational or aggressive like corporate leaders are supposed to be. Instead they need to be able to synthesize, to innovate and be perceptive, and, like the best school leaders, take an unhurried, careful approach to change.

Some of these points are potentially helpful from a critical point of view. For instance, the last arguably reminds school leaders that while managerial reforms may be constantly asked of schools, they do not have to be embraced. But it is also possible to not contest managerialism and still see the need to synthesize, to innovate and be perceptive. A critical perspective, if that is what is intended, is not explicit enough here. The seven basic principles of leadership which follow (pp. 5–14) are similarly problematic. Here school leaders are told to act in the following ways:

1. Invert the rule (schools are really culturally tight and managerially loose). This 'places emphasis on the school's culture' (but note that student culture does not get a look in).
2. Consider causes and consequences. This stresses reform which focuses directly on what needs to be achieved rather than just assuming that some more distant organizational change will have the intended consequence.
3. Think amoeba. This stresses the need for a theory of school leadership which fits the way the world of schooling works using a metaphor of the difficulty of trying to get a giant amoeba to move from one side of the road to the other in the direction intended. Sergiovanni (2001b: 7) comments:

    How different is this view from the one offered in the literature and the one assumed by policymakers – a view that would have us attempt the crossing of the street by first specifying our destination as a highly specific outcome and then implementing an explicit linear and managerial chain of planning, organizing, directing, controlling and evaluating as if context were fixed and people were inanimate.

4. Emphasize sense and meaning. Sergiovanni says his principles are certainly non-organizational views of schooling but not non-leadership views. 'If what matters most to teachers and students, parents and other locals are values and beliefs, patterns of socialization and norms that emerge in the school, then these are the characteristics which must be considered as key to school improvement efforts' (p. 8). As an example, Sergiovanni points to the limits of rewards – 'the power of calculated involvement pales when compared with the power of moral involvement' (p. 9).
5. Build with canvas. Like decoys of tanks built in canvas during the war, when change will create too much resistance, 'building in canvas' allows a doable option. Sergiovanni (2001b: 10) suggests that this can help with the issue of legitimacy since schools have to respond to demands and pressures from external audiences which require that schools look the way they are 'supposed to'.
6. Be humble in decision-making. This is about building in time for reflection through incremental change. Sergiovanni suggests that trial and error is acceptable provided it is focused and not random.
7. Remember the moral aspects of leadership. Part of what Sergiovanni suggests here is that the preceding ideas may be seen as deceptive and have no place in the theory and practice of leadership but that moral questions are raised when we ignore human realities by continuing to push an ill-fitting, rationalistic management theory on to school

leaders and constantly trying to shape human nature to fit this theory.

It will again be apparent that many of the points Sergiovanni is making could chime with a critical perspective. For instance, the amoeba theory undoubtedly provides a critique of a managerial conception of schooling. Lurking around point 4, 'emphasize sense and meaning', is a great critique of contractualism. Point 5, 'build with canvas', could be seen as a helpful strategy for building in flexibility for resisting managerial interventions: while pursuing more clearly educational goals, school leaders could fabricate what is publicly required of them. Point 6, 'be humble in decision-making', offers good guidance for anyone pursuing alternatives in education. And point 7, 'remember the moral aspects of leadership' again surely provides a potentially powerful critique of managerialism.

But here we are putting words into Sergiovanni's mouth. What he provides is potentially very helpful but not *necessarily* so because the discussion is so general that while a critical reading is possible, it is not required: it is possible to take many readings. The same is true of the book as a whole; for instance, we liked the following:

- The chapter 2 discussion about the importance of substance over style in leadership and the notion of ideas-based leadership drawing on the authority of shared ideas rather than personal authority or bureaucratic authority. But what ideas are to become the common ground?
- The chapter 3 discussion of the vacuous nature of educational change: 'we are so concerned with change that we neglect substance . . . Let's face it, some ideas are not worth advancing. We would be better off if some heads knew less about the change process than they do. When ideas are not worth advancing, less effective leadership may be a virtue and teachers who resist change may be heroes.' But the value of the consequent 'competencies for leadership' – management of attention, meaning, trust, self, paradox, effectiveness and commitment – all depend on the school leader having a grasp of the key political and social issues facing schools, and here Sergiovanni leaves the reader guessing.
- The chapter 4 discussion of 'communities of responsibility' with its point that,

    unfortunately, considering students as clients and considering students as customers does not help. Whether we intend it or not, 'client has a technical ring to it that suggest teaching and learning are about delivery – the delivery of expert services to customers who are dependent on our expertise . . . Since delivery is so different from leading, it distances teachers from their role as pedagogues and reduces them to roles as technicians. Having been distanced themselves, students assume little or no responsibility in this image for the success of teaching and learning. Success rests entirely on the teachers' shoulders.

(Sergiovanni 2001b: 73)

There is surely at least an oblique critique of the market here. But it is also suggested in this chapter that establishing schools as communities of responsibility is a way in which schools can reclaim the trust of central governments and the general public. But surely if Sergiovanni's ideas realized their critical potential they would make schools less trustworthy to central government, not more?

• The chapter 5 discussion of school 'lifeworlds' which need protecting and therefore a layered approach to setting standards. But here there is an oddly apolitical discussion of the politics of performativity.

Overall, we are left in no doubt there is much critical *potential* in Sergiovanni's work (and we have taken that potential seriously, see the final section of this chapter). It also comes as no surprise that Grace (2000) regards Sergiovanni's work as one of a number of critical leadership studies (see below). However, we would not go this far with Sergiovanni's writing as it stands. This is because while Sergiovanni's approach is infinitely better than clearly problem-solving or overtly apologist accounts of school leadership, it fails to use research and scholarship to directly inform the reader's understanding of neoliberal education policy and its impact on schools. Part of the problem here may be the popular style Sergiovanni chooses to write in to reach his audience. A more explicit critique would be more contentious and also less subject to multiple readings, and hence more challenging to the managerialist trends in education which Sergiovanni clearly finds distasteful.

Finally, as noted earlier, Sergiovanni's work may be seen as part of a visionary or motivation strand of literature on school leadership. In some of its manifestations this literature does not deserve to be taken too seriously. Epitomizing this trend is the leadership writing of Terrance Deal. His book (with Petersen) *The Leadership Paradox* is about resolving the 'technical' and 'artistry' elements of school leadership, hence chapter 3 about the 'bifocal principal' who can combine managerial tasks with symbolic sensitivity and passion, and chapter 5 about 'the balanced school' where this happens. An important problem with all this is that the tensions between technicist and more educational perspectives are frequently less resolvable than Deal and Petersen suggest and their account once again encourages the reader to work with, rather than challenge, managerialism because there is only fleeting mention of wider structural or political factors. Nevertheless, it is an entertaining read and it is not surprising to find that Deal is also an author of several more generalist leadership books with his long-time collaborator Lee Bolman. One of them, *Leading with Soul: An Uncommon Journey of Spirit* (Bolman and Deal 2001), invites readers

> to join Steve Camden, a highly successful fast-track manager who has run into an existential wall, as he works with Maria, a spiritual mentor. Many readers, both men and women, have told us they identify with Steve – his confusion, his yearning, his sense of being lost and stuck. Many have also told us they were fortunate enough to have a Maria who provided them critical guidance at key moments in their lives. Other have written to say they desperately need a Maria and wonder if we know where to find one. This story is a parable drawn from the authors' own lives and the lives of others we have known. We hope it speaks to you. To assist your reflections, we punctuate the story with a series of interludes – meditations on the issues and questions raised in the story.
>
> (pp. 12–13)

This is 'pop philosophy' at its most obvious and, for us, it points up the difficulties of working in an applied area where generic leadership fads also come and go and may hold considerable sway. School leaders might enjoy this kind of thing but it is an awfully long way from the rigorous empirically, theoretically and politically informed educational perspectives we think they should be reading.

The textual dissenters

In the school leadership area, textual dissent tends to centre on alternative accounts of leadership rather than on detailed critique of textual apologism. Grace (2000: 235–6) sums up the concerns of dissenting authors as follows:

> The critics of the dominance of Education Management Studies . . . believe that the colonisation of the life-world of school leaders is in process as a result of the imperialism of market culture in education and of the hegemony of the new managerialism. The effects of this colonisation, they believe, will be detrimental to humane and ethical values in education, to educative and pedagogical values, to social and professional relations within the school, to constructs of educational community and collegiality and to commitments to greater social equity and inclusiveness . . . It must be made clear that this oppositional position is not based upon resistance to the insights and functional value of Educational Management Studies *per se* but rather

upon their current constitution as a new hegemony in the formation of school leaders. The perceived problem is that school leadership which is a major agency of cultural, moral intellectual and political education in society is in danger of being reduced, in Wright Mill's (1973) terms, to a form of 'abstracted empiricism' and to a set of technical manoeuvres.

As noted at the outset, we think the distinction to be drawn is not between management and leadership but between critical and uncritical leadership studies seen in turn as part of a wider debate around critical and uncritical education management. We also think that many critics (ourselves included) *would* want to resist the insights and functional value of educational management studies *per se* because as a way of thinking about and framing education they are so inadequate and potentially damaging. Nevertheless, the concerns identified here do go to the heart of the dissenting perspective and Grace goes on to identify a corpus of writing which has reacted against the perceived dominance of mainstream educational texts in various ways. These include books and chapters by Bottery (1992), Greenfield (1993) and Ozga (1993), as well as a collection edited by John Smyth (Smyth 1989) and, most recently, Jill Blackmore's book *Troubling Women* (Blackmore 1999).

We will come back to Blackmore's account but it should also be noted that Grace's own *School Leadership: Beyond Educational Management – An Essay in Policy Scholarship* (Grace 1995) has also done much to emphasize the need for a more critical approach to school leadership. First, it starts by contrasting problem-solving 'policy science' with more critical 'policy scholarship' and by arguing that to resist the study of school leadership being reduced to a set of technical considerations, it needs to be 'historically located and . . . brought into a relationship with wider political, cultural, economic and ideological movements in society' (p. 5). Second, Grace illustrates how the construction of English headship and discourses of leadership and management have been related to wider socio-political changes over time (chapters 1 and 2). Third, various critical perspectives on school leadership are reviewed (chapter 3). Fourth, the book reports a raft of empirical findings on the changing culture of English school headship in the areas of power relations, curriculum and educational leadership, self-management and market relations, moral ethical and professional dilemmas, Catholic headship and gender relations (chapters 5–10). Finally, it points to the need for more democratic and inclusive forms of school leadership and governance (chapter 11, discussed further below).

The book therefore covers a great deal of ground. However, what sets it apart most from the kind of leadership literature discussed in previous sections is the way it grounds headship firmly within England's distinctive social and political history. It stresses, for instance, how, in the nineteenth and early twentieth century, a period of 'explicit class-cultural control of provided schooling', headteachers of state schools held subordinate class positions and role status in relation to school managers and governors. In contrast, however, the public schools had a powerful 'headmaster' tradition which allowed their school leaders more autonomy. The 'social democratic' period of English schooling (1940s to 1970s) saw a version of this headmaster tradition taken up by headteachers in state schools who began to take substantive operative and 'professional' leadership of schools. During the 'market accountability' phase of the 1980s and 1990s, Grace perceives headteachers losing their power as professionals but gaining new forms of management and enterprise power. The result is that

> Those headteachers who are drawn by the image of managing director, or skilful player of the education market place, will experience the excitement of new roles to be practised on what is sure to be called 'a new playing field'. Those for whom the professional aspects of headship were especially important, particularly in the cultural, pedagogical and pupil relations sectors, have to face the challenge of adjustment or flight from the field.
>
> (Grace 1995: 23)

One important effect of this kind of analysis is that it highlights the way English school leaders have generally worked towards conservative interests, apart from the 'blip' of the social democratic period (and, as Grace points out, this had its limitations in terms of the continuing hegemony of 'strong leadership'). Thus by highlighting features of school leadership in different eras which have been 'dynamic, contested, historically and culturally situated' (p. 192), the analysis is able to be exceptionally insightful about the current tensions within school leadership, what desirable features of leadership are being lost with the shift to post-welfarism and also, just as importantly, realistic about the contradictions in the welfarist settlement it replaced.

Helen Gunter's book *Leaders and Leadership in Education* (2001) is another important example of textual dissent in the area of school leadership.[6] Like Grace, Gunter immediately debunks decontexualized and asocial, or what Wilson (1999) refers to as 'sanitised' management models and 'theories'. Indeed Gunter (2001: vii) argues that

> leadership is not an 'it' from which we can abstract behaviours and tasks, but is a relationship . . . Consequently, leadership is highly political and is a struggle within practice, theory and research. Furthermore, leadership is not located in job descriptions but in the professionality of working for teaching and learning.

She suggests that in managerialist times the dominant model of leadership is 'a conduit through which individualising markets are installed in education, rather than a dialogic process located in civic democratic values connected with social justice and equity' (p. 17). The ascendant model of leadership is firmly located in neo-liberal versions of the 'performing school', where leadership is being defined around notions of controlling uncertainty through charismatic behaviours and strategic tasks, whereas management is defined around system maintenance. Gunter suggests three interrelated strands in the preferred leadership model for educational institutions. They are: leadership of systems, which concern strategic development and operational action planning; leadership of consumers, which involves target-setting and outcomes-monitoring; leadership of performance, which enjoins the control of embodied identities and approaches to work.

Gunter goes on to examine the conceptions of leadership used within education management by the school effectiveness and school improvement, education management and critical studies (chapter 3). The key concern here is how writers in the area of education management and school effectiveness and school improvement unreflectively accept charismatic transformational leadership and the school as a unitary organization. This model lacks the necessary radicalism needed to pursue greater equity in managerialist times. Gunter also argues that for leadership to be *educational* leadership, it must encompass pedagogy, in which teachers and students engage in a leadership relationship where, as Gunter argues, the emphasis is on 'problem-posing' rather than 'problem-solving'.

Following this are chapters on the ways in which leaders and leadership in education are being researched, theorized and taught, particularly in England (chapters 4–6). Discussing research, Gunter critically dissects current emphases on 'what works' and 'evidence-based/informed policy'. She also points to the predominance of 'laboratory epistemology' that underpins leadership research, where the researcher is presented as a neutral data-gatherer and interpreter. Whether and how leadership might impact on learning outcomes can be measured in isolation from the local setting is rightly queried. In relation to theory, Gunter argues that (a) a leader may have contractual authority for being a leader, but may not necessarily exercise leadership; (b) leadership is a relationship that all are capable of exercising, and (c) leadership within education should be directly connected to attempts to realize democratic forms and practices. In particular, she provides a critique of transformational leadership (pp. 72–5) and, following Smyth (1996), argues for the restoration of 'educative leadership'. When it comes to training for school leadership, Gunter also notes the trend in the UK towards prescriptively determined learning and towards competences. However such competences are disconnected from pedagogical relationships and in the National Professional Qualification for Headship (NPQH), for example, other key elements such as the culture and values of the school are missing.

Towards the end of the book, Gunter uses qualitative data gathered from and about headteachers regarding their experiences to illustrate how New Labour's modernization programme is moving headteachers away from educational values and collegial processes towards what Gunter calls 'marketised performance' (chapter 7). As she puts it:

> Certainly the mandated model of headship as presented within current government documents does not see the headteacher as a head *teacher*, but as a leader and manager in an educational setting . . . Headship is being reworked around strategic business-like models rather than leadership growing out of pedagogic expertise.
>
> (p. 96)

In essence, Gunter notes that there is resistance to the new managerialization of education, but for how long and to what extent is difficult to assess. Indeed, Gunter ends the chapter thus: 'Teachers have to turn their backs on conceptually informed practice integrated with learning, to a regime of numbers and graphs designed to tell them what does and does not work' (p. 105).

Gunter concludes the book by underscoring the fact that leadership is a highly political issue and any claims to neutrality are unfounded (we would add ideological). She argues that 'education is being ontologically and epistemologically purged, as particular forms of knowledge are privileged in ways that characterise dialogic intellectual work as being disruptive and irrelevant' (p. 141).

On the whole, then, Gunter's work represents a strong example of textual dissent in the area of leadership, albeit one which is hard to follow in places. Nevertheless, she identifies herself as someone who inhabits border territory between the education management arena and its critics:

> Much of my professional practice is the same as other field members, but my research and theoretical interests have shifted from the common-sense problem-solving agenda to that of critical studies and in particular, the historical setting and development of the field. During this intellectual journey I seem to have crossed Popkewitz's (1999, p. 2–3) metaphorical room away from the 'pragmatic-empiricists' who are concerned to make organisations work better towards a position where 'critical' is interpreted as being about understanding and explaining the tensions.
>
> (Gunter 2001: 4)

We think this 'crossing over' is admirable, of course, but Gunter's closeness to the conventional education management arena means she is sometimes let down by the arguments of her collaborators. For instance, *Living Headship*

(Tomlinson *et al.* 1999) begins with a quite critical account of headteacher education by Gunter and colleagues which includes its own critique of textual apologism. Gunter *et al.* (1999: xx–xxi) suggest six characteristics of what is being sold to educational professionals as leadership through their training and educational literature:

- Leadership which seems to float free of educational values and professionalism reconstructed as management processes.
- Leadership presented as a consensus where culture is managed.
- Effective leadership which is strongly normative and based on a construction of what ought to be rather than the day-to-day experiences of headship.
- Leadership methodology which is often ahistorical and where the biographies and narratives of headteachers are often marginalized.
- The agency of headteachers being emphasized at the expense of the structural context within which their work is located.
- Children and teachers being constructed as objects to be managed, related to follower status.

This is all good stuff – and there is more – but this collection also gathers some terribly instrumental chapters by headteachers; indeed, one contributor notes:

> It has always been part of my thinking that whatever the rules of the game I will play to win using them. It does not mean I always agree with them or would not seek to change them but it does stop me wasting a lot of time achieving something the system does not value. Perhaps it might be argued that this is a lack of principles but at the end of the day – a vision of higher standards of education for all students – is difficult to argue with even though the systems and mechanisms for achieving it might be flawed.
>
> (Cain 1999: 104)

In their introduction Gunter and colleagues only comment about this: 'It is important to accept the reality of the current environment as a headteacher and to succeed within the current policy framework' (Gunter *et al.* 1999: xxxi). However, Cain's perspective is what Grace (2002) calls that of a 'pragmatic survivor' and it is problematic from a critical perspective where school leaders must be prepared to put a lot of energy 'into achieving something the system does not value' because they have a view of success which centres on educational and social justice perspectives above and beyond those encouraged by the current policy environment. The risk here is one of celebrating the voices of school leaders who are caught up in managerialist education rather than trying to resist it as highlighted in Grace's (2002) book (see below).

There is no such problem around Jill Blackmore's work. *Troubling Women* (Blackmore 1999) is particularly concerned with feminist leadership and the way it is placed at risk in managerialist times. It frames the problem of leadership from a radically different slant, rooted in feminist post-structuralism, albeit with a 'materialist bent' (p. 16). Although she does not discuss the general limitations of the mainstream school leadership literature at any length, Blackmore provides a powerful summary critique of the way 'educational administration as a field of practice and disciplinary technology ... has "othered", subsumed or ignored the "feminine" ' (p. 44). She argues that

> Throughout the twentieth century, leadership has been continuously reinvented as *the* solution to political and management problems, rather than the means to democratically negotiated educational ends, through the effective schools literature of the 1970s, the 'visionary leadership of strong corporate cultures' of the 1980s, and now 'best practice' in the 1990s. Thus 'the vast, repetitive and intellectually stultifying literature on leadership recycles idealised masculine virtues of decisiveness, incisiveness and strength'.
>
> (Blackmore 1999: 49, citing Ozga and
> Walker 1995: 37, Blackmore's emphasis)

Blackmore goes on to argue that feminist leadership discourses such as those to do with 'women's styles of leadership' remain too constrained within the discursive parameters of educational administration. Drawing on case studies from a range of Australian research projects, she argues that those discourses are able to 'rework, co-opt, subvert and incorporate potentially oppositional feminist leadership discourses' (p. 18). For instance, there are the contradictions involved in leadership of self-managing schools. Blackmore points out that while feminists find postmodern discourses of education self-governance seductive because the local is thought to be more democratic, in reality women's experiences of self-managing leadership is very modernist – controlling and conforming. While this may be the case for both men and women, women find this 'doubly difficult' since they are overseeing the feminization, casualization and deprofessionalization of teaching, are more likely to be located in poor, multicultural 'failing' schools, and having to perform 'strong leadership' and 'managed change' roles which are hostile to their preferred mode of collegiality and genuine debate (p. 156). Blackmore also illustrates how women leaders end up doing a lot of what she calls 'emotional management', where they are supposed to 'manage' productively for the school the unproductive emotions of anger, disillusionment and alienation among students, teachers and themselves (see pp. 162–5).

In essence, then, Blackmore offers an account of feminist leadership in managerialist times which fundamentally unsettles uncritical and problem-solving accounts of leadership. The 'greedy organisations' of the post-welfarist era have a negative impact on those who work in them, especially women, that is not adequately acknowledged in the literature around transformational leadership. In relation to this point, Christie and Lingard (2001: 5) have commented:

> To focus exclusively on positive aspects of leadership and organisation is to limit understanding of their complexity, particularly in terms of their social relations . . . we would argue that the 'management of meaning' so often listed as a leadership task, also needs to be considered in its negative instantiation, as does the notion that leaders and managers should shape organisational culture. Read differently, these practices may come close to indoctrination and manipulation by those in power. Whereas it may be possible to argue that indoctrination and manipulation are not strictly speaking elements of 'leadership', it could be counter-argued that the conceptual boundaries of activities as complex as leadership cannot so easily be drawn in practice. While theories of transformational leadership add the important dimensions of vision and vision-building to leadership studies, it is also necessary to 'deromanticise' these concepts.

Deromanticizing leadership is what Blackmore does superbly. To avoid being caught up in the disempowering 'regimes of truth' around post-welfarist leadership, she suggests that feminists in educational administration

> need to focus beyond the issue of women and leadership, to contextualize it and to politicize it by linking leadership more transparently to wider educational debates about social inequality, educational reform and issues of social justice. We also need to theorize gender change better – to consider both its textual nuances and the power of discourse in meaning making, but also to consider more often the material and cultural conditions that produce particular leadership discourses that constrain women. It also means problematizing leadership as a key concept in educational administration and policy – redefining it and even rejecting it – for perhaps the focus upon leadership is itself the biggest barrier to gender equality.
>
> (Blackmore 1999: 222)

It is interesting that, like Davies (1990), Blackmore ultimately comes back to the question of whether we really want leadership, even if reconstituted. Indeed, when she talks about a feminist post-masculinist politics of educational leadership she is really inviting us to join a critically informed feminist *educational* project rather than a leadership one and she provides a lot of ideas, at a general level, about how such a project might be pursued (see below).

Some recommendations for practitioners

While we would clearly want to encourage practitioners to seek out the kind of critical approaches to school leadership offered by the textual dissenters, they usually focus on alternative principles and concepts rather than providing specific advice about leadership in an era of post-welfarist educational reform. Grace (1995) suggests moving past previous conceptions of 'strong leadership' to one which opens up the schooling process to the scrutiny and participation of all local citizens including school pupils (pp. 201–2). While he admits to intrinsic tensions between notions of professional school leadership and notions of democratic school governance, and notes that some have suggested doing away with leaders altogether (for example, Davies 1990), Grace argues that some form of substantive leadership is here to stay for a long time yet and that democratic school leadership 'can begin, even in present structural and ideological circumstances, because potentiality for such change exists in the contradictions of contemporary education reforms' (Grace 1995: 204).

Grace's latest book provides some important empirical findings about how school leaders in Catholic schools are trying to resist market 'realities' and work towards the common good (Grace 2002). Grace found 'explicit condemnation of the potentially corrupting effects of market values and market forces in Catholic education' characterized the stance of at least half of the 60 heads he interviewed in London, Liverpool and Birmingham between 1997 and 1999 (p. 197). These heads were 'searching for forms of association and collaboration which would meet reasonable demands for efficiency and accountability . . . while not involving the "win or die" imperatives of unregulated market competition in schooling' (p. 204). Grace points in particular to the Birmingham Catholic Secondary Partnership involving formal collaboration among ten schools over enrolments, school improvement and a host of other matters and which he suggests acts as a 'developed countercultural force' to the market in education. Such collaboration does not have to be just a feature of the Catholic school system, and indeed many of the Catholic heads in Grace's study were much more pragmatic about surviving as market competitors.

Gunter's (2001) recommendations are very general. She focuses on a fundamentally different type of leadership from the one currently on offer, which at the same time anticipates a different student–teacher relationship (chapter 9). She hammers home the need for *educational* leadership that is *distributed*: 'What we need is less emphasis on restructuring hierarchical leadership and more courage to enable teachers and students with managers to work on developing learning processes . . . Such an approach would politicise schools around pedagogy rather than around glossy manifestos' (p. 138). Yet, by using such general concepts, Gunter is at risk of having her arguments co-opted by those who bring much less critical meanings to these ideas. Just as she refers to Smyth and Shacklock's (1998) argument that the 'spraying' around of 'aerosol' words like empowerment, collegiality, collaboration and participation has devalued the potential meaning we could draw from them, the same is true of many terms used by textual dissenters.

Of the three textual dissenters featured, Blackmore has the most substantial discussion of the way forward at a tactical level. She draws on her research to recommend that local feminist leaders revisit their conceptualization of leadership, reactivate Equal Employment Opportunities (EEO) networks which have been dismantled or taken over by men and create new sites for critical leadership training work for women. Feminist leaders can also exploit the discourses of the market, managerialism and contractualism, for instance by arguing that school-based policies and practices and school leader professional development must address equity, diversity and fairness as these are legal requirements in decentralized employment relations. Blackmore suggests that women can challenge men or work with them as appropriate and that they should reinvent feminist politics to take more account of political and social differences among women. Finally, feminist leaders can keep abreast of gender research and also take advantage of the way they are being discursively constituted while holding dear their feminist principles. They can, for instance, '[learn] to play with management discourses in ways that make it difficult to position them as extreme feminists, being loud and strong when necessary, but often quietly achieving their ends' (p. 214).

Our own initial recommendation would be for school leaders to be extremely wary of the way that school leadership training courses, in addition to school leadership texts, tend to act as relaying devices for managerialism, and so to get involved in these courses as little as possible. In England, as Raab has put it, the

> Government's hope must be that the implantation of the systems and ethos of management will take root sufficiently to legitimise new mechanisms and routines and to make them appear to be self-imposed, or collaboratively adopted, from top to toe. In this headteachers are pivotal, and a massive reaffirmation of their role as managers is being undertaken.
>
> (Raab 1991: 16)

There have been several critical analyses of headteacher training courses in England along these lines (Ford 1996; Hextall and Mahony 1998; Gunter 1999; Male 2000; Fragos 2001); however, even mainstream education management writers express concern about these courses. Peter Ribbins has suggested the NPQH is 'highly prescriptive and focussed narrowly on the delivery of a package of material developed centrally and, initially at least, produced in haste' (Ribbins 1999: 80), while Bush (1998: 330) talks of 'the pretentious claim that only the NPQH can prepare aspiring heads'. On the other hand, these courses are also often seen much more benignly (Lodge 1998; Blandford and Squire 1999; Johnson and Castelli 1999; Parsons *et al.* 1999), and some of those whose arguments are critiqued here (Fullan, Southworth and Caldwell) are all connected with the most recent initiative, the National College for School Leadership (NCSL). They had the role of visiting professors over the 2001/2002 academic year, part of the college's stated aim at 'establishing a "think tank" to act as a catalyst in developing thinking about a new leadership development framework' (Nclsonline 2001).[7]

Second, good school leadership in managerialist times would involve the kinds of practices we have suggested in other chapters, but we are also sure that leadership is one of those areas where actions speak louder than words but where actions also have to be explained if the support of fellow staff is to be gathered and held. It therefore needs a reasonably eloquent critique of the limitations of managerial schooling and a public commitment to doing things differently – where possible. Put another way, while there is much hollow talk of moral purpose in the school leadership literature (and also in the school change literature – see the next chapter) the key 'moral purpose' of school leadership at the current time should be to invest no more significance or energy into managerial activities than is strictly necessary. Towards this end, school leaders should be open and honest about unpalatable decisions they have to make around school budgets, staffing, marketing and the like so as to problematize managerialism rather than obscure it by absorbing these problems themselves. They should also be well informed (what does research show us?), savvy enough to assess the political risk of particular activities (what can we get away with?) and able to use a mix of convincing argument, humour and sarcasm to get their message across (why is this kind of reform not to be taken seriously but also very seriously?).

Some examples may help here. The head who is able to talk with confidence to parents about the limitations of market, managerial, performative and prescriptive reforms in education and is able to convincingly illustrate how the school is trying to take a more clearly educational stance should be able to gather considerable support even in aspirant, middle-class communities. The head who prepares for an impending Ofsted review by fabricating where possible (such as 'borrowing' Ofsted-suitable material from other schools) and 'keeping the temperature down' among staff helps to prevent the hijacking of school culture and subsequent values-drift towards managerialism. Similarly, the head who comes into the staffroom and begins the discussion of some 'important' activity such as SATs testing with the quip 'more pig weighing today unfortunately folks' (as in the Confucian saying 'No matter how often you weigh a pig it doesn't make it any fatter') is delivering the message to staff that 'we are doing this because we have to but I want you to keep a wider perspective'.

However, all of this is to focus too much on the actions of the head or principal as the formally constituted leader. Thus Bottery (1994: 150) has commented that, 'whilst an essential function of a leader is to present to pupils and teachers their own personal vision of where the school and society should be going, another is to provide a forum in which other visions are debated and resolved. Participation and dissent are then essential features of any educational organisation worthy of the name.' We agree, and so whether one is talking about 'distributed' leadership (Gronn 1999; Gunter 2001) or 'democratic' leadership (Grace 1995), the ability for interested parties to *genuinely* have their say must be the proof in the pudding. However, such power-sharing will also be difficult to organize in a managerialist context which favours a chief executive model of leadership and where workloads are intensifying. Whether manifested in formal or informal ways, if power-sharing is to be more than contrived, it presents a substantial challenge.

Finally, and as a short-cut to a more detailed set of recommendations, it may help readers to say that we can support much of Sergiovanni's general approach to leadership. For instance, what is being talked about above is what Sergiovanni would call 'ideas based leadership' (Sergiovanni 2001a: 142–3) and 'leadership by outrage' (pp. 154–5), and we indicated earlier the critical potential in Sergiovanni (2001b). However, we also want to see these ideas harnessed to what, frankly, should be called *anti-managerialist leadership*. Put another way, because of the risk of taking a quite different, uncritical reading of Sergiovanni's work, reflective practice for teachers and school leadership has to include explicit reflection on wider issues of social structure and politics and their impact on schools, not just implicit as much of Sergiovanni's work encourages.

9 School change

There are two reasons why school change is the final area of education management considered in this book. First, writers in this 'field' draw extensively upon the areas already discussed and criticized. Second, it is important that we carefully unpack the cases of subtle and not-so-subtle apologism in this area because some of the most influential educational authors align themselves here. As with previous chapters, there are (often contradictory) degrees of textual apologism – hence our continuum. The crucial questions here are why change and why now? The answer is very simple: the rise and consolidation of the (educational) change literature is inextricably bound up with the rise of (new) managerialism in the public sector globally. It is hardly surprising, then, that school change is the education-sector equivalent of the so-called change management literature for business, which draws upon issues of managing culture, developing strategy, human resource management, leadership, and so on. At present, school change is fundamentally about extending and legitimating the neo-liberal managerialization of education, and not about change (for example, curricular) that promotes real learning and engenders creativity in pupils and students.

Each of the authors chosen here draws, to varying degrees, on the issue of 'reculturing' (or what management schools prefer to describe as 'managing culture'). The apparent novelty of the need for 'reculturing' (as championed in particular by Michael Fullan) uncannily parallels the rise of culturalism in business and management schools in the 1980s. In fact, the literature used by Fullan and others is explicitly taken from the culturalist business gurus of the 1980s. This chapter thus begins by delineating the rise of culturalism during the 1980s, highlighting the academically dubious and politically managerialist nature of the literature here. We then examine key writers in the school change field. The overt and subtle apologists are dealt with in that order, though, again, given the contradictory nature of apologist texts, it is not always a simple either/or. Either way, they legitimate the managerialist status quo.

One of the central themes underpinning the school change literature is the unashamed assault on bureaucracy. Hargreaves (1994) and Fullan (1999, 2001a) are especially scathing about the lack of innovation engendered by bureaucratic school structures. Unwittingly or not, such decrying parallels the arguments of the New Right. It will be argued that we cannot dispense with bureaucratic organizational forms (or what we call degrees of bureaucratization, which is context-specific), and that in turn, this places limits on the speed with which educators can make educational progress. Indeed, the oft-chanted call for 'continuous improvement' is necessarily limited in this regard. More fundamentally, however, the championing of continuous change in an uncertain, volatile educational climate is inherently flawed as a means of engendering creativity and educational success in order to meet the needs of advanced economies. This will bring us back to Chapter 2, where we argued for the (transcendental) need to avoid market colonization of the educational sphere and the concomitant need to fund it adequately and avoid volatility and uncertainty.

Equally, there is an individualist bias that permeates the literature, in turn distracting us from wider socio-economic material structures and cultures that necessarily delimit educational 'success'. 'Moral purpose' and 'energy–enthusiasm–hopefulness' (Fullan 1999, 2001a,b) are content-less slogans that individualize (on the part of educators) educational failure. Such slogans are regularly repeated in the change literature, to the extent that any failure is deemed immoral.

The rise of culturalism

The notion of culturalism has been recently coined by Parker (2000: 9) to draw attention to what he refers to as the 'breathlessly enthusiastic works that use the term "culture" to suggest a prescriptive analysis of management in organizations'. Such works are largely practitioner-oriented and are referenced and cited liberally by education management writers. Parker looks in some detail at three books, the first of which has been most referenced in the school change (and other education management) literature, namely Peters and Waterman (1982), Deal and Kennedy (1988) and Ouchi (1981). There is a consensus that these books were central to stimulating the growth of popular managerial interest in organizational culture. At the same time, Parker usefully places culturalism in its social context, namely the marketizing (neo-liberal-cum-conservative) reforms of the Thatcher and Reagan 1980s combined with the economic and cultural threat of Japan. It is not surprising then that such texts are now widely used as sources by education management texts that legitimate and/or buttress the marketization of education. It was the combination already mentioned that provided the fertile ground for a form of description and prescription that privileged entrepreneurial values and elevated managers into heroes.[1] Parker goes on theoretically to rescue culture from managerialism in the rest of his book (which Willmott 2002a also does for theorizing about education policy).

The purpose of this section is to underscore the managerialist nature of the texts on culture, since they have been directly transferred, uncritically, to management texts in education (see Bennett *et al.* 1992; Whitaker 1993; Hargreaves 1994; Stoll and Fink 1996; Fullan 2001). Some of the writing on culture had begun to appear in US management books and journals from the mid-1970s. However, the wider dissemination began at the end of the decade, initially through the US business magazines *Business Week* and *Fortune*. In 1980, *Business Week* published a piece on 'excellence' by Tom Peters, which outlined the bestselling book he was to co-author two years afterwards. This book, *In Search of Excellence* (Peters and Waterman 1982), is, according to Parker, probably the most influential text of recent times and has claims to be the first of a new kind of popular and populist management writing (such popularity is evident in the school change literature, as will be seen later). By 1985, it had sold over 5 million copies and been translated into 15 languages. It is subtitled 'Lessons from America's Best-Run Companies' and ostensibly contains a study of 43 high-performing US corporations, such as Hewlett-Packard and Procter and Gamble. It is also a story of how Peters and Waterman found companies in America that behave very much like the celebrated Japanese companies that US businesses were having to compete with from the late 1970s. As Parker notes, the Japanese problem for American business is illustrated with an anecdote about a 'Honda worker who, on his way home each evening straightens up windshield blades on all Hondas he passes. He just can't stand to see a flaw in a Honda!' (Peters and Waterman 1982, cited in Parker 2000: 11).

Peters and Waterman suggest that this level of employee dedication must also be widely achieved in the USA in order for any kind of long-term economic and cultural renaissance to occur. As Parker notes:

> Rather fortuitously, they then discover that the best US companies already have it. Their central assertion is that all these 'excellent' companies possess certain cultural qualities that ensure their success . . . The authors argue that the companies they studied were actually repositories of myths, symbols, stories and legends that reflected and reinforced the central (and positive) aspects of the organization – caring about customers, being innovatory, focusing on quality and so on. This allowed for less dependence on a bureaucratic rulebook because every one shared a strongly held 'philosophy'. From this collection of stories, the authors distil eight neat maxims for a successful culture and corporation.
>
> (Parker 2000: 11)

The comment about attenuated dependence on a bureaucratic rulebook is a leitmotif of New Right thinking and public choice theory, which will be addressed later in our discussion of the work of Fullan and Hargreaves. It is worth flagging it up now since it resonates with the management literature of the 1980s, which only emphasizes the inefficiencies of bureaucracy, without acknowledging both its unavoidability and its efficiencies. However, Deal and Kennedy's (1988) *Corporate Cultures* draws more explicitly on the anthropological dimensions of culture, but its message is nevertheless almost identical to that of *In Search of Excellence*. Of a surveyed 80 companies, only 18 had clearly articulated sets of (non-financial) beliefs and these companies were outstandingly successful. Like *In Search of Excellence*, the style is heavily anecdotal, 'glossily written, smugly managerialist and, in social scientific terms, not particularly persuasive' (Parker 2000: 13). We will return to the latter shortly. William Ouchi's *Theory Z* (1981) was another bestseller. Its similarity is reflected in the subtitle: 'How American Business Can Meet the Japanese Challenge'. Ouchi constructs a typology of three types of firm: American (type A), Japanese (type J) and an American version of the Japanese (type Z). The book is populist. It began as a comparative study of US and Japanese organizations and became an investigation of specific American companies that (unsurprisingly) are discovered to perform like Japanese companies. Ouchi emphasizes the organization's mission as expressive of its deepest values: the reader is provided with a vision of a 'new kind of company, one that satisfies both its employees and the demands of the marketplace . . . Once again . . . [a] formula for the salvation of American industry . . . is attached to the emphasis on the importance of values and meanings for understanding the internal workings of the organization' (Parker 2000: 15).

Parker then notes that these three books have more in common with a long tradition of business self-help texts than they do with contemporary academic literature. Crucially,

> The writing is chatty and anecdotal, presumably intended to be read rapidly by people who would like to be too busy to have their time wasted with academic sophistry. Standard academic conventions are avoided in favour of shock tactics, cultural and disciplinary eclecticism, flip chart subheadings and the seduction of a clever turn of phrase.
>
> (Parker 2000: 15)

We can see this in the educational change literature, too. Thus to Fullan (1993: vii), 'Change is ubiquitous and relentless, forcing itself on us at every turn'; 'We have argued in our *What's Worth Fighting For Out There?* that this position is no longer tenable (or desirable). The "out there" is now in here, in your face' (Fullan 1999: 45). To Hargreaves (1994: 235), 'In a postmodern world which is

fast, compressed, uncertain, diverse and complex, balkanised secondary structures are poorly equipped to harness the human resources [sic] necessary to
create flexible learning'. And, finally, to Stoll and Fink (1996: 3), 'Simply
stated, we are living in a postmodern world . . . The postmodern world is fast,
complex, compressed and uncertain'. Scary stuff indeed. Change is relentless,
in our faces. We now live in a postmodern world that is fast, compressed and
uncertain. Schools have to change – and quick. But let's pause a moment. It
does not, or rather must not, have to be like this. Such scaremongering feeds
off the neo-liberal public sector reforms that have occurred globally; for they
do increase systemic uncertainty, work intensification and stress. Frankly,
such apologism is unacceptable; moreover, as we will argue, it undercuts the
visionary futures these writers envisage.

Equally, such texts feed off the insecurity generated, which is exacerbated
by the palpable lack of practical help and use of eclectic quasi-theoretical
sound-bites (such as 'leading on the edge of chaos'). The salient point here is
that Fullan and others draw, albeit eclectically and superficially, upon the
change management literature quite simply because they argue that schools are
not that different from businesses. Indeed, we would argue that Fullan should
be 'more true to himself', which would involve establishing his own educational equivalent of McKinsey & Co., since his latest book *Leading in a Culture
of Change* (2001b) is about marketing a new consultancy product: reculturing,
which is liberally peppered with the need for 'moral purpose' and an understanding of complexity theory (which, regrettably, Fullan barely elucidates).
Indeed, as Parker remarks, Peters commented in an ironic aside that he charges
an obscene amount of money because corporate culture consulting is 'one of
the most legalised ways of stealing'. 'Organizational culture was hence an idea
for selling, so successful that even its leading guru could ironize it . . . In general,
this is material written to be read and remembered easily and there is very little
concern for fidelity to dull academic convention' (Parker 2000: 16). Now,
readers should not infer that we are accusing Fullan of 'legalised stealing'. The
point is that, whatever his intentions, his work – particularly his more recent
work on 'reculturing' – has palpable resonance with the guru culture texts of the
1980s, which conceal the unavoidable reality of winning *and* losing. Our argument, basically, is that Fullan's work exemplifies subtle apologism.

The problem is that despite a last-minute and incomplete recognition of
the problematic nature of such texts as *In Search of Excellence* on Fullan's
(2001b: 47) part, the glaring methodological problems are not recognized (see
Whitaker 1993; Stoll and Fink 1996, among others). In essence, the sample
used has been limited to companies in high-growth markets with large numbers of professional staff:

> Whether the same would apply to organizations in stagnant markets
> with a high proportion of working class employees is a questionable

point. After all, it may be that these companies were able to use expensive personnel techniques because they were successful and if their profitability declined then so would their investment in them. In other words, soft human resource management is something you can afford if your organization is making money.

(Parker 2000: 16)

Indeed, as seen in Chapter 7 on strategic HRM, solvent schools are able to adopt a soft HRM approach; not-so-solvent schools are required to adopt the so-called hard approach. As we argued, this state of affairs should never have been constructed in the first place, since it undermines educational opportunities for children, for whom the reality of LMS is not of their making or choosing. Furthermore, 14 of the 43 'excellent' companies were experiencing severe difficulties three years after the Peters and Waterman book was published. Crucially,

> In general then, there are problems with the culturalist thesis which could be summarized as *wishful generalization from very doubtful research*. There is simply no compelling evidence here that organizational culture – whatever it might be – is related to profitability, efficiency, job satisfaction and so on.
>
> (Parker 2000: 17, our emphasis)

Parker then adds that arguments about the importance of cultural change are empirically impossible to demonstrate unless culture and structure can be unambiguously disentangled and separately operationalized. Stoll and Fink (1996) also echo this (cf. Willmott 2002a).

More important for our purposes is not the conceptual poverty of culturalism in both management and education management texts, but the effects of such literature on its readers.[2] As Parker suggests, at a general level these books legitimate a version of organizations in which a managerial standpoint is accorded primacy, practically and morally. 'The reader is given a vantage point that smoothes any contradictions between the personal and economic imperatives of corporate life' (Parker 2000: 18). Finally, Parker argues that the absence or weakening of bureaucratic control systems does not mean that no control is being exercised, or that 'freedom' is being enjoyed, which means that we should treat with caution the post-bureaucratic narrative. This is basically correct and we will return to the feasibility of post-bureaucratic organizational forms when we look at the work of Fullan and Hargreaves.[3] So far we have introduced the rise and phenomenon of culturalism within the business and management literature essentially because of its uncritical and ready incorporation by school change academics. Indeed, the very reason for such incorporation derives from the professed similarity between business organizations and schools.

School change and overt apologism

As noted earlier, placing texts in an either/or form of apologism is not straight-forward, since such texts are almost invariably contradictory in their assessment of managerial techniques and processes. The extent to which texts in the school change literature may be placed within the respective poles of overt versus subtle apologism is a relative matter. However, there are two recent texts that are reasonably viewed as overtly apologist, namely James and Connolly's (2000) *Effective Change in Schools* and Morrison's *Management Theories for Educational Change* (1998).

Effective Change in Schools (James and Connolly 2000) seemingly adds new insight by virtue of its foray into emotions and psychoanalytic theory. However, as we will see, such 'insight' is due to the reality of what the authors call 'emotional pain' and how to contain it in order to succeed in manage-rialization. Furthermore, James and Connolly discuss the importance of school effectiveness and school improvement without any critical reflection. Indeed, they happily acknowledge that 'the pressure of the "new public management" on schools, especially the obligation to manage their performance, is causing them increasingly to focus on ways of improving pupil achievement [read: exam scores]' (James and Connolly 2000: 38). Moreover, they accept the utility of the 11 'key factors' or effectiveness correlates propounded by Sammons *et al.* (1995) and go on to endorse the 10 characteristics of school improvement distilled by Stoll and Fink (1996).[4] But, such recipes for effectiveness or improvement are deeply problematic (Thrupp 1999, 2001a; Willmott 1999; see also Chapter 6 of this book).

James and Connolly delineate the neo-liberal background to their book as if it were unproblematic:

> In the contemporary setting, the management of educational institu-tions exposes schools to the three sharp prongs of the so-called 'new public management'. The first of these is the establishment of a quasi-market in education which exposes schools to 'market type mechan-isms' . . . In this competitive arena, there is a pressure on schools to be effective and to improve their effectiveness so that they maintain their competitive advantage. The second element . . . is the decentral-isation of power and control . . . schools are expected to optimise the use of their own resources, to flourish and to improve. The third element of the new public management for schools is performance management, where the work of schools is monitored and made public.
>
> (James and Connolly 2000: 1–2)

Moreover, they argue that

> [In the] early days of this era of educational accountability, some schools needed to change. Over time, there is no doubt that some schools, for a variety of reasons, were not giving their pupils the kind of educational experience that many (often neighbouring) schools were able to provide. Also some schools were underperforming and *needed to change quite substantially and very quickly* . . . Opening up the work of schools to greater public scrutiny has forced many schools to improve the quality of many aspects of their activities. Also, schools have been exposed to other trends in the non-educational world, such as *quality management and the growing importance of communicating with and responding to the needs of the customer.*
>
> (James and Connolly 2000: 2, our emphasis)

The extent to which schools adequately educate our children is not the issue here. Rather, the issue is how best to improve such schools in terms of authentic educational outcomes, which is not achieved via managerialist techniques, i.e. performance management. Note the emphasis on speed and substantial change. This is congruent with the shock tactics mentioned above: we have to change and now! Note also the uncritical acceptance of 'non-educational' trends such as quality management to which schools have been exposed and the elision of parents and/or children and customer, whose 'needs' are presumably those of examination success. Indeed, the need to 'go strategic' underpins the text, which involves the whole school in identifying measurable goals, which include quantitative and qualitative success criteria. Typically, there is an emphasis on the need for leadership and the need to develop 'human resources' (here, James and Connolly (2000: 115) praise the Investors in People framework for integrating human resource strategy with organizational strategy, 'which appeared to be particularly helpful in the newly amalgamated schools we studied'). Contradictorily, the authors on the one hand emphasize leadership as a key determinant 'if not the key factor in accelerating the performance of schools', yet, on the other hand, suggest that at best 'all we can say is that the leadership capability of the headteacher is probably important and necessary' (James and Connolly 2000: 140–1).

The acceptance of managerialism in this text is not in doubt. But what is novel here is the *managerialist* emphasis on emotions and how ostensibly they can be managed via a creative use of open systems theory. James and Connolly are keen to make explicit the real emotional pain involved in change and contend that such emotional pain must be 'contained'. Unhelpfully for those accepting of, or forced to implement, performance management, 'aspects' of the management of change are only considered in *general* terms.

Such aspects constitute the two central themes of the text, namely 'institutional transformation'.

> The first theme essentially embraces the non-rational emotional responses of individuals and institutions. This psychodynamic perspective therefore includes the influence of the unconscious, the defences of individuals and institutions against emotional pain . . . The second major theme is open systems theory, which provides a useful way of thinking about groups and their roles in institutions . . . The combination of these two perspectives is crucial, since the open systems theory perspective helps the understanding and resolution of the issues revealed by the psychodynamic perspective.
>
> (James and Connolly 2000: 4–5)

Apparently, this is meant to be 'useful and helpful to all those who work to change and improve schools' (James and Connolly 2000: 6). First, the perspectives delineated are not without their problems, as will be seen in a moment. Indeed, the exact nature of an open system is not explained; moreover, we are not told practically how to relate it (notwithstanding lack of elucidation) to managing change (read: implementing top-down managerialist practices). Second, and more importantly, even if the nature of an open system had been elucidated, its practical import cannot be assumed to follow unproblematically. We are not criticizing the authors for not providing a prescriptive list, since such a list would be managerialist in nature. Instead, what is needed is a clearer discussion of open systems, their properties and powers, and why they are open.[5] Moreover, we would want to ask the authors to think about why educational systems globally have been rendered more open, creating uncertainty, and whether such considerably increased systemic openness is educationally valuable for children and conducive to economic growth and sustainability. We have argued to the contrary.

However, we have indicated the novelty of the text in virtue of the primacy it accords to emotions. For James and Connolly (2000: 161), 'non-rational influences are the dominant force on the life of schools. Emotions, particularly anxiety, have a significant effect on the processes of organising and the structuring of organisations'. Despite the (contradictory) emphasis on the leadership capabilities of the headteacher, we are told, ultimately, that 'the burdensome nature of the containment of projected anxiety may be one explanation as to why shared leadership is an attractive notion' (2000: 165). For James and Connolly (2000: 17), 'emotional responses are essentially non-rational by definition'. There are two main problems here. First, we are not provided with any evidence for the dominance of non-rational influences on schools. Given the focus on anxiety, anger, projection and such like, we will assume that the latter are such influences. Second, then, how anxious are teachers and children now? Were they anxious prior to (new) managerializa-tion and quasi-marketization? Indeed, we are not told why teachers are likely to exhibit anger and frustration. Might it not be that such teachers are angry precisely because managerialization contradicts the very educational values that underpin their everyday work?

It is refreshing in one sense that James and Connolly acknowledge the reality of emotions, for the majority of organizational behaviour texts used globally in management and business schools tend only to focus on power, conflict, class, politics and ideology. Consequently, as Wilson (1999: 2) puts it, 'there is a very tidy and sanitized view of what goes on in organizations, yet we all know that work issues and behaviour are much more than this. There is . . . uncertainty, chaos, and confusion'. Indeed, Wilson argues that organizational behaviour could profitably draw from the area of emotion and feeling: 'a scan of the indexes of textbooks on organizational behaviour and theory reveals few, if any, entries under emotions or feelings. Yet gripes, joy, drudgery, anger, anxiety, frustrations, glee, embarrassment . . . are part of the social creation and personal expression of work and organizational life' (Wilson 1999: 3). However, James and Connolly's text acknowledges the reality of emotional life in order for it to be managerially manipulated. Telling us that emotional responses are non-rational by definition does not tell us where they come from or whether they can be 'contained' by school managers.

Following Archer, we see emotions as commentaries on human concerns: 'The central assumption made here is that our emotions are among the main constituents of our inner lives. They are the fuel of our internal conversation and this is why they matter' (Archer 2000: 194). In essence, emotions involve a sense of our situation. We now get back to the point above about why teachers are angry: *underpinning their concerns as teachers is the welfare and education of their students, which is damaged by the performance management characteristic of current educational performativity.* Emotional responses can certainly subvert rationality, but to define them as non-rational is inadequate. James and Con-nolly are certainly aware of the emotional pain, yet do not address the locus of such pain. This is hardly surprising in view of their overt apologism. Thus, the role of the manager is to help teachers to cope with such pain and to contain it. Precisely how is not mentioned. At the same time, James and Connolly enter the field of psychoanalysis. For us, the crude and hurried use of such concepts as 'denial' and 'repression' simply individualizes schools and pathologizes 'unsuccessful' or 'failing' schools (notwithstanding the glaring fact that not all schools can succeed in a competitive educational arena). For James and Connolly on denial, for instance:

> Feelings associated with the under-performance of a school, for example, can be repressed and thereby ignored. The need for change is thus removed, and so is the anxiety that goes with it. Poor

> performance in the 'league tables' of GCSE results may be denied on
> the basis that such tables are meaningless or that 'You can't expect
> anything different with the kids we get'.
>
> (James and Connolly 2000: 55)

Who's in denial now? The crucial point to be made here is that James and
Connolly's text, like the majority of the school effectiveness and school
improvement literature (which, as we have seen, they endorse without qualification) denies the reality of socio-economic-cultural factors that delimit the
extent of 'improvement'. Simply adding a psychological gloss in echoing the
charges of 'low expectations' is untenable.

Morrison's book *Management Theories for Educational Change* (1998) is
similarly problematic. He argues:

> The reach of this new business mentality extends beyond simply
> financial concerns. One of the significant developments in the field of
> education has been the view that the worlds of business and educa-
> tion are not mutually exclusive . . . The business literature has a
> wealth of contributions to make to understanding and developing
> individuals and organizations for effective change . . . The strength of
> the business literature is that, far from advocating the austere,
> dehumanized and objective pursuit of profit at all costs, it suggests
> that the effective management of change is an affirmation of the
> humanity of businesses. That clearly is a message of great significance
> for education.
>
> (Morrison 1998: x–xii)

This is accepting of the wholesale shift towards the employment of business
models, which underpin (new) managerialism. However, it seems that Morrison would rebut the latter, since such business literature emphasizes
humanity. We will return to this extraordinary claim shortly. The salient
point here is that Morrison, while immediately recognizing that there are
fundamental differences between the worlds of business and education, suggests that 'nevertheless practices for the management of change in business
and industry have a vast amount to offer the worlds of education in its management of change' (Morrison 1998: 1). Moreover, the issue of marketization
of education is a 'non-issue' for Morrison, 'because 1) market forces are
already operating because of funding arrangements; 2) public perception of
several aspects of a market mentality (e.g. consumerism, information
accountability, efficiency, "standards") is here to stay – it is embedded in the
broader current of social and economic change' (Morrison 1998: 7). Despite
recognition of some of the problems of the business models, we would not
characterize Morrison's text as subtle apologism mainly because any concerns

expressed are glossed over and also because of his unacceptable *non sequitur* that extant practices should remain so because they are extant. However, it is salutary to remind readers that categorizing texts is not a straightforward matter, since Fullan's work – especially his more recent work – might also be characterized as overtly apologist. However, as we will see, this is not the case, for Fullan is more aware of the critical literature and makes some attempt to engage with it.

However, like Hargreaves and Fullan especially, Morrison champions the applicability of business and management models, since, apparently, education and businesses are not that different after all. As with all texts critically surveyed here, there is an acceptance of uncertainty and change as inescapable. For Morrison, uncertainty and change are ubiquitous and apparently the case for having to cope with change does not need to be made. He goes on to write that 'Hammer . . . suggests that new technologies are being used not to render existing practices more efficient . . . but to revolutionize the way we think about things' (Morrison 1998: 1). We have already discussed the nascent technocratic totalitarianism that permeates Hammer's work on business process reengineering in Chapter 7. It is a pity that Morrison does not engage with the critiques drawn upon here. Like Stoll and Fink, Hargreaves and Fullan, Morrison underscores the so-called move away from 'modernist' society, exemplified by the decline of large-scale factory system. As Morrison puts it, 'Flexibility, responsiveness, consumerism and client satisfaction are the order of the day, with flatter management organization' (Morrison 1998: 2). This is due, in part, to responses to what Morrison calls 'rampant bureaucratisation'. Equally, Morrison underscores the metaphorical value of chaos and complexity theories, yet as with Fullan, such metaphorical value is not cashed in practically.

We return to the issue of bureaucracy when Hargreaves and Fullan's work is discussed. We now want to question Morrison's justification of business practice transfer to education:

> The view that business and educational practice are, in very many areas, compatible entails a shift of perception and, perhaps, an abandonment of prejudice on the part of educators who might hold a negative view of business as being essentially exploitative, driven by thirst for naked profit, dehumanized and dehumanizing . . . boring, repetitive . . . that is, an outmoded view of business that was characterized by Taylorism . . . many companies are far more person-centred.
> (Morrison 1998: 9)

The problem here is that Morrison's somewhat positive discussion of management practices does not match reality. Morrison would clearly deny the charge of overt apologism, yet we will argue below that Taylorism is not only alive and well in education but is reflected in the national numeracy and literacy hours. Indeed, we have to remember that Morrison argues that the business community 'is at the forefront of change because not to be so would be to court failure, closure and demise. The logic of survival leads to the logic of managing change' (Morrison 1998: 10). Actually, the logic of survival (which derives directly from market-based competition) leads to the logic of failure for some, which is not appropriate for education. Perhaps this is why Morrison talks in terms of degrees of 'person-centredness', since a hard approach in HRM-speak is unavoidable for firms (and schools and colleges) that are not so successful or moribund.

Morrison does not define Taylorism and we are left with the (implicit) assumption that it is about dehumanization and repetitive, boring work. While this is correct, more detail is needed, especially about the nature of work design and ideological manipulation (managing culture). Furthermore, Taylor's scientific management is very much in practice in many organizations. Extending our discussion of Taylorism in Chapter 2, Taylor believed that the best management was true science, 'resting upon clearly defined laws, rules and principles' (Taylor 1911: 7). For Taylor, it was the manager's job to gather all the traditional knowledge, hitherto possessed by workers, and then classify, tabulate and reduce such knowledge to rules, laws and formulae. As Wilson (1999: 21) notes, from a job design perspective, Taylor's scheme is predicated upon the principle of division of mental and manual labour: '(a) a general principle of the maximum decomposition of tasks; (b) the divorce of direct and indirect (setting up, preparation, maintenance) labour; (c) the mimimization of skill requirements leading to minimum job learning time'. Is this not familiar? Is it not the case that the numeracy and literacy hours are prescribed, delimiting considerably the scope for professional creativity on the part of teachers?

It might be the case that Morrison is conflating the technical aspects and the cultural aspects of Taylorism, whereby the point of human resource management is to use a battery of techniques (ideologically) in order to manipulate employees – yet notions of 'empowerment' are ideological-cum-rhetorical devices to conceal the reality of inequality and (often) boredom. The point is that Taylorist practices are prevalent. As Wilson rightly notes, despite the limitations of Taylorist job design and its negative effects, there are many benefits to be gained. She gives the example of United Parcel Service, which employs industrial engineering managers who stipulate, for example, how fast their drivers walk; they are expected to walk at 3 ft per second. 'Until recently drivers were instructed in how to move in an effort to maximize efficiency. Packages were to be carried under the left arm and the driver stepped into the van with the right foot while holding the van's keys on the middle finger of the right hand' (Wilson 1999: 24). The irony of Morrison's assertions is that while we would argue that the mechanistic conception of people needs to be replaced with an alternative approach, education policy is mechanistic in its underpinning, the emphasis on 'standards' and the ostensible 'one best way'. It must be remembered that if you are producing a continuous standardized product with homogeneous throughput for a mass market, Taylorism is extremely efficient.

Indeed, the routinization to be found at McDonald's is congruent with the logic of Taylorism, that is, maximizing managerial control of work and breaking down work into its constituent tasks that can be preplanned. In order to provide fast service, hot food and clean restaurants, McDonald's needs to use the principles of scientific management as well as centralized planning, centrally designed training programmes, automated machinery, meticulous specifications and systematic inspections. Ofsted? Centralized curriculum control? Timed standardized tests? Ritzer (1993) argues that fast-food restaurants like McDonald's are the new model of rationalization – what he calls McDonaldization. He believes that McDonaldization affects education, work, travel, the family, basically every other sector of society. Despite the determinism, it is the case that education has been influenced by consumerism. Both at the school and university level, pupils and students are positioned and position themselves as customers. University students are increasingly looking for low price, convenience, efficiency and absence of hassle (Wilson 1999: 45).

However, the above is not recognized by Morrison. Indeed, fancifully he writes that 'The business literature is redolent with references to agreement, involvement, need, assistance, consultation, reward, support . . . celebration of success – terms that reinforce the need to view change *not through the mechanistic lenses of Taylorism but as focused on people*' (Morrison 1998: 41, our emphasis). At best this is naïve; at worst, insidious legitimation of the ideology of 'empowerment'. Indeed, there is a point at which we get a sense of subtle apologism when Morrison discusses Japanese working practices.

> The notion of persistence is important . . . for the Japanese model is scrupulous – or relentless – in achieving goals. In Japanese companies, this is evidenced in terms of production targets, quality assurance targets and comparatively easily operationalized goals . . . How straightforwardly this can be translated into education is, perhaps, a moot point, for educational goals are multiple non-uniform and sometimes tension-ridden (Pollard, 1982) and cannot be operationalized straightforwardly, e.g. simple figures-based views do not address the unmeasurable, but equally valuable, aspects of education.
>
> (Morrison 1998: 46)

Note the equivocal 'perhaps': the issue of translation cannot be approached in this manner and is a debatable point. Indeed, instructively Morrison immediately adds that, 'Nevertheless, the single-mindedness of the exhortation to "persistence" is, perhaps, a salutary reminder for schools to "stick to their knitting" (Peters and Waterman, 1982)'. Note again the equivocality. Also note the reference to Peters and Waterman, whose 'excellence' work has been discussed. Equally instructive is the assertion that

> the message in education is very similar to the Japanese model: teachers receive a prescribed national curriculum and strive to 'deliver' it most effectively, efficiently and with the maximum level of assessed outcomes and achievements . . . Education, then, has some affinity to the Japanese model but transcends it in many respects.
>
> (Morrison 1998: 49–50)

Taylor would be proud. It is a pity, yet unsurprising, that we are not told how and in what ways education 'transcends' the Japanese model. In fact, somewhat contradictorily, we are told later that many elements of the Japanese model commend themselves to education. Either they do or they do not. This brings us to our final criticism, namely equivocality and denial of responsibility. It is such equivocality that distracts from the charge of overt apologism, since Morrison is clearly in favour of the neo-liberal reforms and the elevated role of business and management approaches. What is particularly problematic in our view is the abdication of responsibility.

> This book has avoided making specific, detailed prescriptions for educational institutions. This has been deliberate, for the overwhelming message is that these are matters for the people involved in the organization. This is not to avoid responsibility or invite criticism that academics are long on theory and short on practice. Rather, it is to identify where responsibility for certain decisions about practice should and do lie.
>
> (Morrison 1998: 227)

To proffer specific management techniques and practices that impact upon human beings and then disclaim responsibility for such proffering is both contradictory and unacceptable.

School change and subtle apologism

In this section we consider the works of Whitaker, Stoll and Fink, touch on Hargreaves (and Fullan) in relation to their treatment of bureaucracy, and then devote most space to Fullan whose writings are not only particularly well known but raise and exemplify a number of important concerns, including the championing of 'reculturing' and the reductive individualization of social problems.

Whitaker

Despite the typical prefacing comment that change is ubiquitous, Patrick Whitaker's *Managing Change in Schools* (1993) is initially redolent of textual dissent. It is worth quoting him at length here:

> It is unfortunate that so much of what happens in education is affected by the competitive ethic – being brighter than someone else, getting higher marks, achieving a landmark first. It applies in the rivalry between the state and private sectors, and now within the state sector itself as Local Management of Schools links school survival with pupil recruitment. One of the common polarized arguments hinges on the belief by one side that competition is the essence of progress and the belief by the other that competition merely sustains inequality of opportunity and inhibits successful learning. A concern with rivalry – of winning, or at least not losing – can cloud attention to the more fundamental purposes of education.
>
> (Whitaker 1993: 5)

Here, we expected a 'does' rather than a 'can': LMS as part and parcel of the (new) managerialization of education *does* cloud (or, rather, divert) attention from the more fundamental purposes of education. In fact, the apologism is subtle here at the outset: 'well, it's unfortunate and there are arguments for and against . . . but'. Indeed, on the next page, he writes that while improvement is constantly needed, it is 'sad that many of the reasons forwarded for wishing to improve are so connected with tangential issues' (Whitaker 1993: 6). Such issues range from proving experts wrong to increasing the competitiveness of British industry. So, continuous improvement *is* required because, he now adds, 'the world is different than it was, *and is changing fast. For an educational system to be in tune with change it needs to be flexible, adaptable and responsive to constantly changing circumstances and needs*' (Whitaker 1993: 6, our emphasis). This nicely complements the arguments of Stoll and Fink, Hargreaves and Fullan – which is why their texts have also been used in this part of the chapter.

Whitaker rightly argues that one of the difficulties facing those charged with the management of change is 'the rigid context for education envisaged by the reformers. Educational change is approached in strictly rational terms . . . This manifestly fails to realise that education and learning are characterised by complexity and an infinite range of variables' (Whitaker 1993: 6–7). Furthermore, a 'worrying characteristic of the debate has been the increasing tendency to denigrate educational specialists – "experts" – those who dare to offer an opinion based on first-hand experience and systematic study' (Whitaker 1993: 8). Moreover, he notes that in all the documentation of the National Curriculum, none of it has been written and offered to the pupils. The problem, however, is the lack of firm conviction. In the opening quotation, Whitaker laments the prevalence of the 'competitive ethic' but does not discount it unequivocally, merely noting the arguments for and against.

Equally, he does not question the need for continuous, unremitting change nor, indeed, does he ask what kind of change and why specifically now? Certainly, teacher professionalism has been virtually expunged, replaced instead by top-down neo-Taylorist mechanisms. Crucially, Whitaker, like all the textual apologists surveyed here, does not pause to question whether schools should in fact be protected from the vicissitudes and uncertainty of the market or globalization precisely because the latter presupposes a stable functioning over time. The point is that stress and uncertainty cannot exist at every level. However, we are told that the world is now characterized by 'turbulence, systemic stress, boundary blurring and temporary expediency. In attempting to create a culture of change it is necessary for educational managers to help their colleagues develop a psychological metabolism sturdy enough to cope with increasingly higher levels of disorder and uncertainty' (Whitaker 1993: 12). Indeed, the problem with the National Curriculum derives from its 'inhibiting the capacity of schools to introduce programmes geared to a world in which constant change and uncertainty are the norm' (Whitaker 1993: 15).

Thus, instead of recognizing the need for schools to be buffeted (or protected) from insecurity, uncertainty and 'chaos', Whitaker simply evades the latter and individualizes the (potentially devastating) problems thereby generated. Such individualization is psychological, as we have seen. In soft HRM-speak, he argues that 'traditional styles of management have tended to reinforce the suppression of potential, and senior staff . . . have tended not to concern themselves with building the psychological climate in which this directional tendency can be promoted' (Whitaker 1993: 42). Furthermore, he cites Peters' (1988) *Thriving on Chaos*, which considers how an increasingly unstable economic environment presents challenges to commercial organizations. This is indisputable: what is at dispute is the necessity of not eliding educational and commercial organizations. Whitaker, in quintessentially apologist fashion, writes:

> A fundamental part of school management is developing an appropriate relationship to the forces created by the changing structural environment. Schools . . . are faced with a plethora of prescriptions, setting requirements for their work and creating tighter systems

of accountability . . . These environmental forces not only condition the *strategic process of schools, they impact on each individual teacher* . . . The third strategic process is concerned with assessing outcomes and end results. The *productive school is one that succeeds in bringing about purposeful and planned change in its participants.* The quality of management and leadership is judged on results rather than intentions . . . ERA [Education Reform Act 1988] has placed new emphasis on assessment and evaluation, imposing a set of tight requirements on schools. *It is essential that schools incorporate these new elements into their own more comprehensive procedures for evaluation.*

(Whitaker 1993: 113–17, our emphasis)

Back to familiar managerialist territory now: 'strategic process', the 'productive' school, purposeful and planned change, tighter systems of accountability, and unavoidability of responding to external mandates. Moreover, Whitaker maintains that for school leaders this will be

a daunting task and that most of all they will have to be fascinated with change and comfortable in confusion. In a world where flexibility is strength, the challenge to personal equanimity comes through learning to expect ambiguity, working confidently in complexity and operating creatively in flux.

(p. 143)

Finally, while Whitaker is right that 'chaos' is about uncovering hidden patterns of order under the surface of random complexity, the point is that schools should not be enjoined to respond to, and be shaped by, state-created uncertainty via quasi-market mechanisms and processes. In other words, Whitaker should not accept as given the inordinate stress that is necessarily placed on the individual teacher – as we have seen he does.

Stoll and Fink

We have already indicated that Stoll and Fink (1996) indulge in scaremongering, specifically drawing our attention to the 'postmodern' world in which we live, which is fast, compressed and uncertain. It has also been indicated that their text, *Changing Our Schools*, alongside the texts surveyed here, draws superficially upon the business and management literature. Nevertheless we regard Stoll and Fink's text as subtly apologist in view of their sensitivity to the difficulties of improving schools, which derive from genuine educational reasons. We have already mentioned the untenable way in which Stoll and Fink approach the correlational studies of school effectiveness research (this chapter, note 4). As Thrupp (1999: 171) argues, Stoll's work is more contextually aware than most in the effectiveness and improvement literature, but still offers rather mixed messages (Stoll and Fink 1996, 1998; Stoll and Myers 1998). Now, as already noted, the educational change management literature focuses largely on reculturing (cultural change). Before addressing Stoll and Fink's discussion of reculturing, it is worth briefly highlighting their apologism, which is contradictory.

'Schools must balance increased school autonomy with national, provincial or state government controls to deal with the demand made of them, while at the same time not being controlled by these demands' (Stoll and Fink 1996: 64). This is a clear contradiction since schools are being controlled by government – which Stoll and Fink maintain is an unavoidable 'must' – yet at the same time must not be controlled by them. Contradictorily, again, they write that

> While external accountability appears to be a perennial favourite of politicians, many people view empowerment, teacher development and school improvement as more important. The question is, are the two incompatible? From our experiences, the twin pillars of accountability and empowerment (Gluckman 1990) are compatible.
>
> (Stoll and Fink 1996: 168)

Well, they are fundamentally incompatible and the question should be which do we want? Indeed, we concur wholeheartedly that 'there is substantially more evidence of their [performance and accountability] negative effects on teaching . . . and many examples of "teaching to the test" where test content drives what is taught' (Stoll and Fink 1996: 166). Thus they then immediately ask: 'Why have non-educators determined a narrow range of outcomes on which schools are to be judged?' What is needed here is a critique and rejection of managerialism – and quasi-marketization. Instead, the text contradictorily (and thus rather frustratingly) proffers managerialist solutions to the lack of commitment engendered by the reforms. They write that, 'While opening mandated doors will certainly get people's attention, there is little evidence that they engender commitment on the part of the people who have to implement the change' (Stoll and Fink 1996: 48). Indeed, Stoll and Fink (1996: 37) note that most studies have identified between 8 and 14 per cent of the variance in pupils' achievements is attributable to the school; but, as we have noted, the flaws of the effectiveness studies are by-passed and it is argued that a high proportion of school effectiveness efforts on a global scale have collapsed because of resistance to imposed change. The need here is to change the message.

This brings us to the generic thrust of the educational change literature: 'managing culture'. 'Changing the message' is, in reality, about imposing contradictory values (i.e. managerialist versus child-centred values). Stoll and Fink dedicate a whole chapter on the 'power of culture'. Following Deal and

Kennedy (1988) – discussed above – they argue that when culture works against you, it is nearly impossible to get anything done. It is hardly surprising that teachers have resisted the values that underpin the (new) managerialization of education. Crucially, Stoll and Fink write that, 'Frequently, however, school improvement efforts only focus on change of behaviours or technology and, therefore, do not touch the cultural core of the school' (Stoll and Fink 1996: 89). Instructively, they conclude that

> In terms of change, underlying values are much more difficult to reach than surface behaviours, and yet it is vital to understand them and how they motivate norms and actions. This is particularly important in that norms, beliefs and values also influence teachers' perceptions and definitions of what it means to be effective. Culture, therefore, defines effectiveness (Rossman *et al.* 1988). The leadership of the principal in shaping culture is highly significant.
>
> (p. 100)

It is interesting that Stoll and Fink omit to ask why? Why are underlying values difficult to reach? The message is clear: there is a need to change values since effectiveness (instrumentally redefined) contradicts values that underpin effectiveness defined non-instrumentally. It is not surprising that the authors emphasize the significance of the leader and also restructuring in order to effect 'cultural change', since, of course, power comes to the fore. That is, if you cannot change values (teachers' hearts and minds, stated simply) then you must use structural power to change 'surface behaviours'. Stoll and Fink are not making explicit that the business literature they draw upon is empirically and theoretically dubious, to say the least. As we have said, a large and profitable literature has capitalized on the idea that culture can be diagnosed and changed to improve organizational effectiveness. But what is almost invariably left out is the fact that

> employees are not passive objects of control . . . They may accept, deny, react, reshape, rethink, acquiesce, rebel, or conform and create themselves within constraints imposed on them. Research . . . on employee values and norms reflected in everyday practices . . . shows direct conflict with the aims and objectives of management.
>
> (Wilson 1999: 103)

Hence the oft-lamented need for coercion when all else fails. Finally, Stoll and Fink conclude:

> We hasten to add, before anyone concludes that here is another 'sloppy' plea to love the children but allow academic failure . . .

> Caring requires expectations of quality work from *all* children. To do
> less is uncaring. To decide that pupils cannot learn important things,
> like reading, because they are deprived, handicapped in some way or
> not academically bright, is to be uncaring and inhumane. Caring
> teachers expect pupils to do well.
>
> (Stoll and Fink 1996: 192)

Frankly, this is unfair to both students and teachers. Unfair to students because
the educational reality is that not all pupils are equally 'bright'; to teachers
because to recognize and deal with the latter reality is not uncaring. At best, we
accept the need in the abstract that we must have the highest expectations.
However, at the concrete level, it must be equally accepted that pupils and
students are reflective young people with varying backgrounds, interests and
emerging intellectual and social powers that may or may not gel with the
state's (and/or parents') educational priorities. At worst, the primacy accorded
to morality at the end of *Changing Our Schools* is a recipe for stress and guilt. We
return to the question of morality when we discuss Fullan.

The postmodern anti-bureaucrats: Hargreaves and Fullan

As mentioned at the start of the chapter, a significant leitmotif of the school
change literature is the assault on bureaucracy. Hargreaves and Fullan are
scathing about the lack of innovation engendered by bureaucratic school
structures. Unwittingly or not, this assault contingently complements the
lamentations of the New Right, which underpin social policy globally. Public
choice theory, for example, baulks at the putative benevolence of bureaucrats
and politicians. Public choice theory's critique of the state rests on the claim
that assumptions made by economists about the nature of the economic agent
in the marketplace are universal in the scope of their application: be it politics,
the family, scientific community or any other association. Applied to the political domain, public choice theory is aimed against attempts to rectify market
failure by state action. As O'Neill puts it:

> For public choice theorists state action does not and could not pro-
> duce the optimal outcomes of 'ideal markets' by other means. State
> actors act to maximise their own interests not the 'public interest'.
> Bureaucrats are taken to aim at maximising their bureau budget . . .
> Once economic theory is applied to politics, the state no longer
> appears as a beneficent representative of the public good . . . The pub-
> lic choice theorist typically appeals to a free-market economic policy,
> which attempts to rectify market failure . . . by institutional changes
> within the market.
>
> (O'Neill 1998: 161–2)

We agree with O'Neill that while there is something right about the public choice critique of state benevolence, the general claim it makes about the universality of the self-interested economic agent should be rejected. However, more important is the smuggling-in of the material reality of institutions that provide the very backdrop to economic activity. As O'Neill sums up: 'the new institutionalism has failed in any case to carry out its eliminative project of deleting references to institutions within its explanans. Reference to institutional contexts is smuggled in at the level of its assumptions about individuals' conceptions of their interests' (O'Neill 1998: 165).

While O'Neill provides a trenchant critique of the narrow conception of self-interest assumed by public choice theory, we are concerned to underscore the contingent compatibility with the anti-bureaucratic thrust of Hargreaves and Fullan – both of whom have impacted substantially on the educational world. In essence, the critique of bureaucracy and its material constraints complements the neo-liberal ideational corpus. Whatever the authors' intentions, the critique of bureaucracy is congruent with the Right's critique and also with the business literature, which does not recognize bureaucracy's (a) necessity, (b) efficiency, and (c) materiality. Indeed, the focus on the issue of bureaucracy is significant here, since its material constraints necessarily delimit the urgent calls for fast and responsive change on the part of schools. In other words, a recurring theme of the apologist literature is an implicit denial of the material constraints of structure and culture that necessarily delimit the managerialist calls for continuous improvement or 'success for all'.

Thus, to Hargreaves, 'teachers continue to cling to crumbling edifices of bureaucracy and modernity; to rigid hierarchies, isolated classrooms' (Hargreaves 1994: x). Moreover, 'especially in times of rapid change, modernistic structures of the secondary school kind inhibit innovation, delay organisational responsiveness, restrict professional learning' (p. 256). Indeed, he concludes that

> The challenge of restructuring in education and elsewhere is a challenge of *abandoning or attenuating bureaucratic controls*, inflexible mandates, paternalistic forms of trust and quick system fixes . . . What I have tried to make clear throughout this book is that while the prospects for the future remain uncertain, *the one sure thing is that we cannot cling to the crumbling edifice of the modernistic and bureaucratic present with its departments, hierarchies and cubby-hole structures of schooling.*
>
> (Hargreaves 1994: 260–1, our emphasis)

Hargreaves and Fullan (1998) argue together that bureaucracies have become 'rigid and faceless'.

Characteristic of both authors' work is a palpable lack of definition, rigorous assessment and argument. Rather, in the populist manner of the management and business 'culture gurus' discussed above, we are offered sweeping generalizations and inadequately elucidated fashionable theories, which are of little practical import. Clearly, for Hargreaves, bureaucracy is a major problem inhibiting innovation and change in schools. But we are not told what it is and how it might be avoided. Indeed, as above, we are told that the 'challenge' is to abandon *or attenuate* bureaucracy. Can it therefore be abandoned? Hargreaves does not even briefly consider the arguments against abandonment. It is important that we spell out the nature of bureaucracy and its inevitability in both public and private organizations in any advanced economy, since the calls for its abandonment complement neo-liberal market reforms. However, we want to make clear that there are problems with bureaucracy and we agree with Hargreaves that we should avoid inflexible mandates (such as the National Curriculum and standardized testing).

Although bureaucracy is not the only possible form of organizational structure, it has tended to dominate large, modern organizations. Coincidentally, while Hargreaves and Fullan decry the stifling reality of bureaucracy, there is a continuing questioning within business of the appropriateness of bureaucratic forms of organization to the objectives of companies and the individuals within them. The concept of bureaucracy has dominated the field of organization theory and is almost invariably held to be synonymous with any large-scale organization. One of the key scholars associated with the concept is the German sociologist Max Weber. The literal meaning of bureaucracy is 'rule by office or officials'. It is to Weber that most commentators turn when considering modern developments of the concept. As Hales puts it, 'Weber's "ideal type" bureaucracy (Weber, 1964) stands as a kind of totem which many writers on organisation feel obliged to dance around if their aim is ultimately to knock it down' (Hales 1993: 87). The main characteristics of bureaucratic organization as specified by Weber are: job specialization; authority-hierarchy; formal rules and regulations; impersonality; formal selection; career orientation. As Buchanan and Huczynski (1997) note, Weber used the term to describe a type of formal organization which was both impersonal and rational. For Weber, bureaucracy 'emphasised speed, precision, regulation, clarity, reliability and efficiency' (Buchanan and Huczynksi 1997: 366). But in everyday usage the term bureaucracy has pejorative connotations – 'red tape' or 'meddlesome bureaucrats'. However, it is argued here that bureaucratic forms or degrees of bureaucratization are unavoidable. This is not to deny that bureaucratic structures have their problems and inefficiencies.

There is considerable evidence that questions the existence of one, unitary bureaucratic type. As Hales (1993) notes, to some extent the discovery of bureaucratic variation is a function of the tendency to regard bureaucracy and organization as synonymous, and hence to regard alternative forms of organization, even decentralized forms, as variations of bureaucracy. He also points out that the unitary form of bureaucracy that some writers attempt to refute is something of an artificial construction – Weber's original concept admits of variation, in forms of authority, expertise and centralization. However, our concern is whether bureaucracy is inevitable. It is argued that management of work on an increasingly large scale necessitates differentiation and specialization, in turn necessitating vertical differentiation and delegation of responsibility to coordinate these diverse efforts, and standardization and formalization to control them. Bureaucracy is seen as the inevitable consequence of size. A central debate is about whether this is a technical necessity, that is whether it is the only possible way of coordinating work on a large scale or the result of the needs of the powerful to control work. Hales is right to reject the idea that bureaucracy is inextricably bound up with size.

This brings us to our rebuttal: instead, one needs to ascertain the level of informational and material throughput. As Sayer (1995: 16) argues:

> Bureaucratic control, in Weber's non-pejorative sense, is the norm for organizations of any scale, whether operating in markets or outside. It is by no means exclusively associated with public ownership; private organizations need a significant degree of bureaucratization if they are to cope with large throughputs of information and materials. Though bureaucracy has well-known deficiencies, especially with respect to flexibility and motivation, it is efficient, and even the most post-Fordist of firms need significant degrees of hierarchization and routinization of activities in order to function.

Bureaucratic structures have both unintended and intended consequences, which are conducive to both efficiency and inefficiency. For Hales, the impatience of many writers on bureaucracy to proceed to its detailed indictment means that its strengths are often by-passed or played down. It is thus ironic that Hargreaves refers to the fast, post-Fordist nature of postmodern society, since so-called post-Fordist organizations need significant degrees of bureaucratization. The indictment of bureaucracy chimes with both the public choice theorists and the business writers, who have argued, rather like Hargreaves and Fullan, that bureaucracies simply cannot survive in today's fast-changing world – they have to be replaced by more flexible organizational structures. Mintzberg, for example, has argued for what he terms 'adhocracy' (as opposed to bureaucracy). This is a loose, flexible organizational form that is tied together by lateral rather than horizontal communication. Adhocracies dispense with traditional hierarchies, job titles and rules. As Buchanan and Huczynski put it: 'Instead of coming up from the top, strategy "bubbles up", emerging from the decisions made by different units at different levels' (1997:

386). Unsurprisingly, they immediately note that actual examples of adhocracies are rare. It is unsurprising for the reasons Sayer alludes to above, that is, how is it in fact impossible not to have job titles and rules, since the latter are necessarily constitutive of any organization.

Buchanan and Huczynski cite the example of Apple Computer, which considered itself in its early days as '*nearly* an anarchic organization. However, following an increase in size, revenue and shareholder concern, the rational bureaucratic principles were established. The informal, *structureless organizational forms can cause staff anxiety*. It can result in conflict and chaos as separately begun projects overlap and bump into each other' (1997: 386, our emphasis). We have two brief points to make here. First, is not an increase in size due to the pressures for bureaucratization? Of course, demand creates jobs, but the extent of bureaucratization is not directly linked to the increase in jobs (again, it depends on the nature of the work and the informational requirements; for instance, a painting firm may increase its employees from 10 to 25, yet the firm may still operate successfully without any increase in bureaucratization; it may still operate with previous staff of secretary and assistant). Second, it is contradictory to speak of a 'structureless organizational form': the recognition of staff *per se* begs the question of the possibility of dispensing with job titles. Finally, the literacy and numeracy strategies adopted in England that are largely accepted by Fullan have involved significant degrees of *further* bureaucratization. Indeed, what is particularly lamented about the strategies is exactly their unwieldy bureaucratic impulse that results in work overload and stress. One of the many ironies of the neo-liberal critique of planning and bureaucracy is the fact that markets are regulated institutional entities: the neo-liberal Hillgate Group's idea of providing vouchers for parents, for example, would itself, if implemented on a wide scale, have required significant planning.[6]

Fullan (1): nodding but not really listening

We said towards the end of our discussion of Stoll and Fink that we would return to the issue of morality in relation to Fullan. It is apposite that Fullan has been left to the end of this chapter because of his considerable impact on the educational world. Now, Fullan's work is not solely about what he calls 'moral purpose'. Our subtitle above is intended to mean that Fullan acknowledges the problems and dangers that derive from neo-liberal, global education policies yet barely incorporates the policy implications, which enjoin a *reversal* of extant policy. In fact, we considered 'the reality and the rhetoric' as a subheading for this section about Fullan's work since upon scrutiny it extends and legitimates the neo-liberal restructuring of education globally. As pointed out in Chapter 4, it is important not to take out of context statements and propositions that seem to legitimate and extend neo-liberal restructuring – no easy task in Fullan's work given his lack of engagement with the deleterious reality of neo-liberal public sector policies. In Fullan's work we do however find – and concur with – statements that are critical of policy, such as the numeracy and literacy strategies in England, and the use of top-down mechanisms. Nevertheless, a reading of his texts evinces congruence with the neo-liberal restructuring of education.

The crucial task here is to go beyond the rhetoric of such notions as 'moral purpose'. We do not intend to subject to critical scrutiny every facet of Fullan's texts. In particular, while we would like to address in depth the serious lack of theoretical elucidation that characterizes, for example, Fullan's celebration of complexity and chaos, this would detract from some of the more pressing issues, particularly his reductive individualization of social problems and his championing of 'reculturing', which is inextricably linked to his claim that schools are not that different from business organizations. A good example of subtle apologism is clear from Fullan's discussion of the trenchant critiques of school effectiveness contained in the Slee *et al.* collection:

> Similarly, Slee, Weiner and Tomlinson (1998) and others launch a fundamental critique of school effectiveness and school improvement . . . They argue that social class is relegated to a control variable and not treated as problematic in its own right, that there is a failure to focus on power and that school effectiveness research tends to focus on power, and that school effectiveness research tends to concentrate on management issues and broad generalizations rather than on the complexity of the issues faced by teachers operating in disadvantaged circumstances. Slee, Weiner et al. themselves *are short on solutions*, but along with Oakes and her colleagues they are essentially right in calling for a more critical preoccupation on the part of researchers, policymakers and teachers . . . These problems . . . *may seem insurmountable. And critical theorists, as correct in their analysis as they may be, have offered little by way of strategy beyond brute sanity* (to be sure, this is an enormously difficult issue to address strategically). *There may, however, be other resources and ideas available for accomplishing more comprehensive and equitable reform, which brings us to complexity and evolutionary theory.*
>
> (Fullan 1999: 2–3, our emphasis)

A close reading here shows the sleight of hand that is characteristic of subtle apologism. That is, yes, Slee *et al.* are right to be critical, *but* not only are they 'short on solutions', the problems that call for such solutions *may* be insurmountable. And, in fact, such critical theorists *may* be right but even if they are right, they have not provided an appropriate strategy. Moreover, while such problems are 'enormously difficult' to address strategically, there *may* be other resources and ideas available for accomplishing equitable reform. Well, either there are or there are not other ideas and resources. Equally, either Slee *et al.* are right or they are not or there are specific areas of concurrence for Fullan. However, notwithstanding this irritating equivocality, it is clear that Fullan is suggesting that complexity and evolutionary theory fill the theoretical-cum-practical gap, which the critical theorists fail to do.

However, both complexity and evolutionary theory are not properly elucidated. By this we mean that the discussion is exceptionally brief and does not attend to the complexity (no pun intended) of the subject matter. At the same time, it does not provide the practitioner with practical advice, contrary to the claims made in *Change Forces: The Sequel*. Fullan writes that:

> Complexity and chaos theory are the same thing, but I prefer the former label because it is more accurately descriptive. This new science of complexity essentially claims that the link between cause and effect is difficult to trace, that change (planned and otherwise) unfolds in non-linear ways, that paradoxes and contradictions abound and that creative solutions arise out of interaction under conditions of uncertainty, diversity and instability.
>
> (Fullan 1999: 4)

He then quotes heavily from Stacey (1996a,b), who emphasizes that the science of complexity studies the properties of non-linear feedback networks, particularly complex adaptive systems. For Fullan this is 'rocket science', which can be used to cope with change. He approvingly refers to Brown and Eisenhardt's (1998) study of twelve global businesses, which employed complexity theory to differentiate successful from unsuccessful cases. Of course, this is not the issue, since schools should not be operating in a competitive environment. Fullan then discusses evolutionary theory, the import of which for Fullan lies in the need for cooperation. Instructively, in responding to the question of how to achieve narrower economic income distribution and better social cohesion, Fullan writes thus: 'No one has the answer, but it is likely that a combination of political, moral and self-interested forces will be needed' (p. 9).

Who's 'short on solutions' now? However, Fullan, with characteristic brevity, asserts that concerning the first of the three forces – political will – 'the power politics of recognizing that social cohesion, better health and economic productivity are closely associated . . . It is capacity building that counts, such as investment in early childhood development. Clearly, the moral purpose of educational reform must include capacity-building' (p. 9). Second, in evolutionary terms,

> some appeal to the common good and the welfare of others is essential. There is a greater commitment to the common good than there

was a century ago (but maybe not greater than five years ago). Moreover, moral purpose and social cohesion can be made more explicit
and can be fostered . . . More focus and discussion of moral purpose
and more instances of fostering relationships are needed to enhance
social cohesion.

(p. 9)

Third, 'and again in evolutionary terms, we *may* all be better off if greater
equity prevails' (p. 9, our emphasis). It is this recurrent equivocality that opens
up Fullan to the charge of subtle apologism: the importance of equity is not a
matter for equivocation. Indeed, he immediately adds that, in educational
terms, moral purpose and complexity 'play themselves out in the relationship
between public schools and democracy. In many ways this represents the
unfinished legacy of John Dewey' (p. 10). Such 'playing out' is not described,
nor, moreover, are we given evidence as to the 'greater commitment to the
common good' and why it was probably attenuated five years ago; such
unsubstantiated statements are academically inadequate. However, while
there is a normative emphasis (albeit equivocal) on social democracy and
equity, the generic themes of Fullan's work belie such normativity, namely the
vacuity that underpins his discussion of democracy, equity and moral purpose; the espoused urgency that he attaches to 'reculturing'; the individualization of social structure. It is both the vacuity of Fullan's populist 'forces' and
elision of education and business organizational values and purposes that
facilitate his reductionism of irreducible socio-cultural properties that delimit
the possibilities for equity and reform.

Essentially, while Thrupp (1999) has enjoined 'Let's be realistic!' in the
context of school effectiveness and school improvement, we would enjoin
Fullan to 'Get back to reality!' Fullan would no doubt decry the latter; it is thus
incumbent upon us to outline and defend this perspective. Again, on his work,
it does not help when we are confronted with contradictory statements; however, what we are really concerned about in Fullan's work is the undefended
championing of business-style 'reculturing' and the individualization of structured inequality. Despite the populist invocation of democracy and equity,
Fullan ultimately adopts a reductionist social ontology, which, coupled with
his undefended championing of business models and values, resonates with
the neo-liberal global restructuring of education. Such restructuring involves
standardized testing of which Fullan basically approves (see below) and
the considerable increase in stress and work, which, equally, Fullan plays
down. The point is that if Fullan took seriously, among other things, the non-
reductionism of complexity theory he would have to rethink such statements
as 'schools mired in inertial bureaucracy' (Fullan 1999: 31), since, as we have
argued, some degree of bureaucratization is unavoidable, in turn placing real
constraints on social interaction.[7] Indeed, the testing arrangements in England

have increased the level of bureaucratization: the accountability regimes glob-ally cannot avoid it. Furthermore, even if Fullan acknowledged the real material constraints that derive from school systems and the wider polity, we still need to reject the comparison between schools and businesses in terms of their 'tumultuous, uncertain and increasingly intrusive' environments.

Fundamentally, this is not to argue that schools should not be responsive to changing economic and technological circumstances. Instead, it is to reject the neo-liberal framework within which schools are located. Equally, it is to reject the crude, narrow and reductionist 'standards' approach that many countries now adopt. For Fullan (1999: 9), 'well-implemented equity-based reforms (such as achieving literacy standards for all children) may be in all our interests as they result in economic growth in the society as a whole'. Fullan recognizes that the focus on literacy and numeracy for all in the case of England is not problem-free. As he puts it:

> We have no doubt that the targets of 80 percent and 75 percent will be achieved by 2002, although I do not present it as a problem-free case because a preoccupation with achievement scores can have negative side effects, such as narrowing the curriculum . . . and burning people out as they relentlessly chase targets.
>
> (Fullan 2001b: 19)

Furthermore, he writes:

> Most people would agree that the public school system is in a state of crisis. It needs authoritative leadership before it disintegrates, but the system is still out of line with its environment, which calls for acceler-ated change and learning. There can be a fine line between coercive and authoritative leadership. Certainly the strategy in England has elements of coercive as well as pacesetting leadership. Is this degree of pressure required to get large-scale change under way? We don't really know, but I would venture to say that the strategy moved the English school system from near-chaos to a modicum of success is not the same strategy that is going to create the transformation needed for the system to thrive in the future. For that you need plenty of internal commitment and ingenuity. School systems all over the world, take heed.
>
> (Fullan 2001b: 47)

This is quite incredible: where is the evidence that the public school system is in a state of crisis? This chimes rather well with the scaremongering tactics we discussed at the beginning of this chapter. In what ways is this so-called quasi-disintegrating system out of line with its environment? What is its environment? What should be accelerated precisely, and is any acceleration practical? Apparently Fullan does not know whether external pressure is sufficient, though we are told, albeit equivocally in *Change Forces: The Sequel* (1999), that a judicious mixture of moral purpose and an understanding of chaos and complexity theory should do the trick. We are told that the answer lies in plenty of internal commitment and ingenuity. Yet this is so vague as to verge on vacuity. Furthermore, since Fullan (rightly) wants schools to be responsive to changing economic realities *and* to pursue and sustain social equity, he should not be asking whether any educational system should need to thrive: again, states need to protect their educational systems from competition precisely in order that they can provide high-quality education. This brings us to two issues that Fullan inadequately addresses, namely material causality and high-quality education. The latter will be dealt with first since it continues our discussion of the English numeracy and literacy strategies.

Fullan (2): complexity theory, standards-based reform and the lack of feasible alternatives

The charge of apologism is difficult to spell out because the literature is 'slippery'. Fullan is by no means immune here. We find statements that recognize the problems with, in this instance, the English numeracy and literacy strategies, yet their considerable limitations are (inconsistently) played down or simply glossed over. We have already seen that the English case is not 'problem-free'. Later in *Leading in a Culture of Change*, Fullan writes that

> in an era of high-stakes testing in schools and with a sense of urgency to show short-term results, leaders in a culture of change require a quality that all long-term effective leaders have – the capacity to resist a focus on short-term gains at the expense of deeper reform where gains are steady but not necessarily dramatic. Unlike businesses that go for immediate profit, schools should resist going for an immediate boost in test scores.
>
> (Fullan 2001b: 63)

Here, Fullan should query the policy reality of high-stakes testing at the outset, rather than encourage 'effective leaders' to resist short-termism. Why is there no critical discussion of the educational value of testing: how does or, rather, will such testing improve or sustain the competitive advantage of nation states? What are the possibilities for resistance? The point is that Fullan should not be responding; rather, he should be proactively critical of extant managerialist education policies. Also, characteristic of Fullan's work is a generic sloppiness, theoretical aspects of which will be discussed in a moment. Let us first consider his final comment quoted above regarding profit.

Although the capitalists' interests may best be served by striving for immediate and/or ever greater profits, this tells us little about precise corporate strategy, the mode of management or the precise structure of the firm (Hodgson 1999).[8] This applies with equal force to schools and their 'leaders'. Fullan needs to climb down from the abstract to the concrete level, where we find that schools are differently placed to circumvent or resist top-down standardized testing arrangements. Moreover, he does not acknowledge that the management mechanisms presented here are explicitly managerialist. As Willmott (2002a) argues, the trend now in England is towards organizational isomorphism, which involves a narrowing of the curriculum and teaching to the test in order to meet the shifting numerical sands of target-setting. This development hardly augurs well for the creativity and difference required of an advanced competitive economy.

Furthermore – and crucially – Fullan is not against top-down accountability: 'The politics of moral purpose can also help. Oakes *et al.* (1998) remind us that while top-down change doesn't work, *we still need the force of top-down mandates*' (Fullan 1999: 19, our emphasis). The logic is far from impeccable here. At the same time, 'the conceptualisation of infrastructure must be driven by a philosophy of moral purpose and human development *in which capacity-building and accountability learn to work together*' (1999: 60, our emphasis). This is an enforced union of two contradictory 'forces', which ineluctably undermines the capacity-building that Fullan, in fact, does not define or develop. The point here is that Fullan recognizes the reality of the stringent pressures to narrow the curriculum and teach to the test, yet denudes this of any practical contra-policy import. Indeed, a front-page headline of the *Times Educational Supplement*, 'Literacy test "gains" challenged' (May 2002), underscores the serious inadequacies of top-down target-based testing arrangements. But this should come as no surprise and the point is not how best to work with it but to reject it and think through feasible alternatives that develop children's social, cultural and intellectual capacities.

While Fullan rightly places a number of direct question marks over the English strategy, ultimately he does not question its fundamental rationale and champions, following Michael Barber, standards-based (as opposed to standardized) reform, approvingly quoting Barber extensively in his third edition of *The New Meaning of Educational Change* (2001a) and *Leading in a Culture of Change* (2001b). For Fullan:

> Standards-based reform is more complicated. On the one hand, witness McNeil's devastating account of the consequences of standardized testing in Texas ... On the other hand, we will discuss in subsequent chapters the new potential of standards-based (not standardized) reform (see Barber, 2000; Elmore, 2000; Hill and Crevola,

1999). We will conclude that standards-based reform . . . is an essential strategy for achieving meaning and coherence.

(Fullan 2001a: 37)

We are not sure what is the difference between standards and standardized: is not standards simply one practical step away from standardized practices? The problem with Fullan's approach here is that he completely ignores the neo-liberal, performativity and 'audit culture' principles that underpin the standards-based reform in England, which we will discuss shortly. Despite reference to McNeil's work, Fullan 'in any case, [is] willing to conclude that the combination of accountability and incentives produces results' (Fullan 2001a: 224). In fact, earlier on the book, he argues, contradictorily and without providing evidence, that despite reason to believe that hard-won successes over a period of 5 to 10 years cannot be sustained under current conditions, 'successful change is possible in the real world, even under difficult conditions' (Fullan 2001a: 104). The real problems with standardized reform and the standards-based reform in England are glossed over. Indeed, what he calls the collateral damage resulting from the English strategy is held not to be causally linked. Fullan readily discusses the chief components of Barber's reforms, such as the modernization of the teaching profession, the strengthening of leadership (cf. Gunter 2001), Ofsted and the Hay McBer report. Ultimately, while Fullan believes that the English results do not constitute 'deep and lasting change', nevertheless

[the] gains are real and they represent not a bad day's work – to get millions of pupils reading and engaged in numeracy. But they do not represent the kinds of transformation in teaching and learning . . . or the closing of achievement gaps by disadvantaged groups. [In England] they have blended accountability incentives effectively to produce gains in literacy and numeracy.

(Fullan 2001a: 231)

But Fullan never considers the fact that competitive, quasi-market mechanisms can never result in closure of achievement gaps by disadvantaged groups. Moreover, while we are not told what kinds of transformation in teaching and learning Fullan would like to see, the English strategy inherently encourages, and actively rewards, technicist teaching practices, thereby stifling innovation and meeting the real needs of children and students. Crucially, the point is that, as we mentioned earlier, the wider neo-liberal backdrop to the New Labour reforms in England, for example, is not discussed. This omission is not a mere peccadillo: together with the fact that Fullan openly welcomes Barber's reform programme in England and champions the need for 'reculturing' (changing ideas and beliefs and concomitant practices), it represents a clear case of subtle apologism.

However, we do not wish to suggest that the reforms in England are wholly deleterious. Here, we agree with Fink, who writes that the literacy and numeracy strategies do provide teachers with some good materials and appropriate assistance. Equally, we share his deep reservations: 'Many questions remain, however. One that interests me is how testing and other accountability measures will affect the intent of the strategy. When senior British policy officials use North Carolina and particularly Texas as exemplary change models there should be reason for profound concern' (Fink 2001: 231). What Fullan does not acknowledge is that the McNeil evidence he cites indicates irrevocably that such accountability measures discriminate further against minorities and the less advantaged, as Fink notes. Nevertheless, contrary to Fullan, it needs to be stressed that there is evidence that

> technicist approaches based on a behaviouristic view of learning promote some basic skills and raise test scores . . . This narrow and shallow perspective on teaching and learning, however, contributes little to pupils' desire to imagine, create, appreciate, and think critically . . . There is, unfortunately, not a great deal of room in most of the test-driven reform agendas internationally for pupils to construct knowledge, and to demonstrate their creativity, imagination and innovativeness.
>
> (Fink 2001: 232)

The recognition of the international thrust of education policy-making is important and is something, again, that Fullan does not acknowledge. What needs to be emphasized here is the global neo-liberal restructuring of education, which Fullan readily consolidates in his championing of the Barber reforms and, of course, the 'reculturing' necessary for their implementation, not just in England. Since Fullan approvingly and uncritically discusses Barber, it is important to spell out the overtly managerialist nature of the programme and its (global) neo-liberal underpinning.

As we have seen, the change literature generically decries so-called inefficient bureaucratic systems of governance within the public sector. As Elliott (2001a: 192) rightly points out, under New Labour the previous Conservative administration's project of replacing such inefficient bureaucratic systems with New Public Management, 'based on ideas derived from the private sector, has proceeded with a much firmer and more confident resolve'. Here, Fullan's latest work fits rather well. Indeed, blissful ignorance is not a defence here, since considerable critical literature is readily available. Of course, the paucity of critical literature Fullan uses is speedily dismissed or glossed over. Fullan must acknowledge that his own championing of reculturing is congruent with the changes enjoined by the English reforms, since here, as elsewhere, the reforms are underpinned by new managerialism. The professed need here is for school cultures to become *performative* organizational cultures. As we have seen in Chapter 2, within performative organizational cultures, 'quality' is defined as the best equation between inputs and outputs: the organization's overriding goal is to optimize performance by maximizing outputs (benefits) and minimizing inputs (costs) and thereby provide 'value-for-money'. As Elliott notes, Lyotard calls this the 'principle of performativity', which is well captured in Barber's account of the government's 'important strategy innovations' in education:

> Each year the professional development programme will be based on an analysis of what pupils and teachers have (and have not) been able to do well the previous year. Precision-targeting of professional development across a system is, I believe, one of our most important strategy innovations, ensuring both quality and cost-effectiveness.
>
> (Barber, cited in Elliott 2001a: 193)

As noted in Chapter 2, performative cultures presume that the performance of core activities can be made transparent on a continuous and sustainable basis through highly selective objectifications of performance known as performance indicators. The language of indicators underpins the reengineering approaches discussed in Chapter 7. Barber is explicit about the use of social engineering techniques in relation to the Excellence in Cities programme: 'Ultimately the programme should result in a complete reengineering of secondary education. Instead of fitting students into the system as we did in the 20th century, we would build the system around the needs and aspirations of students' (Barber, cited in Elliott 2001a: 194–5). What both Barber and Fullan do not acknowledge is that the social engineering of performance to meet human needs is paradoxical. As Elliott puts it: 'The more activities are shaped by "the timeless logic of standardised indicator" the less they meet the real needs they are intended to serve. People's needs change over time and circumstance' (Elliott 2001a: 195). Elliott cites the example of services to the elderly. The more the elderly ask their local authority to respond to their need for meals, the more the authority responds by attempting to match its performance to the standardized indicator of 'home helps per thousand of population'. 'The problem is that the elderly want microwaves and freezers rather than home helps at this particular point in time. Similarly, one could argue that meeting school attendance requirements and attaining good GCSE grades is not well matched to the learning needs of adolescents at a time when they are preoccupied with 'emotional work' (Elliott 2001a: 195).

Moreover, the crucial point is that the more totalizing the 'engineering' of the educational system around standardized performance indicators becomes, the more difficult it is for schools and teachers to provide flexible responses to their students' learning needs. Here, then, we reach one of the poignant ironies of Fullan's critique of the inflexibility of bureaucratic educational systems: the standards strategy increases the level of bureaucracy at the same time stifling the very creativity required of an advanced economy. Indeed, if international governments were to take seriously the devolution of decision-making to (properly funded) schools, unencumbered by stringent account-ability, quasi-market mechanisms (such as league tables, Ofsted and so on), then inevitably teachers would be better placed to teach with flexibility and sensitivity. As discussed above, the educational change management literature apes its business counterpart in creating a sense of urgency in fending off an impending crisis. Unsurprisingly, Barber writes thus: 'The sense of urgency comes, not just from the belief that every passing day when a child's education is less than optimal is another day lost, but also from the belief that time is running out for public education to prove its worth' (Barber, in Elliott 2001a: 198).

As Elliott rightly underscores, there is an intolerance of time, which was discussed in Chapter 2. This is characteristic of Fullan's work and comple-ments our argument that Fullan woefully neglects the materiality of social reality, in turn perpetuating work overload and stress, since such materiality necessarily places limits on what can be done. Indeed, time itself is a con-straint, which is equally neglected in social theory (Archer 1995). However, the point that Fullan does not (again) acknowledge is that there is no time for teachers in England to reflect upon and develop their practice. In fact, what Elliott calls 'the constant state of activation' (engendered by Ofsted) has been reinforced by the new performance management (see Chapter 2). Here, Barber has been pivotal, particularly in his calls for performance-related pay. Fullan also refers to the Hay McBer research. Briefly, such research represents the construction of more layers of indicators to supplement National Curriculum targets and attainment levels. Such research was carried out over a period of ten months to the cost of £4 million. What Fullan does not acknowledge is that the methodology of the research is shaped directly by a policy context that demands 'a technology for auditing teaching as a basis for implementing its performance-related pay proposals. From the outset, the researchers pre-sumed that the outcomes of effective teaching could be measured against pre-standardized outputs in the form of exam/test results and classroom climate variables' (Elliott 2001a: 199–200).

As Elliott argues, the researchers do not question the ambiguous idea of quality and the conceptual conflation of outputs with outcomes and do not ask what the layers of indicators conceal and whether the professional self they construct will have dysfunctional consequences for education. Barber's com-ments must also be placed in a broader neo-liberal politics about sustaining economic growth in the face of international competition. Elliott succinctly summarizes thus:

In English-speaking countries, like the UK, governments tend to deal with their anxieties about globalisation by continuously reaffirming the belief that sustainability depends on their capacity to re-engineer and re-regulate every sphere of society, including the public services, by introducing market mechanisms. Such reaffirmations of belief to ward off anxiety about the consequences of globalisation involve the 'continual re-intensification of available instruments of regulatory control'.

(Elliott 2001a: 200–1)

Earlier, we mentioned the issue of causality. To recap, Fullan advocates complexity theory as the (albeit equivocal) means of implementing change successfully. However, as already argued, his exposition of complexity theory is hardly complex. Moreover, we are not served what is promised, namely how to use it in practice for the purposes of 'continuous improvement'. The point we wish to make here, briefly, is that Fullan's approach to social theorizing is at best sloppy when he implicitly asserts a direct causal link between improved literacy and economic growth. The empirical reality of disaffected graduates working in McDonald's is sufficient rebuttal here. Of course, such populist-cum-managerialist writing is likely to proffer sloppy, unsubstantiated causal relationships. Furthermore, what makes such statements likely – especially in Fullan's case – is reductionism. That is, the reduction of irreducible social and cultural properties to individuals and their interpersonal relationships (as opposed to impersonal relations in and between organizations). In turn, this facilitates the putting aside of the materiality causal efficacy of bureaucratic forms and time itself.

A far more sophisticated grasp of complexity theory should lead to questions about material (social) causality. Here, Fullan does not recognize the stringency of constraints that derives from incongruence between (usually managerialist) change-ideas and material reality. Indeed, crucially, Fullan never discusses the feasibility of his (unarticulated) normative championing of social equity, which ironically cannot be achieved via quasi-market mechanisms and standards-based reform.[9] His inability to address the issue of feasibility is, of course, evident in the critique of bureaucracy. There are problems, but can we avoid it? The so-called alternative of 'adhocracy' simply highlights the fact that it is not feasible to replace bureaucracy with some wishful, highly responsive, highly flexible alternative. Despite the irritating equivocality that haunts Fullan's texts, he does champion 'the good life', specifically democracy and greater social equity. Here, we are not offered any thinking about plausible causal chains, which would immediately throw up the issue of feasibility. Even Brian Caldwell (co-author of the highly problematic *The Self-managing School* (1988) discussed in Chapter 3) laments the 'seductive and incomplete' nature of Fullan's *Change Forces* texts. As he puts it:

> It is seductive because the 'lessons' are friendly, the language is access-
> ible, and the author has high credibility. The reality is that the prom-
> ising reforms of which he writes have been difficult to achieve . . . In
> every setting, these reforms have been professionally and politically
> contentious, and have proceeded in a climate of escalating expect-
> ations for schools, unprecedented social transformation, and *chronic*
> *under-resourcing. The book is incomplete . . . because there is no detailed*
> *account of what capacities are to be developed, especially at the school and*
> *classroom levels.*
>
> (Caldwell 2000: 208, our emphasis)

What Fullan has yet to acknowledge is that, for example, the costs of democratic control may well outweigh the benefits. As Sayer (1995) notes, electoral
democracy is limited to voting either for simple single issues or for whole
packages of issues, since disaggregation is extremely costly. It is worth quoting
him at length here:

> Where interests are diverse and the tasks complex, the degree of con-
> trol can only be loose, not least because of the division of knowledge
> . . . It is in the very nature of an advanced economy that society comes
> to depend on arcane bodies of specialist knowledge which are largely
> beyond the understanding of even highly educated outsiders. How
> many voters can be expected to understand the options open to the
> Chancellor of the Exchequer? This also presents problems of account-
> ability for any mode of coordination: how can central planners assess
> whether the specialists' bids for resources are reasonable?; how can
> consumers know whether the providers of a specialist service like
> medicine can be trusted? As in economics, so in politics: the scope for
> effective democratic control is limited not only by class, by minority
> control of the means of production, but by the division of knowledge.
> Dunn identifies this as the 'central paradox – that we have all become
> democrats in theory as just that stage of history at which it has
> become virtually impossible for us to organise our social life in a
> democratic fashion any longer'.
>
> (Sayer 1995: 111)

Sayer is not suggesting, however, that within the technical divisions of labour
of institutions and among groups with similar interests there is not more scope
for democratic determination. Notwithstanding the hierarchical and bureaucratic nature of specific organizations, their design and rules may still be subject to democratic control. The point is that the calls for social democracy
on Fullan's part are so general that they are vacuous. Moreover, in markets it is
not democratic principle but profit and price that determine development:

individuals do not have the power to decide how resources in general are allocated – they can only spend their own money.

> For liberals, this is how it should be, for you – and not others casting their votes – are the best judge of your interests, and similarly you and no one else should be responsible for your own property. Clearly, this assumes an atomistic view of interests and fails to acknowledge that many goods cannot be provided through markets because of conflicts between individual and collective interests.
>
> (Sayer 1995: 112)

Fullan (3): individualization and neo-liberalism

This brings us to our final criticisms of Fullan, namely his reductionist individualization of social reality, specifically social inequality. Even if Fullan provided the sorts of fine-grained detailed analysis for change that Caldwell (above) quite properly calls for, his analysis would be fatally flawed simply because he does not acknowledge, and adequately theorize about, the material limits (structural, cultural and temporal) to change (read: standards-based reform). In essence, he adopts an undifferentiated, 'flat' social ontology, which, whether he recognizes it or not, complements the individualist ontology of neo-liberal marketers and public choice theory. Let us flesh out his individualist (reductionist) strategy. In the first book of the *Change Forces* trilogy, he writes:

> At a policy level, growing concerns about educational equity and economic performance mirror the more particular issues just described . . . Poverty, especially among children and women, racism, drug abuse, and horrendous social and personal problems all make the equity and excellence agenda more serious and poignant day by day (Hodgkinson, 1991). My main point, however, is not to consider these matters at the institutional level – at least not at this time. The building block is the moral purpose of the *individual* teacher.
>
> (Fullan 1993: 10, emphasis in original)

Near the end of the book, he reiterates his individualist focus:

> Paradox is standard fare in the complexity of change processes, and it shows itself here in the realization that personal change is the most powerful route to system change. In *Prisons we Choose to Live Inside*, Lessing (1986) says, 'It is my belief that it is the individual, in the long run, who will set the tone, provide the real development in society'.
>
> (Fullan 1993: 140)

It does not follow that individual moral purpose or change will result in greater equity. Indeed, such an abstract proposition really does not hold up to concrete (empirical) scrutiny for the very reasons discussed above, namely material and temporal constraints. The emphasis upon the moral purpose of the individual teacher complements Stoll and Fink's emphasis on individual caring. This leitmotif is also evident in Hargreaves and Fullan's *What's Worth Fighting for Out There?*:

> When love and care extend to inclusion, this advances the interests of equity and social justice as well . . . Once teachers really put a priority on care, justice and inclusiveness as moral purposes underpinning their teaching, everything starts to change.
>
> (Hargreaves and Fullan 1994: 35–6)

Fullan implied above (in 1993) that we would receive an institutionally based analysis. However, in 2001 he remains unequivocal: 'In the final analysis, it is the actions of the individual that count' (Fullan 2001a: 84). This is very poor social theorizing: the concept of agency – the ability to act – presupposes social contexts that delimit action to varying degrees. Has Fullan not heard of collective (agential) action (that also fails)? For all his (brief and unarticulated) talk of theory, Fullan's secreted sociology is methodically individualist. The point here is not to outline a robust theoretical framework that acknowledges the irreducible power and properties of structure, culture and agency (see Willmott 2002a), but simply to emphasize Fullan's individualism, which can never be a practical starting-point for any envisioned change programme. Put simply, it is not surprising that Fullan does not provide us with any detailed programme, since his social theorizing precludes it.

Indeed, we should not be surprised that he 'does not spend a great deal of time elaborating his view of moral purpose' (Gitlin 2000: 211). In tandem with Fullan's lack of social theorizing, again, it comes as no surprise that Gitlin takes Fullan to task for not acknowledging the lessons of the 'new sociology of education':

> Another example of the ambiguity caused by the facile articulation of moral purpose, is Fullan's discussion of social capital. This discussion is limited primarily to a list of desired dispositions such as civility, compassion, fairness, trust, collaborative engagement and commitment. In Fullan's view, the role of the school is to develop these dispositions in students. Unfortunately, without further articulation of social capital, it would be easy to assume that he sees these dispositions as a sort of universal good. If we have learned anything from the new sociology of education, however, it is clear that all dispositions

reflect particular dominant perspectives ... which provide advantages for middle class students.

(Gitlin 2000: 212)

Furthermore, Gitlin rightly points out that Fullan's borrowing from business allows 'the taken-for-granted morality of business to be imported into schools and does not highlight the different aims of these organisations' (Gitlin 2000: 215). We want to underscore the fact that such borrowing is part and parcel of the neo-liberal quasi-marketization of education. Indeed, all the apologist literature conveniently ignores discussion of power and the stringent critiques of quasi-marketization. Therefore Gitlin is right to note Fullan's lack of focus on relations of power, which raises serious concerns about Fullan's claim that learning communities should embody conflict and operate collaboratively within and across institutions, since 'collaboration may be nothing more than a guise to legitimate hierarchical relations of power, and "better knowledge" constructed as nothing more than a confirmation of the dominant position of particular groups within the educational community' (Gitlin 2000: 216).

Indeed, Gutierrez rightly argues that Fullan

> fails to deal head-on with the fact that schools' cultures exist within and must contend with the society's culture, which is driven by market forces and industrial models. The trends of educational reform have been market-oriented. We need to be savvy and wary of market trends that conflict with and erode quality teaching and learning practice.
>
> (Gutierrez 2000: 220)

We argue that Fullan actually legitimates and extends it, albeit at the same time recognizing its deleterious effects on teachers and their students and children. Essentially, Gutierrez shows what Fullan should be thinking and advocating, thereby underscoring the charge of subtle apologism. Gutierrez counters the manic scaremongering that erases the conditioning temporality of educational structures and processes. As he puts it:

> Practical conditions need to be worked on constantly to involve ways for people to move at a pace that is reasonable. This means slowing down at times, in order not to let the fast pace of change generate freneticism, fragmentation, and undue exhaustion ... Currently, conditions demand teachers to do more and more things, trying to get the young to know more and more 'stuff' contained in too many 'high standards' ... [they] *demand that one does too much too fast at a*

> *faster and faster pace, which leads to doing little or less over all, incurring unnecessary stress.*
>
> (Gutierrez 2000: 220–1, our emphasis)

Again, Gutierrez hammers home the point that Fullan ironically misses a 'capital opportunity' to counter the market and industrial forces. Finally, regarding the fulfilment of moral purpose, Gutierrez notes that 'we need to confront the fact that in the United States, as in many other societies, we have vested our sense of democracy and freedom in private property and capitalism, endorsing private achievement' (Gutierrez 2000: 223). Here, we would again reiterate not just that Fullan is committing a sin of omission – none of his texts explicitly discuss and criticize the marketization of education globally and the imposition of accountability measures that do not address children's needs and learning abilities – but also that Fullan does not criticize the prevalence of business thinking precisely because he champions its transposition to education.

Why reculturing and why now?

This brings us back to the beginning of this chapter: why the need for change (reculturing) and why now? For Fullan (2001b: 5), 'reculturing is the name of the game', where

> Effective leaders know that the hard work of reculturing is the sine qua non of progress. Furthermore, it is a particular kind of reculturing for which we strive: one that activates and deepens moral purpose through collaborative work cultures . . . Reculturing is a contact sport that involves hard, labour-intensive work.
>
> (Fullan 2001b: 44)

Now, this suggests that Fullan is about competition, played out 'on the edge of chaos', as he likes to put it, in which business practices and models not only are appropriate but also may save your school from failure in an increasingly fast-moving 'postmodern' world. It is a pity that Fullan does not tell us precisely the 'particular kind' of reculturing for which he strives: we have seen that moral purpose is ultimately vacuous, and that any attempt to improve the educational lot of disadvantaged children is seen as an individual matter for individual educators. The point is that we are compelled to infer the particular ideas that need to be put into practice (hence *subtle* apologism). Such ideas are ideological in that they (a) individualize social problems; (b) champion business and managerialist ideas and practices, and (c) accentuate the putative benefits of standards-based reform. They are ideological precisely because they conceal the fact that they promote and consolidate neo-liberal quasi-marketization of education. It is, regrettably, all too easy to make the causal link between the neo-liberal globalization of education policy and its consolidation and acceptance among influential education academics: this is the reason for reculturing now. In all of the school change texts surveyed above, the imposition of new managerialism is not explicitly rejected and there is no reflection upon the uncanny similarity between their exhortations and those of the business culture gurus of the 1980s. Instead, we find simply degrees of apologism. Whatever the claims of the school change authors to the contrary, their texts do not – or rather cannot – provide ways of attenuating social inequality.

Finally, since the 'school change' message is both overblown and counter-productive, we would draw from it no particular implications for practice in schools over and above those already drawn in the more grounded areas of school improvement, school leadership and the like. Rather, the key messages of this chapter for practitioners are not to accept individualized and hence reductionist accounts of social inequality and to avoid being panicked into embracing changes which are not genuinely educational, feasible and equitable.

PART III
Conclusion

10 Education management: where to now?

Our critical response to the education management literature is now all but complete, at least for now. In Part I we discussed how our concerns about education derive from both theory and empirical evidence: how theoretically (transcendentally) education should not be subject to market colonization; how empirically, the effects of quasi-markets and managerialism are deleterious. Following this, Part II illustrated many times over that education management writers do not take these concerns seriously enough: the problem of textual apologism. If we have provided examples to the extent of labouring the point it is because we have wanted readers to be quite clear about the way the education management literature may be read and why it concerns us. Furthermore, in each chapter of Part II we have tried to spell out some implications of our analysis for practitioners, ways in which educators can reflect upon the nature and extent of managerialism and pursue, within differentially constrained limits, alternative educational paths.

We wish to use our conclusion for just three more purposes. First, we will provide an overview of the Part II chapters to remind readers of our main conclusions about textual apologism in relation to the literatures discussed. Second, and especially because we have criticised Fullan for not discussing the feasibility of his normative championing of social equity, we want to go beyond the school-level strategies already suggested to briefly engage with the normative general policy implications of our critique. Third, we would like to comment briefly on how we think education management *as an area of academic study* needs to respond to the arguments we have made.

Our findings about textual apologism: an overview

Our review began by examining how education management academics were dealing with *educational marketing* – a highly precarious area of academic scholarship given marketing's problematic ethical foundations and history of unsuccessfully trying to overcome them, as well as empirical evidence about the damaging impact of educational quasi-markets (discussed in Chapter 3). It was argued that, while presenting itself as 'the discipline of exchange behaviour', marketing fails to adequately consider how asymmetrical power relations mediate exchanges. Far from securing consumer sovereignty and satisfaction, many marketing methods frustrate or undermine the realization of this ideal. Commodified education permits people with sufficient money to buy educational services without any justification to others who have equal, if not more, need for them. The market renders its subjects adiaphoric, and marketing involves the 'removal of the face'. In this process the individual is no longer regarded as a moral agent, but as someone to whom something must be done; that is, as a target for the marketing mix. Despite all this, we found those in the educational marketing area generally embraced marketing in an opportunistic way which fails to give much weight to research-based critiques. It lacks discussion of the historical limitations of marketing as a business discipline, or critiques of it from within business and management studies, and reflects an inadequate philosophical and ethical understanding of the market. Indeed, some educational marketing texts were found to be problem-solving to the extent that they do not even raise the possibility that educational marketing might be politically or ethically problematic (e.g. Barnes 1993), while other overtly apologist texts strongly champion the role of marketing in today's schools while glossing over its implications for authentic learning and social justice (e.g. Davies and Ellison 1997). Subtle apologists in this area, such as Foskett and Hemsley-Brown (2000), tend to draw on the softer notion of 'relationship marketing', however it was shown that this approach fails to save marketing from its mired history of unethical foundations. Rather than 'bringing the (moral) face back in', relationship marketing involves the instrumentalization of emotions and thus undermines the conditions for authentic trust and commitment.

In the introduction to Chapter 6, we noted that in recent years in England the *school improvement* literature has become marked by an extraordinarily close interrelationship with educational policy. Whereas a previous review had pointed to most school improvement writers being subtle apologists, because they lacked an adequate critique of neo-liberal politics or much concern with the sociological limits of school improvement (Thrupp 1999), increasing interest in the impact of social and political context was noted (e.g. Harris 2001, Maden 2001). We welcomed this development but suggested it had not yet gone far enough. Despite close links to policy, school improvement remains an area with some primarily problem-solving texts (e.g. Walsh 1999). There are also texts which are overtly apologist in the way they actively 'sell' recent official school improvement policy (e.g. Brighouse and Woods 1999). However, most school improvement texts exemplify more subtle apologism by indicating concern with wider social and political context but still offering predominantly decontextualized analyses. We argued that the net effect of this would be to give the reader an insufficiently critical perspective on post-welfarist reform, and encourage them to go along with policy rather than contest it. It was suggested that the continued emphasis on decontextualized approaches probably reflects the problem that even leading school improve-ment writers have yet to find ways of breaking out of the generic discourses which have dominated school effectiveness and improvement for so long. The discussion focused particularly on the recent arguments of John Gray and David Hopkins. We supported much of what Gray (2001) was arguing but felt his criticisms of policy are understated. Hopkins (2001) takes a technicist 'pol-icy science' rather than 'policy scholarship' approach to education policy. This has led to an over-rational understanding of the policy-making process, and has allowed him to view national policy as merely ineffectual rather than damaging.

Chapter 7 examined the *school development planning (SDPing)* literature as well as the *(strategic) human resource management (HRM)* literature which has begun to incorporate and overshadow it. Starting with SDPing, we pointed out that there is nothing wrong with planning and target-setting *per se*, but that they should be educational aids rather than tools of managerial account-ability if we are to avoid narrow and inauthentic schooling processes. Yet SDPing is increasingly about the latter. Its overt apologists see it as an over-rational process and largely accept the market and accountability regime as a given (e.g. Hargreaves and Hopkins 1994, Leask and Terell 1997). Meanwhile SDPing's subtle apologists, such as MacGilchrist *et al.* (1995), recognize some of the risks but do not go far enough in scrutinizing the wider context. They also fail to consider the contradictory manner in which they mix the need for both educational and accountability practices linked to planning. Our discus-sion of the strategic HRM literature began with a discussion of Seifert (1996), who raises a number of concerns about HRM, especially its managerialist co-option of the appraisal mechanism and its support for performance-related pay, because of its alleged effectiveness. Again Seifert points out that there is nothing wrong with appraisal *per se*, but argues that it needs to be part of a wider scheme of genuine professional development. Moreover the evidence on performance-related pay reveals a strong pattern of discontent and failure. However, overt apologists underplay the dangers highlighted by Seifert (1996). Writers such as Hall (1997) advocate HRM, but ignore its critiques from within business and management studies. We went on to note how the strategy talk favoured by many education management writers wishes away material constraints and allows conventionally manipulative HRM tech-niques to be employed. Moreover, while Business Process Re-engineering is seen as part of the strategic way forward by education management writers, such as Davies and Ellison (1999), it has been roundly criticized for its highly coercive approach to organizational change. Drawing on Alvesson and

Willmott (1996), this chapter concluded by pointing to the colonizing tendencies of strategy and its self-disciplining effects, as employees subordinate themselves to its implications.

The *school leadership* literature was considered in Chapter 8, and here we argued that this literature had become so linked to managerialism that it should not be seen as a phenomenon distinct from education management. Managerial colonization occurs when leadership texts are overtly framed within managerial government policy, and when school leaders are asked to take advice from texts for effective business leaders. However, in the school leadership area education management also reaches some of its most thorough treatment by including historical, sociological and philosophical analyses, and the school leadership area has important elements of textual dissent including critically informed alternative accounts. The chapter went on to consider a spectrum of apologetic and dissenting school leadership perspectives. It used Ramsay's (1997) text with its checklists of 'tips' to illustrate a primarily problem-solving approach, and Davies and Ellison's (1997) account of how to work within a managerialist framework as an example of overt apologism. However, most discussion was devoted to subtle apologism, exemplified in the work of Leithwood (Leithwood *et al.* 1998), Southworth (1998) and Sergiovanni (2001b). Each of their accounts was distinctive but it was argued that none were sufficiently critical to challenge managerialist models of leadership. In the case of Sergiovanni this was not because his work lacks critical potential, but because it does not inform the reader's understanding of neo-liberal education policy and its impact on schools explicitly enough to avoid uncritical readings. Finally, textual dissent in the area of school leadership was examined, particularly the work of Grace (1995), Gunter (2001) and Blackmore (1999). Some of the key strengths of these accounts were the way they historically contextualized post-welfarist school leadership, underscored its highly political nature, and deromanticized it.

The last of the Part II chapters, Chapter 9, was concerned with the *school change* literature. We argued that school change is inextricably bound up with the rise of managerialism and is the education-sector equivalent of the so-called change management literature for business. In particular, we pointed out that 'reculturing' in the school change literature has paralleled the rise of culturalism in business and management schools in the 1980s, and draws on the same business gurus. The chapter therefore began by delineating the rise of culturalism during the 1980s, and highlighting the conceptual poverty and politically managerialist nature of this literature, which has been uncritically incorporated by school change writers. One of the central themes underpinning the school change literature is the lack of innovation engendered by bureaucratic school structures, but we argued that it is not possible to dispense with degrees of bureaucratization. In turn, we noted that this places limits on the possibilities for 'continuous improvement', which in an uncertain and volatile educational climate is inherently flawed as a means of engendering creativity and educational 'success'. Equally, an individualist bias permeates the school change literature, distracting the reader from wider socio-economic material structures and cultures that necessarily delimit educational 'success'. Chapter 9 also considered cases of (relatively) overt and subtle apologism in the school change literature. Examples of the former are James and Connolly (2000) with their distinctive managerialist emphasis on emotions and psychoanalytic theory, and Morrison (1998) who especially champions the applicability of business models to education but mistakenly argues that Taylorism has had its day. Our discussion of subtle apologism in the school change literature focused mostly on the work of Fullan (e.g. 1999, 2001b). We argued that, while Fullan acknowledges the problems and dangers that derive from neo-liberal, global education policies, he barely incorporates the policy implications, which demand a *reversal* of extant policy. Rather, his work involves the undefended championing of business models and values in education and the individualization of social problems in ways which complement rather than challenge neo-liberalism.

At its broadest, the key problem with all these education management literatures is inadequate attention to the wider social and political dimensions of education management. However, while our review of education management texts found much to confirm our initial concerns as listed in the introduction to this book, it is also apparent that these problems have been manifested in many different ways and to greatly varying extents. Not all texts are problematic in all respects, and our review has also indicated that some are far more so than others. This limits the usefulness of such intermediate generalizations as those outlined in the introduction. Rather, it seems to us, especially in cases of subtle apologism, that it is the detail which counts, and this returns us to the point made in Chapter 4 in relation to our categorization of apologism, the importance of interrogating the arguments of particular writers. Yet we have also found some discussion to be slippery or equivocal in a way which makes it hard to be precise about what is actually being argued. Here we should not only ask for clarification, but also consider the work being done by such slipperiness or equivocality in terms of trying to satisfy different policy, academic and practitioner constituencies.

Normative policy issues: towards the 'learning economy'?

In this section we want to sketch some ways in which policy should (the normative) and could (the feasible) be refashioned in order to enhance social equity and develop individuals' intellectual, social and moral capacities in order to facilitate the development and consolidation of the so-called learning economy. As Hodgson (1999) argues, policy has to engage with, and build upon, generalities, although it should not be confined to them. Furthermore, it should be borne in mind that all policies are fallible and thus must be explicitly provisional and practically adaptable. While, for reasons of space, we cannot provide detailed policy prescriptions, and thus our normative discussion here is brief, important things can and will be said.

Immediately, it is painfully clear that the global neo-liberal restructuring of education (and public organizations and institutions generically) hardly augurs well. Indeed, in the UK context, we have seen how New Labour's so-called modernizing strategy has consolidated and extended the managerialist project with its imposition of performance management. We have also seen how, in the UK context, the primacy accorded to education's role in contributing to economic competitiveness rests on a set of pedagogical strategies, the effects of which are antithetical to the needs of a 'high skills' economy. Nevertheless, matters remain such that it is not too late. Any possibility or feasibility for change, however, has two aspects. First, whether a certain desired end state can be realized, for example, how people can be politically mobilized to make it happen. Second, whether, assuming enough people are willing to make it happen, the end state is feasible in itself. We have seen in Fullan's case that normative rejection of bureaucracy does not mean that we can replace it. Indeed, we provided a counter-balance, highlighting both its efficiencies and material necessity. Nevertheless, Bottery (2000) shows how, even at stage one, matters are not auspicious in the UK context. He notes that those in government and other positions of power 'need to believe that their positions exist primarily for the pursuit of democratic purposes and the creation of a more just and equitable world' (Bottery 2000: 215). Moreover, he describes the reactions of teachers themselves:

> It is then not unfair to say that most public sector professionals – and particularly those in education – are constrained in what they must do and how they must think to a much greater extent than at any time in the last 40 years. Now it would be easy to blame this situation on governments too keen on control, and insufficiently reflective upon the ultimate effects of such control. *Yet the reactions of teachers to this legislation have been . . . very cautionary . . . they exhibited a potentially dangerous mixture of overwork and indifference towards an understanding of why these changes had come about, and what they as professionals should do in reaction to them.*
>
> (Bottery 2000: 223, our emphasis)

Bottery points out that the vast majority of teachers in his research saw their role as centrally concerned with either 'the kids' or 'the subject', and were uncomfortable about taking a political stance, particularly in the light of the damaging strikes of the 1980s. Further, he suggests that the situation may be worse than this. Research conducted during the 1990s (see Bottery and Wright 2000) uncovered evidence that strongly indicates that not only do teachers often have little understanding or interest in wider 'ecological' areas, but also that schools do little in terms of their staff's continuing professional development in relation to them.

Bottery then argues that we need to revitalize a sense of 'public good', advancing conditions for making democracy possible. He rightly argues that privatization fails in many respects to advance these concerns. Equally, he argues that we cannot avoid state intervention and fiscal redistribution. 'Markets, and the practice and language of privatisation, then, are forces which are deeply damaging not only to a wider vision of responsibilities within the wider society, but also to the conception of education as being a crucial base for the values of civil society' (Bottery 2000: 229). Bottery ends his book by providing an account of two sets of principles, one for duties and one for rights. While we agree with both sets of principles, we want to put a little more flesh on the analytical and policy bones, albeit (necessarily) at a general level. At the same time, in delineating a plausible causal future chain, following Hodgson (1999), we wish to underscore the limits to democratic participation (an issue touched upon in Chapter 9).

Evotopia and the learning economy

This section relies solely upon the work of Geoffrey Hodgson, specifically his *Economics and Utopia: Why the Learning Economy Is Not the End of History* (1999). In brief, we find Hodgson's highly sophisticated grasp of economics and social theory immensely useful in the context of how we can change current social and economic policy, globally. In essence, what Hodgson calls 'evotopia' is about the challenge for the twenty-first century, which is not the construction of a fixed and final utopia but of evotopia – 'a system that can foster learning, enhance human capacities, systematically incorporate growing knowledge and adapt to changing circumstances' (Hodgson 1999: 24). The evotopian schema embraces the following principles (taken from Hodgson):

- Reigning uncertainty and incomplete knowledge make any fully rational, social or economic, policy or design impossible.
- Much policy should be formulated by experimentation, and with a variety of routines, institutions and structures. Only on the basis of such a variety can policies and institutions be given any comparative and pragmatic evaluation.
- In-built variety is important for helping the system deal with, and adapt to, unforeseen changes.

We will return to the policy priorities for the development of evotopia. One of the central themes of Hodgson's work is the positing of plausible future causal chains or scenarios. The scenarios that Hodgson considers derive from the belief that modern, developed economies have entered, over the 1980s and 1990s, a long process that can lead to immense transformations of historical proportions comparable to the Industrial Revolution. Hodgson assumes the following broad and interlinked developments within modern capitalism. First, in core sectors of the economy, the processes of production and their products are becoming more complex and sophisticated. Second, increasingly advanced knowledge or skills are being required in many processes of production. Levels of skill are being raised to cope with growing complexity and difficulty.

Crucially, Hodgson is emphatic that the above is not inevitable. The point is that the 'knowledge-intensifying scenario discussed here has a high level of plausibility' (Hodgson 1999: 182). Now, as complexity increases, and the required skill levels rise, workers require more intensive training. New specialisms emerge to deal with the multiplying facets of the increasingly complex socio-economic systems. In essence, this is a scenario of enhanced skills and growing knowledge intensity. 'Uncertainty increases because calculable estimates of future events are more difficult in a more complex world . . . Democratic institutions also have difficulty coping with the complexity, bringing further uncertainty' (Hodgson 1999: 183). Thus, on the issue of democracy, we need to be realistic about its limits, if the appropriate policy initiatives are adopted (to be discussed) that continue and enhance this scenario, which is already manifest. In a complex and evolving, knowledge-intensive system, agents have to learn how to learn and to adapt and create anew.

Hodgson points out that the assumptions here regarding increasing skill levels concern the most knowledge-intensive, technologically advanced and dynamic core of the capitalist system. Importantly,

> [this does] not rule out the possibility, as today, of a substantial underclass of unskilled or unemployed workers. Today, many workers in developed countries are confined to low paid, part-time, insecure or menial 'McJobs', often in the service sector. To some degree this may result from, as well as persist alongside, the above developments . . . Nevertheless, at first we are considering a scenario where the developments at the dynamic core overwhelm and dominate other tendencies.
>
> (Hodgson 1999: 186–7)

The alternative route Hodgson calls the 'omega scenario', which is a world of McJobs, unemployment and robots. This scenario remains firmly within capitalism. Hodgson delineates the epsilon, beta, gamma, delta and zeta scenarios, respectively. Very briefly, the epsilon scenario could be described as beyond capitalism. Here, a form of employment contract remains but is a mere shell of its former capitalist self. In the work process, the degree of control by the employer of the employee is minimal. It is an economy still dominated by private property relations and largely regulated by the market. The beta scenario relates to many of the actually existing developments in the advanced, knowledge-intensive capitalism of the late twentieth century. The gamma scenario is, loosely speaking, state socialism, that is, a centrally planned economy under public ownership, with the machine-intensive technology of the late nineteenth and early twentieth centuries. The delta scenario, with machine-intensive production and worker cooperatives, is genuine market socialism. Hodgson spells out the zeta scenario, which is a further post-capitalist development of the epsilon scenario, involving further increases in the knowledge intensity of production, of human skills, in the economic power of the workforce and in the broadening of share ownership of the corporation by the workforce. Knowledge is more sophisticated and enhanced.

Unquestionably, however, the global neo-liberal restructuring and reculturing of educational systems is wholly detrimental (not only) to the development of evotopia and the learning economy. Indeed, an intimation of the systemic problems that are slowly creating the path towards the omega scenario is gleaned from the fact that teaching to the test in order to perform well in league tables is *not* teaching children and pupils to learn how to learn or how to be creative and adaptable. However, we will not recapitulate the litany of problems, dangers and perversions that necessarily attend neo-liberal marketization – this has already been done. What we want to do now is discuss the policy imperatives that may pave the way towards an evotopian socio-economic system, in which the greatest possible (feasible) social equity and justice prevail.

Policy conclusions

It should come as no surprise that, like Bottery and many others critical of extant neo-liberal policy, we want a complete reversal. An overriding policy conclusion is the need for growing investment in education and training at all stages and levels. In other words, let's have *genuine* devolution of autonomy to schools and colleges, where generous degrees of funding and cooperation, rather than underfunded competition, are the norm. We concur with Bottery that we need an education for citizenship, which requires the development of a politically robust curriculum. Moreover, Bottery argues that we need the introduction of a fundamentally more critical and self-reflective curriculum and the development of a teaching profession that has both the ability and the desire to embrace such a curriculum. We would also add that we need a local and culturally sensitive curriculum, that is balanced with a national curriculum. We need to end performance management, league tables and excessive summative assessment and to show a genuine commitment to children's needs as growing emotional, social individuals. Indeed, as Hodgson argues, the evotopian emphasis is not exclusively or primarily on quantitative measures: quantity can never fully express quality.

One of the many problems with the current testing regimes is the lack of recognition that learning is not simply the acquisition of information. As Hodgson (1999: 248) argues, education for flexibility and adaptability 'requires in general the development of the powers of intuition, comparison, analogy and experimentation. Such second order learning requires the protection and development of individual autonomy, within a secure but stimulating environment'. This brings us back to the transcendental argument against neo-liberal marketization elaborated in Chapter 2. Indeed, Hodgson rightly argues that the market has a necessary but limited role in an evotopian economy.

We also want to reiterate the need for substantial and enduring investment in education, which has immediate implications for income equality. It is worth quoting Hodgson at length here:

> The only substantial and enduring strategy must involve heavy investment in education, to increase the relative and absolute supply of skilled and educated workers . . . In the face of rapid and dramatic global and technological changes, massive increases in effective expenditure on education and training are required both to reduce unemployment and inequality. Countries that have travelled more than others down this road, particularly Germany, have not witnessed a significant increase in income inequality since 1970s, and have been more able to train and relocate workers of relatively lower skill . . . The approach to formal education must be neither narrow nor doctrinal.
>
> (Hodgson 1999: 250–1)

The current competitive market ethic that underpins education policy globally must be replaced with one that facilitates creativity, experimentation and learning how to learn: in the UK context, injecting short-term cash is simply insufficient, considerably so. For instance, the additional £50,000 awarded to each secondary school in England in July 2002 will have helped but it is not the main issue: performance management and the culture of performativity need to be abandoned.

Finally, we fail to see how education can be delivered fairly in such unequal institutions as those we have at present. For, as Dewey put it a century ago, 'What the best and wisest parent wants for his own child, that must the community want for all its children. Any other ideal for our schools is narrow and unlovely' (Dewey 1902: 3). How to achieve a substantial reduction in longstanding segregation when parents are so concerned with positional advantage is a complex issue (see Thrupp 1999). Nevertheless, the most urgent priority is to challenge recent policies which have opened up new opportunities for between-school and within-school segregation under the guise of 'choice' and 'diversity'. To do this we need more debate about the social costs of a highly segregated schooling system and, in particular, a clear public understanding that school choice is not value-free: that where one's own child is enrolled has direct implications for the schooling and subsequent life chances experienced by others.

Academic accounts of education management: the future challenge

Given that we have provided so many examples of what we see as the problem, at one level the implications for writers on education management are self-evident: we need a shift to analyses which provide more critical messages about social inequality and neo-liberal and managerialist policies. Yet how to achieve that as quickly as possible is another matter. We think it requires a change of focus both within and beyond the education management arena.

Internally there is the need to engage more intensively in processes of peer critique and self-examination. We say 'more intensively' because there have been important past and present efforts in this direction which should not be overlooked. For instance, from 1997 to 1999 there was an ESRC (Economic and Social Research Council)-funded seminar series on redefining education management (see Bush *et al.* 1999; Thompson 2000), and another entitled 'Challenging the orthodoxy of school leadership' and organized by Alma Harris, Michael Fielding, Helen Gunter and Geoff Southworth is taking place over 2002–3. Yet such activities, important and worthwhile as they are, represent only one approach to change, the hope that new ideas will be presented, and through dissemination, will gradually overtake old.

What is also needed is more strident internal rejection of primarily problem-solving accounts as being too socially and politically decontextualized, accompanied by an utter refusal to write at the level of 'tips' or in similarly reductive formats or to accept the argument that busy practitioners need only problem-solving texts. There is no point in writing 'simply' if to do so is to present practitioners with an analysis which is fundamentally inadequate. There also needs to be stronger internal challenges to overt apologism on the grounds that there is really no intellectually sound way that managerial reform can be accurately or ethically presented so unproblematically. Indeed, both of these kinds of account are so unacceptable that challenging them should be regarded as a relatively uncontentious activity concerned with ensuring research and scholarly quality. For, as Goldstein and Woodhouse (2000: 357–8) have put it: 'All research fields contain work demonstrating a wide range of "quality". One measure of the health of a field of study is the extent to which it progresses by eliminating the poor quality work, through a shared recognition of what counts as "good".'

Where we envisage more difficulty is in the area described as subtle apologism, since the authors so characterized may well maintain that their work is critical enough. Nevertheless, we hope they will reflect on our arguments and also strengthen their links with writers who take alternative perspectives both within and beyond education management. After all, the literatures we have been discussing are highly self-referential. This is a feature sometimes noted in the education management literature itself; for instance, Fidler (2001: 71) has suggested that school effectiveness involves the 'endless recycling of the literature of a very small number of writers'. Certainly the same names crop up time and again across nearly all of the education management literatures we have considered. We also recognize, however, that there are lesser-known school management writers who offer alternative perspectives. At least some of these would present a significant challenge to textual apologism and it would be good to allow their voices to come to the fore.

The other group which education management proponents should build links with are the 'external' textual dissenters. As we have seen these have done particularly useful work in the area of school leadership and what is needed now is more critical, dissenting accounts in other education management areas as well. However, this would also require more critical scholars to be willing to engage with education management writers rather than just agreeing to disagree as is usually the case at present. While there is no doubt the resulting debates will often be frustrating, to the extent that education management can be encouraged to genuinely incorporate more powerful social and political critiques of structural inequality, markets and managerialism, the literature could send out less apologetic messages and thus become a more potent force for good.

More attention to sociological and political matters will undoubtedly have its costs for those education management writers who take up the challenge since there would be a loss of support in some quarters. At the school level this will be because education management's problem-solving nature is undoubtedly part of what has provided its appeal to many (although not all) practitioners. Similarly, education management frameworks which cannot be easily turned to the cause of managerial reform are not likely to find favour with policy makers in managerialist times. And there can be no doubt that such costs will be borne personally by those education management writers who do seek alternatives. As Ball (1998b: 77) points out: 'the policy entrepreneurs interests in terms of identity and career, are bound up directly and immediately . . . with the success of their dissemination'. Moreover even for those who are not so entrepreneurial it will be harder to construct the individual fabrications which are so much a part of 'getting ahead' as an academic now since research contracts, consultancies and invitations to speak may all become less forthcoming for those who choose to go against the grain.

Nevertheless, it is one thing for academics to unwittingly support damaging and inequitable policy, and quite another to do it knowingly. Given that we – and others – have pointed out the problem of textual apologism in education management texts, the onus is now on those authors critiqued here (and others like them) to shift their position unless they can demonstrate that our concerns are unfounded. Moreover, there would potentially be much to gain in terms of a generally more balanced and rewarding set of research concerns as well as solutions to critical education management problems. Indeed, our various 'implications for practitioners' have been little more than a starting-point for thinking about how those who lead and manage schools might work against, rather than support, managerialism. What is ultimately most frustrating about today's education management literature is that more energy has not gone into thinking about this problem.

Notes

Chapter 1   Introduction: What's wrong with education management?

1   For instance Angus 1993a, 1994; Smyth 1993; Ball 1994, 1998b; Grace 1995, 2002; Gunter 1997, 2001; Hatcher 1998b; Slee *et al.* 1998; Blackmore 1999; Thrupp 1999, 2001a; Willmott 1999, 2002a.

2   See volume 12(1), 2001, also volume 13(1), 2002.

3   Both of us are governors of schools that have faced serious problems of different kinds. Martin Thrupp taught in New Zealand secondary schools for six years and just recently Rob Willmott has moved from the academy to pursue a career in primary teaching.

4   The other reason is because we think school effectiveness has been largely superseded by school improvement; see Chapter 6.

Chapter 2   The market, neo-liberalism and new managerialism

1   Here, it needs to be noted that 'globalization' is a much-debated term – see Green (1997) and Marginson (1999). One of the key points to be bear in mind is that while it is commonplace in the sociology of education in the UK to observe similar market-oriented shifts in educational and social policy in other countries, 'there are considerable differences and similarities in how governments have used the market form. This applies both to the extent of the use of the market form, the purposes it is intended to serve and the precise market mechanisms that governments put into place via legislation . . .' (Gewirtz *et al.* 1995: 4).

2   Ontology concerns the assumptions about social existence (or reality) underlying any conceptual scheme or any theory or system of ideas. For example, methodological individualism's social ontology assumes that the social world consists solely of individuals and their interpersonal relationships in the here and now. See Willmott (2002a) for discussion of social ontology and the realist alternative to individualism (and all forms of reductionism).

3   We discuss the nature and reality of Taylorism further in Chapter 9.

Chapter 3   Inequality, education reform, and the response of education management writers

1   In much the same way as Tomlinson (2001) writes about education in a post-welfare society and Gewirtz (2002) discusses the 'post welfarist education policy complex', here we use the phrase 'post-welfarist education reform' as a kind of shorthand for the market, managerial, performative and prescriptive educational policies and practices of the last decade. Strictly speaking, however, it may be premature to speak of *post*-welfarism when strong elements of welfarism often remain in policy and society.

2   While there are also important ethnic and gender effects related to achievement, social class effects tend to dominate. We are discussing overall trends here – it is certainly possible to point to individuals who for various reasons buck these trends, but unfortunately they are the exceptions who prove the general rule.

3   An Australian study by Hill (1998) suggests that schools and classrooms can be jointly responsible for up to 60 per cent of overall variance in achievement. However, see Thrupp (2002) for a critical response to this claim. The 'school effect' could also be less than 8–15 per cent if, as Thrupp (1999) has argued, some of it actually represents the compositional effects of school mix.

4   Compositional effects have been debated for many years because large-scale studies have produced very little consensus on their size and nature. However, qualitative studies like that of Thrupp (1999) point strongly to compositional effects, and a review by Thrupp *et al.* (forthcoming) argues that the balance of quantitative evidence from the UK, USA, New Zealand and Belgium further supports the presence of important compositional effects.

5   In the UK, Robinson has argued in a similar vein that educational approaches are unlikely to address the impact of social inequality. He has suggested that 'a serious programme to alleviate child poverty might do far more for boosting attainment and literacy than any modest intervention in schooling' (Robinson 1997: 17).

6   For instance, the USA does not have a tradition of school inspection or review while the fact that curriculum prescription has been more marked in England than New Zealand has been reflected in a higher level of teacher concern about control over curriculum content in England (Thrupp *et al.* 2000).

7   This is true, for instance, of the differentiation of students between and within schools, the level of prescription of the curriculum, the amount of testing of students which goes on (according to *The Guardian* (4 August 2000), 'the more educationally successful students [in England] can now expect to take more than 75 external tests and exams during their school careers'), the marketing of schools, and business involvement in schools.

8 There is, however, continuing debate in England about the extent to which quasi-market policies have added to pre-existing levels of social segregation between schools. See Ball *et al.* (2002: 19) who describe the evidence as 'contradictory and contested', also Thrupp (2001b). In New Zealand there has been much more agreement that quasi-markets have polarized schools, see Lauder *et al.* (1999) and Nash and Harker (1998).

9 According to the Notes about Contributors in Davies and Ellison (1997a).

10 According to the Notes about Contributors in Davies and Ellison (1997a). Caldwell had by then been a consultant on about 200 occasions and was also a visiting tutor on an international MBA programme at the University of Southern California for principals of self-managing schools. He has gone on to write books such as *Beyond the Self-managing School* (Caldwell and Spinks 1998) and *The Future of Schools: Lessons from the Reform of Public Education* (Caldwell and Hayward 1998). These promote many of the approaches to school management we criticize in this book (see, for instance, Chapter 7).

Chapter 4   Reading the textual apologists

1 This section is based on a reading of 2001 catalogues from most major US and UK publishers.

2 We also considered a chapter on general education management and educational administration texts but decided there would be much overlap with our chapters on specific areas.

Chapter 5   Educational marketing

1 A good example is Mr Jones, the incoming headteacher in Gewirtz's research at Beatrice Webb School, England. It is worth quoting her observation notes at length here:

> Look at this room, it's down at heel like the rest of the school. We need to give the right impression to middle-class parents who we need to attract if the school is to be saved. It should look more like a chief executive's office. I'm getting rid of these shabby old filing cabinets and getting three spanking new ones and I'm replacing those tables with a round table and comfortable chairs to sit round for meetings. And he wasn't going to use recycled paper like the old head which, he said, was very admirable in environmental terms but hardly gave the right image.
>
> (Gewirtz 2002: 44)

Gewirtz notes that, as with the other headteachers she and her colleagues researched, Mr Jones was very concerned with the semiological subtleties of image, symbols and presentation. Indeed, by the end of his first year in post, Mr Jones had relocated his office to a place that was less accessible to students, staff and parents, creating a formal 'chief executive' style suite consisting of an office with an adjoining meeting room.

2   Indeed, for Sullivan (1991: vi) 'there is no such thing as a market but only people'; for Evans (1995: 7) markets are 'the sum total of all actual and potential buyers of the product'; finally, for Pardey (1991: 8) the market 'is not a homogeneous mass but a large collection of individuals with their own wants and needs'. All three authors cited here are ignoring, like Hayek, the fact that markets are regulated and involve major social structures that are irreducible to the sum total of individual actors. See Willmott (2002a) for further discussion.

3   As Willmott (2002a) found, pressure to 'market' 'Southside' primary school arose from a debilitating financial crisis in 1998 that was independent of school management practices. A firm commitment to child-centred education, buttressed by a strong Catholic ethos, meant that the mooting of marketing was emotionally painful for the staff. Equally, Gewirtz (2002: 40) describes how Ms English's reluctance (in Beatrice Webb School) to embrace the values and practices of the market may have affected the school's income and market position. Whilst Ms English produced a glossy brochure and in 1992 appointed a new deputy headteacher whose main role was to improve recruitment, she refused to countenance trying to attract more middle-class parents by 'massaging the image of the school'.

4   As Kenway *et al.* (1995: 35) neatly put it: 'But the basic point is that markets are not the people-friendly, life-enhancing, neutral processes of exchange that are portrayed in the literature'.

5   See also Foskett and Hemsley-Brown (1999, 2001).

6   See Elliott (2001a) and Smyth and Dow (1998) for excellent critiques of the contractarian model that underpins outcomes-based education policymaking.

7   For example, Evans (1995).

8   Thus, to Susan Robertson (2000: 120):

> The critical point to be made concerning a political economy of consumption is that within the new social settlement, it is increasingly the social rather than the physical property of a commodity that determines patterns of consumption. As a result, the marketing challenge is to commodify and sell desire and need itself. Name and trademark, such as Pepsi, Coke, Converse, Nike, Esprit or Benneton attach youth, chic and vigour to for-profit merchandising [. . .] In much the same way, too, schools in the competitive marketplace are encouraged to sell particular images of desired schooling.

9   For Bottery (2000), managerialism reduces first-order social and moral values to second-order values. 'By doing so, managerialism not only achieves a hegemony within organizations; it also parasitizes and weakens those values upon which the wider society – but also its own existence – depend' (Bottery 2000: 68). This brings us back to the essential properties of markets *qua* markets that operate indifferently *vis-à-vis* persons. Moral behaviour is encouraged only in so far as it serves market demands. In Willmott's (2002a) case study, the troubleshooting headteacher set up a self-esteem programme in order to improve SAT (Standard Assessment Task) results, whereby children were treated as means to managerial ends. However, it is refreshing to note that in Bell's (1999) research, a number of primary headteachers argued that they made use of the press to celebrate the work of their schools, to give children a sense of pride and to locate the school in its wider community, as opposed to advertising or promoting their schools. This is because, as Bell rightly argues, the poverty of the market ideology stems from its inability to recognize the existence of community, personally or organically.

Chapter 6   School improvement

1   We think this is likely given the historical development of the two areas. We have had school improvers make comments to us like 'I don't think I was ever really on the school effectiveness bandwagon', and it would be interesting to find out how many school improvement writers are happy to see their work categorized as part of school effectiveness research. If it is the case that 'school improvement' now fits under the banner of school effectiveness, why have a journal called *School Effectiveness and School Improvement* and an International Congress for School Effectiveness and Improvement?

2   An exception is the chapter by Bottery (Bottery 2001).

3   This section is based on a previous review of this book (Thrupp 2000).

4   In a *Times Education Supplement* interview, Hopkins stated that, 'My educational values are sympathetic to the Government's and I want to help implement policy' (Hendrie 2002).

5   Only the same concern with 'quick fixes': 'school improvement's time in the sun will be short unless it can persuade its new found friends that it is not a "quick fix" response to educational change' (p. 2). Similarly Hopkins talks about policy-borrowing but not the role of education management academics as 'policy entrepreneurs' (Ball 1998b) in the way many proponents of school improvement and related areas tend to be.

6   For instance the section on 'Limits of current reform strategies' argues that 'one cannot be over optimistic about whether current reform initiatives will lead to dramatically enhanced levels of student learning and achievement' (p. 7) because reform is not 'up close', 'system wide' and 'system deep'. But a

more sociological interpretation is that reform is constrained by the deep effects of social structure and this is not mentioned. Similarly, Hopkins is keen to redesign schools around learning (p. xiii) but does not demonstrate a socio-logical understanding that part of the reasons schools are as they are is because of their role in social control and social sorting – roles they carry out all too efficiently.

Chapter 7   School development planning and strategic human resource management

1   They write further that:

> In the UK a whole raft of legislation was passed which was designed to change the education system radically . . . Similar changes are being implemented in other countries too, for example New Zealand, Australia and the Netherlands. The rash of changes has produced casualties and contradictions in the system. Of course, the education system cannot be static; much as teachers, parents and pupils may wish it otherwise. The speed with which society is changing, and with which technology is changing ways of living and working, means that the knowledge, skills and attitudes of yesterday's curric-ulum may not be appropriate today.
>
> (Leask and Terrell 1997: 29)

The stance on global educational change here is that despite the casualties and contradictions, we simply have to move on: change is ineluctable and hence resistance is futile. As we have indicated, school change will be addressed in Chapter 9. However, conspicuously absent in Leask and Terrell's text is the fact that such legislation was underpinned by neo-liberalism. Furthermore, we are not told precisely how deleterious educationally are the contradictions and casualties. While Leask and Terrell are right (albeit implicitly) to see education policy in England and Wales in an international context, they do not adequately take issue with the 'casualties and contradictions'. As Ball (2001b) rightly argues, Labour's education policy thrust is *contradictory in its own terms*: 'the overriding emphasis on education's role in contributing to economic competitiveness rests on a set of pedagogical strategies, the effects of which are actually antithetical to the needs of a "high skills" economy' (Ball 2001b: 46).

2   See also Ball (1994) and Thrupp (1999) for discussions of Hargreaves and Hopkins writing on SDPing.

3   In referring to Riches' (1997) use of HRM discourse, Gold and Evans (1998: 62) write that

some of the language Riches uses . . . must be used with care in education. He writes about 'productivity' and 'optimising own and institutional performance', both of which are terms that seem to rely too
heavily on outcomes which are difficult to measure when the human
relations of learning and teaching are taken into account.

4   The distinction between 'resourceful humans' rather than 'human resources' is
not simply semantic quibbling: the former restores the humanity that HRM,
like managerialism generically, tries to erase or at best play down.

5   However, we would anticipate a managerialist response, along the lines of the
need to change or manage the culture of the school, involving what some
authors irritatingly refer to as 'difficult choices'. Indeed, as we have seen, the
actual messiness of managing and concomitant ethical issues are left to the
manager.

6   Equally, as Bush and Coleman (2000: 2) put it: 'Schools and colleges have to
interpret and implement government imperatives but the greater challenge
arises from the shift to self-management'. A challenge indeed.

7   For instance, 'Dilemmas then concern an ability to bring about change, the
morality of attempting to do so and a consideration of who should be involved
in any decision to change' (Fidler 1997: 102).

Chapter 8   School leadership

1   For more explanation of transformational leadership, see Southworth (1998),
Bush and Coleman (2000), Gunter (2001) and Hopkins (2001).

2   A 'superhead' is a highly paid head brought ('parachuted') in to turn around a
high-profile failing school. Superheads embody a profound confidence in
managerial solutions. The idea clearly draws heavily on the managerial notion
of performance pay and incentives, that to ensure high performance in difficult circumstances and get the 'right' staff it is necessary to pay above usual
rates. On the other hand, the idea of a superhead defies the view that school
context constrains 'effective' school processes in a powerful and unavoidable
way and also implies a considerable distance between the 'strong' head working on behalf of the government or LEA and the 'weak' staff he or she has been
brought in to sort out.

3   See the series editors' introduction to Leithwood *et al.* (1998).

4   See Thrupp 1999: 170–1.

5   Of Sergiovanni's many texts, Sergiovanni 1996 and 2000 probably offer more
critique of markets and managerialism than most; however, they are still quite
limited. In Sergiovanni (1996) there is a critique of Peters and Waterman's
(1982) outcomes-based high performance theory and of TQM as 'a metaphor
for theories and management schemes that we have indiscriminately
imported to education' (p. 15). But overall there is still little discussion of the

politics and social context of schooling and this is true of his own 'theory for the schoolhouse' as well. Sergiovanni (2000) follows Habermas to look at the neo-liberal colonization of the 'lifeworld' of schools. But while there is discussion of post-welfarist education reform in the introduction and at a few other points, it is still not a dominant feature of the book.

6 This section is based on a review of this book published as Willmott 2002b.

7 In late 2002 Southworth became Director of Research at the NCSL. Tim Brighouse and David Hopkins, whose work was discussed in Chapter 6, are also both on the governing council of the NCSL, the latter in an observer role since he took up his post at the DfES.

Chapter 9 School change

1 Interestingly, prior to Fullan's later work that deals explicitly with 'reculturing', Huberman (1992) picked up on the implicit message of the need for supermen and superwomen in schools.

2 Parker notes the contradiction here between the individual manager-hero and the culturalist emphasis on shared values. As he argues, organizational excellence is rhetorically suggested to be a 'matter of both singular vision and collective mission, yet in some sense one surely cancels out the centrality of the other . . . in practical terms it might easily be argued that following either charismatic leaders or common normative frameworks might actually make organizations rather inflexible' (Parker 2000: 18).

3 However, it is worth quoting Parker here:

> Several authors argue that culturalism and its variants were echoed by the Thatcher/Reagan new right rhetoric of enterprise and individualism . . . which Clarke and Newman characterize more specifically as 'the right to manage' (1993). Just as the Japanese 'other' allowed for a rearticulation of versions of nationalism, and a 'return' to the values of gritty entrepreneurship that are suggested to have made the nation great in the first place, so does culturalism stress the centrality of markets, of free consumers and of heroic managers. *Rolling back the bureaucracy, like rolling back the state, became a precondition of encouraging unconstrained enterprise and creativity and allowing the hidden hand of the market to do its benign work.*
>
> (Parker 2000: 24, our emphasis)

The anti-bureaucratic impulse is prominent in the school change literature.

4 On the issue of the effectiveness correlates, Stoll and Fink (1996: 31) write: 'While there are some well-known caveats about correlational studies and generalizability of results, there appears to be a surprising amount of agreement

across studies and more detailed understanding than was first given in Edmonds's (1979) somewhat simplistic five factors of effective urban elementary schools.' Note the equivocal *'appears* to be a surprising amount of agreement'. First, precisely because correlational studies cannot establish causal relationships they at best constitute a tentative starting-point for qualitative analysis over time. Second, to imply that such correlational studies must have some credibility because of academic consensus is a *non sequitur*. Third, the higher the number of factors does not improve chances of grasping the complex nature of educational reality.

5   See Willmott (2002a) for elucidation of the nature of open social (and educational) systems, their irreducible causal properties and powers.

6   The idea here is that money available for publicly provided education would be given directly to parents in the form of a voucher, which could be cashed in for a place at any school that had available space. The voucher could also be used as a contribution to the fees of a private school. But such a system would be bureaucratically unwieldy and involve a substantial increase in the subsidization of private education. This is the logical end result of the neo-liberal ideology. The fact that the voucher scheme requires bureaucratic regulation was (conveniently) by-passed by the Hillgate Group and, indeed, by the then Secretary of State for Education, Keith Joseph.

7   In the *New Meaning of Educational Change* (3rd edition), Fullan writes that 'Complex systems generate overload and confusion, but also contain more power and energy. Our task is to realize that finding meaning in complex systems is as difficult as it is rewarding' (Fullan 2001a: 19). First, the extent of confusion is an empirical matter for investigation, and not one that can be inferred *a priori*. Second, Fullan is quite right that complex systems 'contain' power or 'energy'. It is a pity that Fullan does not tell us why. Let us take the example of bureaucracy (which is pertinent). Bureaucracies can process large volumes of routine information very quickly by virtue of their structure (hierarchical organization, specialization). Here, we need the (realist) concepts of essence and emergent properties (see Sayer 2000; Willmott 2002a). Briefly, as Sayer (2000: 84) argues:

> One purpose is to identify the essence of an object in terms of properties that supposedly determine – or are indispensable for – what it can and cannot do; these are its 'generative' properties. Thus, it might be argued that it is in virtue of the essential features of bureaucracies, such as their division of labour and hierarchical structures, their formalized procedures, etc., that they can process large amounts of routine work more quickly, but find it difficult to provide flexible responses to unforeseen circumstances. The other purpose is to refer to those features of an object which enable us to distinguish it from other kinds of object.

The generative powers of which Sayer talks are emergent powers or properties that are irreducible to, yet ever dependent upon, human actors for their causal efficacy. Such material properties constrain/enable activity. In the case of bureaucracy, they constrain innovation. Now, to reiterate, the necessity of bureaucracy and its attendant constraints are not recognized by change authors.

8   As Hodgson argues, there are two problems with general claims that capitalists who show no concern to maximize profits are liable to cease being capitalists:

> The first is that, in a dynamic context, it is not at all clear what 'maximising profits' means. It would be pointless to maximise profits one year if profits collapse the next. Reasonably, 'maximising profits' would involve future years. It might mean 'maximising the expected value of a future net income stream', where expectations are on the basis of estimated probabilities. But the problem here is that expectations and estimates are necessarily imperfect. *Also they are always culturally and historically conditioned.* 'Maximising profits' leads us to no single or obvious value. The second problem is that in any market economy, competitive selection is haphazard and imperfect, and also depends on cultural norms and interpretations . . . In sum, the *making* of profits is ignored by a capitalist firm at its peril, but the *maximising* of profits is an ambiguous objective, always subject to culture and history.
>
> (Hodgson 1999: 137–9)

This applies to Fullan's recommendation that all leaders should resist short-term gains. All schools operate in a context not of their making, having distinct socio-economic intakes, which differentially condition any form of resistance/accommodation/circumvention.

9   To be fair to Fullan, in general, the positive (descriptive and explanatory) and the normative (critical and evaluative) sides of critical social science are imbalanced: if critical social science is to become more successful it must address normative theory (Sayer 1995). What must be remembered is that the quest for the good is a highly abstract one:

> Up to a point, particular critiques do imply something a little more specific than the standpoint of a better life. The critique of capitalism's anarchic, uneven development implies a critical standpoint or contrast space of an imagined society with a rationally ordered, even process of development. The critique of class implies the desirability of a classless society. But this does not take us very far unless it identifies the determinants of class so that they might be eliminated.

Naturally, society would be better if its illusions, injustices, conflicts and contradictions were reduced, but we need to know how this could be achieved. *The desirability of a life without contradictions or illusions does not make it feasible.*

(Sayer 2000: 161, our emphasis)

References

Adelman, M., Ahuvia, A. and Goodwin, C. (1994) Beyond smiling: social support and service quality, in R. Rust and R. Oliver (eds) *Service Quality: New Directions in Theory and Practice*. London: Sage.

Alvesson, M. and Willmott, H. (1996) *Making Sense of Management: A Critical Introduction*. London: Sage.

Angus, L. (1993a) The sociology of school effectiveness, *British Journal of Sociology of Education*, 14(3): 333–45.

Angus, L. (1993b) Democratic participation or efficient site management: the social and political location of the selfmanaging school, in J. Smyth (ed.) *A Socially Critical View of the Self-managing School*. London: Falmer Press.

Angus, L. (1994) Sociological analysis and educational management: the social context of the self-managing school, *British Journal of Sociology of Education*, 15(1): 79–91.

Anyon, J. (1981) Social class and school knowledge, *Curriculum Inquiry*, 11, 3–42.

Anyon, J. (1997) *Ghetto Schooling: A Political Economy of Urban Education Reform*. London: Teachers College Press.

Apple, M.W. and Beane, J.A. (eds) (1999) *Democratic Schools: Lessons from the Chalkface*. Buckingham: Open University Press.

Archer, M. (2000) *Being Human: The Problem of Agency*. Cambridge: Cambridge University Press.

Archer, M.S. (1995) *Realist Social Theory: The Morphogenetic Approach*. Cambridge: Cambridge University Press.

Armstrong, M. and Murlis, H. (1988) *Reward Management*. London: Kogan Page.

Bagley, C., Woods, P.A. and Glatter, R. (2001) Implications of school choice policy: interpretation and response by parents of students with special educational needs, *British Education Research Journal*, 27(3): 287–307.

Ball, S.J. (1990) *Politics and Policy Making in Education*. London: Routledge.

Ball, S.J. (1993a) Culture cost and control: selfmanagement and entrepreneurial schooling in England and Wales, in J. Smyth (ed.) *A Socially Critical View of the Self-managing School*. London: Falmer Press.

Ball, S.J. (1993b) Education markets, choice and social class: the market as a class strategy in the UK and the US, *British Journal of Sociology of Education*, 14(1): 3–19.

Ball, S.J. (1994) *Educational Reform: A Critical and Post-structural Approach*. Buckingham: Open University Press.

Ball, S.J. (1997a) Policy sociology and critical social research: a personal review of recent education policy and policy research, *British Educational Research Journal*, 23(3): 257–74.

Ball, S.J. (1997b) Markets, equity and values in education, in R. Pring and G. Walford (eds) *Affirming the Comprehensive Ideal*. London: Falmer Press.

Ball, S.J. (1997c) Good school, bad school: paradox and fabrication, *British Journal of Sociology of Education*, 18: 317–36.

Ball, S.J. (1998a) Big policies/small world: an introduction to international perspectives in education policy, *Comparative Education*, 34(2): 119–30.

Ball, S.J. (1998b) Educational studies, policy entrepreneurship and social theory, in R. Slee, S. Tomlinson with Weiner, G. (eds) *School Effectiveness for Whom?* London: Falmer Press.

Ball, S.J. (1999) Labour, learning and the economy: a 'policy sociology' perspective, *Cambridge Journal of Education*, 29(2): 195–206.

Ball, S.J. (ed.) (2000) *Sociology of Education: Major Themes*. London: Routledge.

Ball, S.J. (2001a) Performativities and fabrications in the education economy: towards the performative society, in D. Gleeson and C. Husbands (eds) *The Performing School*. London: RoutledgeFalmer.

Ball, S.J. (2001b) Labour, learning and the economy: a 'policy sociology' perspective, in M. Fielding (ed.) *Taking Education Really Seriously: Four Years' Hard Labour*. London: RoutledgeFalmer.

Ball, S.J., Maguire, M. and Macrae, S. (2000) *Choice, Pathways and Transitions Post 16*. London: RoutledgeFalmer.

Ball, S.J., Marques-Cardoso, C., Reay, D., Thrupp, M. and Vincent C. (2002) *Education Policy in England: Changing Modes of Regulation 1945–2001*, Deliverable 2 of the EU project 'Changes in regulation modes and social reproduction of inequalities in education systems: a European comparison'. London: Institute of Education and King's College London.

Barber, M. (1996a) *The National Curriculum: A Study in Policy*. Keele: Keele University Press.

Barber, M. (1996b) *The Learning Game: Arguments for an Educational Revolution*. London: Victor Gollancz.

Barber, M. (1996c) Creating a framework for success in urban areas, in M. Barber and R. Dann (eds) *Raising Educational Standards in the Inner Cities*. London: Cassell.

Barber, M. (1997) Hoddle showed us how the White paper can succeed. *Times Educational Supplement*, 7 November, p. 21.

Barnes, C. (1993) *Practical Marketing for Schools*. Oxford: Blackwell.

Barth, R. (1990) *Improving Schools From Within*. San Francisco: Jossey Bass.

Bauman, Z. (1988) *Freedom*. Minneapolis, MN: University of Minnesota Press.

Bauman, Z. (1993) *Postmodern Ethics*. Oxford: Blackwell.

Bauman, Z. (1995) *Life in Fragments*. Oxford: Blackwell.

Bell, L. (1999) Primary schools and the nature of the education market place, in T. Bush, L. Bell, R. Bolam, R. Glatter and P. Ribbins (eds) *Educational Management: Redefining Theory, Policy and Practice*. London: Paul Chapman.

Bennett, N., Crawford, M. and Riches, C. (1992) *Managing Change in Education: Individual and Organizational Perspectives*. London: Paul Chapman.

Blackmore, J. (1999) *Troubling Women, Feminism, Leadership and Educational Change*. Buckingham: Open University Press.

Blandford, S. and Squire, L. (1999) An evaluation of Headlamp, *Management in Education*, 13(2): 27–8.

Boisot, M. (1995) Preparing for turbulence, in B. Garratt (ed.) *Developing Strategic Thought*. London: McGraw-Hill.

Bolman, L.G. and Deal, T.E. (2001) *Leading with Soul: An Uncommon Journey of Spirit*. San Francisco: Jossey Bass.

Boothroyd, C., Fitz-Gibbon, C., McNicholas, J., Thompson, M., Stern, E. and Wragg, T. (1997) *A Better System of Inspection?* Hexham: Ofstin.

Boston, J., Martin, J., Pallot, J. and Walsh, P. (1996) *Public Management: The New Zealand Model*. Auckland: Oxford University Press.

Bottery, M. (1992) *The Ethics of Educational Management*. London: Cassell.

Bottery, M. (1994) *Lessons for Schools?* London: Cassell.

Bottery, M. (2000) *Education, Policy and Ethics*. London: Continuum.

Bottery, M. (2001) School effectiveness, school improvement and the teaching profession of the twenty-first century, in A. Harris and N. Bennett (eds) *School Effectiveness and Improvement: Alternative Perspectives*. London: Continuum.

Bottery, M. and Wright, N. (2000) *Teachers and the State*. London: Routledge.

Bourdieu, P. (1974) The school as a conservative force: scholastic and cultural inequalities, in J. Eggleston (ed.) *Contemporary Research in the Sociology of Education*. London: Methuen.

Bowe, R., Ball, S. and Gold, A. (1992) *Reforming Education and Changing Schools: Casestudies in Policy Sociology*. London: Routledge.

Brighouse, T. and Woods, D. (1999) *How To Improve Your School*. London: Routledge.

Brown, P. and Lauder, H. Education, Class and Economic Competitiveness, in A. Scott and J. Freeman-Moir *Yesterday's Dreams: International and Critical Perspectives on Social Class and Education*. Canterbury: University of Canterbury Press (forthcoming).

Brown, S. (1993) Postmodern marketing? *European Journal of Marketing*, 27: 19–34.

Brown, S. and Eisenhardt, K. (1998) *Competing on the Edge*. Boston MA: Harvard Business School Press.

Brundrett, M. (ed.) (1999) *Principles of School Leadership*. Dereham: Peter Francis.

Buchanan, D. and Huczynski, A. (1997) *Organizational Behaviour: An Introductory Text*. London: Prentice Hall.

Bush, T. (1995) *Theories of Educational Management*, 2nd edition. London: Paul Chapman.

Bush, T. (1998) The National Professional Qualification for Headship: the key to effective leadership, *School Leadership and Management*, 18(3): 321–3.

Bush, T. and Coleman, C. (2000) *Leadership and Strategic Management in Education*. London: Paul Chapman.

Bush, T., Bell, L., Bolam, R., Glatter, R. and Ribbins, P. (eds) (1999) *Educational Management: Redefining Theory, Policy and Practice*. London: Paul Chapman.

Butcher, T. (1995) *Delivering Welfare: the Governance of the Social Services in the 1990s*. Buckingham: Open University Press.

Cain, J. (1999) The process of vision creation – intuition and accountability, in H. Tomlinson, H. Gunter and P. Smith (eds) *Living Headship*. London: Paul Chapman.

Caldwell, B.J. (1997a) Global trends and expectations for the further reform of schools, in B. Davies and L. Ellison (eds) *School Leadership for the 21st Century*. London: Routledge.

Caldwell, B.J. (1997b) Thinking in time: a gestalt for schools of the new millenium, in B. Davies and L. Ellison (eds) *School Leadership for the 21st Century*. London: Routledge.

Caldwell, B.J. (2000) Review of Michael Fullan's *Change Forces: The Sequel, Journal of Educational Change*, 1: 205–9.

Caldwell, B.J. and Hayward, D. (1998) *The Future of Schools: Lessons from the Reform of Public Education*. London: Falmer Press.

Caldwell, B.J. and Spinks, J.M. (1989) *The Self-managing School*. Lewes: Falmer Press.

Caldwell, B.J. and Spinks, J.M. (1992) *Leading the Self-managing School*. London: Falmer Press.

Caldwell, B.J. and Spinks, J. (1998) *Beyond the Self-managing School*. London: Falmer Press.

Cassidy, S. (2001) Heads ignore truancy to fiddle the figures, *Times Educational Supplement*, 19 January.

Chang, R. (2001) *The Passion Plan*. San Francisco: Jossey Bass.

Chowdhury, S. (2000) Towards the future of management, in S. Chowdhury (ed.) *Management 21C: Someday We'll All Manage This Way*. Harlow: Financial Times/ Prentice Hall.

Christie, P. and Lingard, R. (2001) Capturing complexity in educational leadership. Paper presented to the American Educational Research Association, Seattle, 10–14 April.

Clarke, J., Gewirtz, S. and McLaughlin, E. (2000) (eds) *New Managerialism, New Welfare?* London: Sage.

Clegg, S. and Dunkerley, D. (1980) *Organization, Class and Control*. London: Routledge & Kegan Paul.

Cockburn, C. (1991) *In the Way of Women: Men's Resistence to Sexual Equality in Organisations*. London: Macmillan.

Coleman, J.S., Campbell, E., Hobson, C. *et al.* (1966) *Equality of Educational Opportunity*. Washington: US Government Printing Office.

Connell, R.W. (1994) Poverty and education, *Harvard Educational Review*, 64(2): 125–49.

Connell, R.W., Ashenden, D.J., Kessler, S. and Dowsett, G.W. (1982) *Making the Difference*. Sydney: Allen & Unwin.

Crawford, M., Kydd, L. and Riches, C. (eds) (1997) *Leadership and Teams in Educational Management*. Buckingham: Open University Press.

Creese, M. and Earley, P. (1999) *Improving Schools and Governing Bodies*. London: Routledge.

Crouch, C., Finegold, D. and Sako, M. (1999) *Are Skills the Answer?* Oxford: Oxford University Press.

Davies, B. and Ellison, L. (eds) (1997a) *School Leadership for the 21st Century*. London: Routledge

Davies, B. and Ellison, L. (1997b) *Strategic Marketing for Schools*. London: Prentice Hall.

Davies, B. and Ellison, L. (1999) *Strategic Direction and the Development of the School*. London: Routledge.

Davies, L. (1990) *Equity and Efficiency? School Management in an Educational Context*. London: Falmer Press.

Davies, N. (2000) *The School Report*. London: Vintage.

Day, C., Harris, A., Hadfield, M., Tolley, H. and Beresford, J. (2000) *Leading Schools in Times of Change*. Buckingham: Open University Press.

Deal, T. and Kennedy, A. (1988) *Corporate Cultures* (1982). Harmondsworth: Penguin.

Deal, T.E. and Petersen, K.D. (2000) *The Leadership Paradox*. San Francisco: Jossey Bass.

Demaine, J. (1993) The New Right and selfmanaging schools, in J. Smyth (ed.) *A Socially Critical View of the Self-managing School*. London: Falmer Press.

Deming, W.E. (1986) *Out of the Crisis*. Cambridge, MA: MIT Press.

Dempster, N. and Logan, L. (1998) Expectations of school leaders: an Australian study, in J. MacBeath (ed.) *Effective School Leadership: Responding to Change*. London: Paul Chapman.

Dempster, N. and Mahony, P. (1998) Ethical challenges in school leadership, in J. MacBeath (ed.) *Effective School Leadership: Responding to Change*. London: Paul Chapman.

Desmond, J. (1998) Marketing and moral indifference, in M. Parker (ed.) *Ethics and Organizations*. London: Sage.

Dewey, J. (1902) *The School and Society*. Chicago: University of Chicago Press.

DfEE (2001) *Schools: Building on Success*. London: HMSO.

DfEE (2000) *Performance Management in Schools*. London: HMSO.

DfES (2001) *Schools: Achieving Success*. London: HMSO.

Docking, J. (ed.) (2000) *New Labour's Policies for Schools*. London: David Fulton.

Donaldson, G.A. (2001) *Cultivating Leadership in Schools*. New York and London: Teachers College Press.

Drucker, P.F. (1995) *Managing in a Time of Great Change*. Oxford: Butterworth-Heinemann.

Duigan, P.A. and Macpherson R.J.S. (1992) *Educative Leadership*. London: Falmer Press.

Dunleavy, P. and Hood, C. (1994) 'From old public administration to new public management', *Public Money and Management*, 14(3): 9–16.

Eagleton, T. (1976) *Marxism and Literary Criticism*. London: Methuen.

Ehrenreich, B. (1989) *Fear of Falling: The Inner Life of the Middle Class*. New York: Patheon Books.

Elliott, J. (2001a) Characteristics of performative cultures: their central paradoxes and limitations as resources for educational reform, in D. Gleeson and C. Husbands (eds) *The Performing School: Managing, Teaching and Learning in a Performance Culture*. London: RoutledgeFalmer.

Elliott, J. (2001b) Making evidence-based practice educational, *British Educational Research Journal*, 27: 555–74.

Evans, I. (1995) *Marketing for Schools*. London: Cassell.

Evans, L. (2001) Developing teachers in a performance culture: is performance-related pay the answer?, in D. Gleeson and C. Husbands (eds) *The Performing School: Managing, Teaching and Learning in a Performance Culture*. London: RoutledgeFalmer.

Exworthy, M. and Halford, S. (1999) Professionals and managers in a changing public sector: conflict, compromise and collaboration?, in M. Exworthy and S. Halford (eds) *Professionals and the New Managerialism in the Public Sector*. Buckingham: Open University Press.

Ferguson, N., Earley, P., Fidler, B. and Ouston, J. (2000) *Improving Schools and Inspection*. London: Paul Chapman.

Fergusson, R. (2000) Modernizing managerialism in education, in J. Clarke, S. Gewirtz and E. McLaughlin (eds) *New Managerialism, New Welfare?* London: Sage.

Ferlie, E., Ashburner, L., Fitzgerald, L. and Pettigrew, A. (1996) *The New Public Management in Action*. Oxford: Oxford University Press.

Fidler, B. (1997) Strategic Management, in B. Fidler, S. Russell and T. Simkins (eds) *Choices for Self-managing Schools: Autonomy and Accountability*. London: Paul Chapman.

Fidler, B. (2001) A structural critique of school effectiveness and school improvement, in A. Harris and N. Bennett (eds) *School Effectiveness and Improvement: Alternative Perspectives*. London: Continuum.

Fielding, M. (2001) Target setting, policy pathology and students perspectives: learning to labour in new times, in M. Fielding (ed.) *Taking Education Really Seriously: Four Years' Hard Labour*. London: RoutledgeFalmer.

Fink, D. (2001) The two solitudes: policy makers and policy implementers, in M. Fielding (ed.) *Taking Education Really Seriously: Four Years' Hard Labour*. London: RoutledgeFalmer.

Fitz, J. (1999) Reflections on the field of educational management studies, *Educational Management and Administration*, 27(3): 313–21.

Fitz-Gibbon, C.T. and Stephenson, N.J. (1996) Inspecting Her Majesty's Inspectors: should social science and social policy cohere? Paper presented at the European Conference on Educational Research, Seville, Spain.

Flynn, R. (1999) Managerialism, professionalism and quasi-markets, in M.

Exworthy and S. Halford (eds) *Professionals and the New Managerialism in the Public Sector*. Buckingham: Open University Press.

Ford, K. (1996) Headlamp: illuminating the way ahead?, *Management in Education* 10(4): 16–22.

Foskett, N. (1999) Strategy, external relations and marketing, in J. Lumby and N. Foskett (eds) *Managing External Relations in Schools and Colleges*. London: Paul Chapman.

Foskett, N. and Hemsley-Brown, J. (1999) Communicating the organisation, in J. Lumby and N. Foskett (eds) *Managing External Relations in Schools and Colleges*, London: Paul Chapman.

Foskett, N. and Hemsley-Brown, J. (2001) *Choosing Futures: Young People's Decision-making in Education, Training and Careers Markets*. London: RoutledgeFalmer.

Fragos, A. (2001) Training for headship in the UK: an analysis of New Labour's approach. Unpublished MA dissertation, Kings College London.

Frost, D., Durrant, J., Head, M. and Holden, G. (2000) *Teacher-led School Improvement*. London: RoutledgeFalmer.

Fullan, M.G. (1991) *The New Meaning of Educational Change*. London: Cassell.

Fullan, M.G. (1993) *Change Forces: Probing the Depths of Educational Reform*. London: Falmer Press.

Fullan, M.G. (1999) *Change Forces: The Sequel*. London: Falmer Press.

Fullan, M.G. (2001a) *The New Meaning of Educational Change*, 3rd edition. London: RoutledgeFalmer.

Fullan, M.G. (2001b) *Leading in a Culture of Change*. San Francisco: Jossey Bass.

Fullan, M.G. (2000) Introduction, in Jossey Bass (ed.) *The Jossey Bass Reader on Educational Leadership*. San Francisco: Jossey Bass.

Gamble, A. (1988) *The Free Economy and the Strong State. The Politics of Thatcherism*. London: Macmillan.

Gates, B. (1995) *The Road Ahead*. New York: Penguin.

Gewirtz, S. (1998) Can all schools be successful? An exploration of the determinants of school 'success', *Oxford Review of Education*, 24(4): 439–57.

Gewirtz, S. (2000) Bringing the politics back in: a critical analysis of quality discourses in education, *British Journal of Educational Studies*, 48(4): 352–70.

Gewirtz, S. (2002) *The Managerial School*. London: Routledge.

Gewirtz, S., Ball, S. J. and Bowe, R. (1995) *Markets, Choice and Equity in Education*. Buckingham: Open University Press.

Gillborn, D. and Youdell, D. (2000) *Rationing Education: Policy, Practice, Reform, and Equity*. Buckingham: Open University Press.

Gitlin, A. (2000) The truth is in the details, *Journal of Educational Change*, 1: 211–17.

Glatter, R. (1987) Towards an agenda for educational management, *Educational Management and Administration*, 15(1): 5–12.

Glatter, R. (1997) Context and capability in education management, *Educational Management and Administration*, 25(2): 181–92.

Glatter, R., Woods, P.A. and Bagley, C. (1997) Diversity, differentiation and hierarchy: school choice and parental preferences, in R. Glatter, P.A. Woods and C. Bagley (eds) *Choice and Diversity in Education: Perspectives and Prospects*. London: Routledge.

Gleeson, D. and Husbands, C. (eds) (2001) *The Performing School*. London: RoutledgeFalmer.

Gold, A. and Evans, J. (1998) *Reflecting on School Management*. London: Falmer Press.

Goldstein, H. and Woodhouse, G. (2000) School effectiveness research and educational policy, *Oxford Review of Education*, 26(3/4): 353–63.

Grace, G. (1995) *School Leadership: Beyond Educational Management – An Essay in Policy Scholarship*. London: Falmer.

Grace, G. (1997) Critical leadership studies, in M. Crawford, L. Kydd and C. Riches (eds) *Leadership and Teams in Educational Management*. Buckingham: Open University Press.

Grace, G. (2000) Research and the challenges of contemporary school leadership: the contribution of critical scholarship, *British Journal of Educational Studies*, 48(3): 231–47.

Grace, G. (2002) *Catholic Schools: Mission, Markets and Morality*. London: Routledge.

Gray, J. (2001) Introduction: building for improvement and sustaining change in schools serving disadvantaged communities, in M. Maden (ed.) *Success Against the Odds – Five Years On*. London: RoutledgeFalmer.

Gray, J. and Wilcox, B. (1995) *Good School, Bad School: Evaluating Performance and Encouraging Improvement*. Buckingham: Open University Press.

Gray, J., Reynolds, D., Fitz-Gibbon, C. and Jesson, D. (eds) (1996) *Merging Traditions*. London: Cassell.

Gray, J., Hopkins, D., Reynolds, D., Wilcox, B., Farrell, S. and Jesson, D. (1999) *Improving Schools: Performance and Potential*. Buckingham: Open University Press.

Gray, I. (1991) *Marketing Education*. Buckingham: Open University Press.

Green, A. (1997) *Education, Globalization and the Nation State*. London: Macmillan.

Green, F. (2000) *The Headteacher in the 21st Century: Being A Successful School Leader*. Harlow: Pearson.

Greenfield, T. (1993) The decline and fall of science in educational administration, in T. Greenfield and P. Ribbins (eds) *Greenfield on Educational Administration: Towards a Humane Science*. London: Routledge.

Grenfell, M. (1998) Language and the classroom, in M. Grenfell, D. James with P. Hodkinson, D. Reay and D. Robbins, *Acts of Practical Theory: Bourdieu and Education*. London: Falmer Press.

Gronn, P. (1999) *The Making of Educational Leaders*. London: Continuum.

Gronroos, C. (1997) From marketing mix to relationship marketing – towards a paradigm shift in marketing, *Management Decision*, 35(4): 322–39.

Gunter, H. (1997) *Rethinking Education: The Consequences of Jurassic Management*. London: Cassell.

Gunter, H. (1999) Contracting headteachers as leaders: an analysis of the NPQH, *Cambridge Journal of Education*, 29(2): 251–64.

Gunter, H. (2001) *Leaders and Leadership in Education*. London: Paul Chapman.

Gunter, H., Smith, P. and Tomlinson, H. (1999) Introduction: constructing headship – today and yesterday, in H. Tomlinson, H. Gunter and P. Smith (eds) *Living Headship*. London: Paul Chapman.

Gutierrez, C. (2000) Teaching and learning are complex and evolutionary but market forces can collide with quality practice, *Journal of Educational Change*, 1: 219–24.

Hales, C. (1993) *Managing Through Organization*. London: Routledge.

Hall, V. (1997) Managing staff, in B. Fidler, S. Russell and T. Simkins (eds) *Choices for Self-managing Schools: Autonomy and Accountability*. London: Paul Chapman.

Hallinger, P. and Murphy, J. (1985) Assessing the instructional management behaviour of principals, *Elementary School Journal*, 86(2): 217–47.

Halsey, A.H., Heath, A.F. and Ridge, J.M. (1980) *Origins and Destinations*. New York: Oxford University Press.

Halsey, A.H., Lauder, H., Brown, P. and Wells, A.S. (eds) (1997) *Education, Culture, Economy and Society*. Oxford: Oxford University Press.

Hammer, M. and Champy, J. (1993) *Reengineering the Corporation: A Manifesto for Business Revolution*. London: Nicholas Brealey.

Hargreaves, A. (1994) *Changing Teachers, Changing Times: Teachers' Work and Culture in the Postmodern Age*. London: Continuum.

Hargreaves, A. and Fullan, M. (1998) *What's Worth Fighting for Out There?* New York: Teachers College Press.

Hargreaves, A, Lieberman, A., Fullan, M. and Hopkins, D. (eds) (1998) *International Handbook of Educational Change*. Dordrecht: Kluwer.

Hargreaves, D. and Hopkins, D. (1991) *The Empowered School: The Management and Practice of Development Planning*. London: Cassell.

Hargreaves, D. and Hopkins, D. (1994) Introduction, in D. Hargreaves and D. Hopkins (eds) *Development Planning for School Improvement*. London: Cassell.

Harris, A. (2000) What works in school improvement? Lessons from the field and future directions, *Educational Research*, 42(1): 1–11.

Harris, A. (2001) Contemporary perspectives on school effectiveness and school improvement, in A. Harris and N. Bennett (eds) *School Effectiveness and Improvement: Alternative Perspectives*. London: Continuum.

Harris, A. (2002) *School Improvement: What's in it for Schools?* London: RoutledgeFalmer.

Harris, A. and Bennett, N. (eds) (2001) *School Effectiveness and Improvement: Alternative Perspectives*. London: Continuum.

Hartley, D. (1999) Marketing and 'the re-enchantment' of school management, *British Journal of Sociology of Education*, 20: 309–23.

Hatcher, R. (1998a) Labour, official school improvement and equality, *Journal of Education Policy*, 13(4): 485–99.

Hatcher, R. (1998b) Social justice and the politics of school effectiveness and school improvement, *Race, Ethnicity and Education*, 1(2): 267–89.

Hatcher, R. and Hirtt, N. (1999) The business agenda behind Labour's education policy, in M. Allen, C. Benn, C. Chitty, M. Cole, R. Hatcher, N. Hirtt and G. Rikowski (eds) *Business, Business, Business: New Labour's Education Policy*. London: Tufnell Press.

Hay McBer (2000) *Research into Teacher Effectiveness*. Report prepared for the Department for Education and Employment. London: Author.

Helsby, G. (1999) *Changing Teacher's Work: The Reform of Secondary Schooling*. Buckingham: Open University Press.

Hendrie, C. (2002) Ain't no mountain high enough, *Times Educational Supplement*, 11 January.

Henry, J. (2001) More heads face claims of test cheating, *Times Educational Supplement*, 10 August.

Hextall, I. and Mahony, P. (1998) Effective teachers for effective schools, in R. Slee, G. Weiner with S. Tomlinson (eds) *School Effectiveness for Whom?* London: Falmer Press.

Hill, P. (1998) Shaking the foundations: research driven school reform, *School Effectiveness and School Improvement*, 9: 419–36.

Hodgson, G. (1999) *Economics and Utopia: Why the Learning Economy Is Not the End of History*. London: Routledge.

Hood, C. (1991) A public management for all seasons? *Public Administration*, 69: 3–19.

Hood, C., Scott, C., James, O., Jones, G. and Travers, T. (1999) *Regulation Inside Government: Waste-watchers, Quality Police, and Sleeze-busters*. Oxford: Oxford University Press.

Hopkins, D. (1987) *Improving the Quality of Schooling*. Lewes: Falmer Press.

Hopkins, D. (1996) Towards a theory for school improvement, in J. Gray, D. Reynolds, C. Fitz-Gibbon and D. Jesson (eds) *Merging Traditions*. London: Cassell.

Hopkins, D. (1998) Introduction: tensions in and prospects for school improvement, in A. Hargreaves, A. Lieberman, M. Fullan and D. Hopkins (eds) *International Handbook of Educational Change*. Dordrecht: Kluwer.

Hopkins, D. (2001) *School Improvement for Real*. London: RoutledgeFalmer.

Hopkins, D., Ainscow, M. and West, M. (1994) *School Improvement in an Era of Change*. London: Cassell.

Horne, H. and Brown, S. (1997) *500 Tips for School Improvement*. London: Kogan Page.

Huberman, A. (1992) Preface, in M. Fullan, *Successful School Improvement*. Buckingham: Open University Press.

Husbands, C. (2001) Managing performance in performing schools, in D. Gleeson and C. Husbands (eds) *The Performing School: Managing, Teaching and Learning in a Performance Culture*. London: RoutledgeFalmer.

Hutchins, L. (2002) English children 'most over-tested in the world', *Times Educational Supplement*, 25 February.

Jackson, P. (1968) *Life in Classrooms*. Chicago: University of Chicago Press.

James, C. and Connolly, U. (2000) *Effective Change in Schools*. London: RoutledgeFalmer.

James, C. and Phillips, P. (1997) Markets and marketing, in B. Fidler, S. Russell and T. Simkins (eds) *Choices for Self-managing Schools*. London: Paul Chapman.

Jeffrey, B. and Woods, P. (1998) *Testing Teachers: The Effect of School Inspections on Primary Teachers*. London: Falmer Press.

Jencks, C., Smith, M., Ackland, H., Bane, M. J., Cohen, D., Gintis, H., Heyns, B. and Michelson, S. (1972) *Inequality*. New York: Basic Books.

Johnson, H. and Castelli, M. (1999) The NPQH: the need for additional support for candidates for Catholic leadership, *Journal of Inservice Education*, 25(3): 519–32.

Jonathan, R. (1997) *Illusory Freedoms: Liberalism, Education and the Market*. Oxford: Blackwell.

Jones, A. (1989) The cultural production of classroom practice, *British Journal of Sociology of Education*, 10: 19–31.

Jones, A. (1991) *At School I've got a Chance*. Palmerston North, New Zealand: Dunmore Press.

Jossey Bass (2000) *The Jossey Bass Reader on Educational Leadership*. San Francisco: Jossey Bass.

Joyce, B., Calhoun, E. and Hopkins, D. (1999) *The New Structure of School Improvement*. Buckingham: Open University Press.

Kell, P. (1993) Managerialism and market-forces in vocational education: 'balkanising' education in the 'banana republic', in J. Smyth (ed.) *A Socially Critical View of the Self-managing School*. London: Falmer.

Kelly, A. (2001) *Benchmarking for School Improvement*. London: RoutledgeFalmer.

Kenway, J. (with Bigum, C. and FitzClarence, L.) (1993) Marketing education in the post-modern age, *Journal of Education Policy*, 8(2): 105–23.

Kenway, J. (ed.) (1995) *Marketing Education: Some Critical Issues*. Australia: Deakin University Press.

Kenway, J. and Bullen, E. (2001) *Consuming Children: Education–Entertainment–Advertising*. Buckingham: Open University Press.

Kenway, J., Bigum, C. and Fitzclarence, L. (1995) Marketing education: an introductory essay, in J. Kenway (ed.) *Marketing Education: Some Critical Issues*. Australia: Deakin University Press.

Knight, J. (1997) *Strategic Planning for School Managers*. London: Kogan Page.

Kotler, P. (1972a) A generic concept of marketing, *Journal of Marketing*, 36: 46–54.

Kotler, P. (1972b) What consumerism means for marketers, *Harvard Business Review*, May/June: 48–57.

Kotler, P. and Levy, S. (1969) Broadening the concept of marketing, *Journal of Marketing*, 33: 10–15.

Kotler, P. and Zaltman, G. (1971) Social marketing: an approach to planned social change, *Journal of Marketing*, 35: 3–12.

Kouzes, J.M. and Posner, B.K. (2000) *The Five Practices of Exemplary Leadership*. San Francisco: Jossey Bass.

Kozol, J. (1991) *Savage Inequalities*. New York: Crown.

Kruchov, C., MacBeath, J. and Riley, K. (1998) Introduction, in MacBeath, J. (ed.) *Effective School Leadership: Responding to Change*. London: Paul Chapman.

Laczniak, G., Lusch, R., Murphy, P. and Patrick, R. (1979) Social marketing: its ethical dimensions, *Journal of Marketing*, 43: 29–36.

Lareau, A. (1989) *Home Advantage*. Philadelphia: Falmer Press.

Lauder, H. and Hughes, D. (1990) Social origins, destinations and educational inequality, in J. Codd, R. Harker and R. Nash (eds) *Political Issues in New Zealand Education*. Palmerston North, New Zealand: Dunmore Press.

Lauder, H., Hughes, D., Watson S., *et al.* (1999) *Trading in Futures: Why Markets in Education Don't Work*. Buckingham: Open University Press.

Law, S. and Glover, D. (1999) *Educational Leadership and Learning*. Buckingham: Open University Press.

Leask, M. and Terrell, I. (1997) *Development Planning and School Improvement for Middle Managers*. London: Kogan Page.

Legge, K. (1989) Human resource management: a critical analysis, in J. Storey (ed.) *New Perspectives on Human Resource Management*. London: Routledge.

Legge, K. (1995) *Human Resource Management: Rhetorics and Realities*. London: Macmillan.

Leiss, W. (1976) *The Limits to Satisfaction*. Toronto: University of Toronto Press.

Leithwood, K. (2000) *Understanding Schools as Intelligent Systems*. Stamford, CT: Jai Press.

Leithwood, K., Chapman, C., Corson, D., Hallinger, P. and Hart, A. (eds) (1996) *International Handbook of Educational Leadership and Administration*. Dordrecht: Kluwer.

Leithwood, K., Jantzi, D. and Steinbach, R. (1998) *Changing Leadership for Changing Times*. Buckingham: Open University Press.

Levin, B. (1995) Education and poverty, *Canadian Journal of Education*, 20(2): 211–14.

Levin, B. (2001) *Reforming Education: From Proposals to Results*. London: Falmer Press.

Lincoln, P. (1999) Improvement policies and LEA strategies in light of the EPSI programme findings, in G. Southworth and P. Lincoln (eds) *Supporting Improving Primary Schools*. London: Falmer.

Lodge, C. (1998) Training aspiring heads on NPQH: issues and progress, *School Leadership and Management*, 18(3): 347–57.

Logan, L., Sachs, J. and Dempster, N. (1994) *Who Said Planning Was Good for Us? School Development Planning in Australian Primary Schools*. Queensland: Griffith University.

Lumby, J. (1998) Understanding strategic change, in D. Middlewood and J. Lumby (eds) *Strategic Management in Schools and Colleges*. London: Paul Chapman.

Lumby, J. and Foskett, N. (1999) Preface, in J. Lumby and N. Foskett (eds) *Managing External Relations in Schools and Colleges*. London: Paul Chapman.

MacBeath, J. (ed.) (1998a) *Effective School Leadership: Responding to Change*. London: Paul Chapman.

MacBeath, J. (1998b) Seven selected heresies of leadership, in J. MacBeath (ed.) (1998a) *Effective School Leadership: Responding to Change*. London: Paul Chapman.

MacBeath, J. and McCall, J. (2001) The policy context, in J. MacBeath and P. Mortimore (eds) *Improving School Effectiveness*. Buckingham: Open University Press.

MacBeath, J. and Mortimore, P. (eds) (2001a) *Improving School Effectiveness*. Buckingham: Open University Press.

MacBeath, J. and Mortimore, P. (2001b) School effectiveness and improvement the story so far, in J. MacBeath and P. Mortimore (eds) *Improving School Effectiveness*. Buckingham: Open University Press.

MacGilchrist, B., Mortimore, P., Savage, J. and Beresford, C. (1995) *Planning Matters: The Impact of Development Planning in Primary Schools*. London: Paul Chapman.

Maden, M. (ed.) (2001) *Success Against the Odds – Five Years On*. London: RoutledgeFalmer.

Male, T. (2000) LPSH – some observations and comments, *Management in Education*, 14(2): 6–8.

Mansell, W. (2000) Flawed Ofsted measure attacked, *Times Educational Supplement* 14 July.

Marginson, S. (1997) *Markets in Education*. St Leonards, NSW: Allen & Unwin.

Marginson, S. (1999) After globalization: emerging politics of education, *Journal of Education Policy*, 14: 19–32.

Marland, M. and Rogers, R. (1991) *Marketing the School*. London: Heinemann.

McCallion, P. (1998) *The Competent School Manager*. London: The Stationery Office.

McLaughlin, M.W. (1990) The Rand Change Agent study revisited: macro perspectives, micro-realities, *Educational Researcher*, 19(9): 11–16.

Menter, I., Muschamp, Y., Nicholls, P. and Ozga, J. (1997) *Work and Identity in the Primary School: A Post-fordist Analysis*. Buckingham: Open University Press.

Metz, M.H. (1990) How social class differences shape teachers work, in M.W. McLaughlin, J.E. Talbert and N. Bascia (eds) *The Contexts of Teaching in Secondary Schools*. New York: Teachers College Press.

Middlewood, D. (1998) Strategic management in education: an overview, in D. Middlewood and J. Lumby (eds) *Strategic Management in Schools and Colleges*. London: Paul Chapman.

Moore, R. (1996) Back to the future: the problem of change and the possibilities of advance in the sociology of education, *British Journal of Sociology of Education*, 17: 145–61.

Morley, L. and Rassool, N. (1999) *School Effectiveness: Fracturing the Discourse*. London: Falmer Press.

Morris, P. (2000) *Practical Guide to Fundraising for Schools*. London: Routledge.

Morrison, K. (1998) *Management Theories for Educational Change*. London: Paul Chapman.

Mortimore, P. and Mortimore, J. (1991) *The Primary Head: Roles Responsibilities and Reflections*. London: Paul Chapman.

Mortimore, P. and Whitty, G. (1997) *Can School Improvement Overcome the Effects of Disadvantage?* London: Institute of Education, University of London.

Mortimore, P., Sammons, P., Stoll, L., Lewis, D. and Ecob, R. (1988) *School Matters*. Wells: Open Books.

Naisbitt, J. (1995) *Megatrends: Asia*. London: Nicholas Brealey.

Nash, R. (1993) *Succeeding Generations*. Auckland: Oxford University Press.

Nash, R. and Harker, R. (1998*) Making Progress: Adding Value in Secondary Education*. Palmerston North, New Zealand: ERDC Press.

National Commission on Education (1996) *Success Against the Odds*. London: Routledge.

Nclsonline (2001) National College for School Leadership web page at http://www.ncslonline.gov.uk

Needle, P. and Stone, M. (1997) *Marketing for Schools*. London: Croner.

Noden, P. (2000) Rediscovering the impact of marketisation: dimensions of social segregation in England's secondary schools, 1994–99, *British Journal of Sociology of Education*, 21(3): 371–90.

Ohmae, K. (1995) *The End of the Nation State*. London: HarperCollins.

O'Neill, J. (1994) Managing human resources, in T. Bush and J. West-Burnham (eds) *The Principles of Educational Management*. Glasgow: Longman.

O'Neill, J. (1998) *The Market: Ethics, Knowledge and Politics*. New York: Routledge.

O'Toole, J. (1999) *Leadership A to Z*. San Francisco: Jossey Bass.

Ouchi, W.G. (1981) *Theory Z*. Reading, MA: Addison-Wesley.

Ouston, J. (1999) School effectiveness and school improvement: critique of a movement, in T. Bush, L. Bell, R. Bolam, R. Glatter and P. Ribbins (eds) *Educational Management, Redefining Theory, Policy and Practice*. London: Paul Chapman.

Ozga, J. (1992) Education management, *British Journal of Sociology of Education*, 13(2): 279–80.

Ozga, J. (ed.) (1993) *Women in Educational Management*. Buckingham: Open University Press.

Ozga, J. (2000a) Leadership in education: the problem not the solution, *Discourse*, 21(3): 356–61.

Ozga, J. (2000b) *Policy Research in Educational Settings: Contested Terrain*. Buckingham: Open University Press.

Ozga, J. and Walker, J. (1995) Women in educational management: theory and practice, in B. Limerick and B. Lingard (eds) *Gender and Changing Educational Management*. Sydney: HodderHeadline.

Pardey, D. (1991) *Marketing for Schools*. London: Kogan.

Parker, M. (2000) *Organizational Culture and Identity: Unity and Division at Work*. London: Sage.

Parsons, C., Welsh, P., Day, C. and Harris, A. (1999) Targeting performance management: some reflections on the leadership programme for serving headteachers, *Management in Education*, 14(5): 11–14.

Perez, A., Milstein, M., Wood, C. and Jacquez, D. (1999) *How to Turn a School Around*. Thousand Oaks, CA: Corwin.

Peters, T. (1988) *Thriving on Chaos*. London: Macmillan.

Peters, T. and Waterman, R. (1982) *In Search of Excellence*. New York: Harper & Row.

Pollitt, C. (1990) *Managerialism and the Public Services*. Oxford: Blackwell.

Purkey, S.C. and Smith, M.S. (1983) Effective schools: a review, *Elementary School Journal*, 83: 427–52.

Raab, C. (1991) Education policy and management: contemporaray changes in Britain. Paper presented to the International Institute of Administrative Sciences, Copenhagen, July.

Ramsey, R. (1999) *Lead, Follow or Get Out of the Way: How to be a More Effective Leader in Today's Schools*. Thousand Oaks, CA: Corwin.

Rayner, S. and Ribbins, P. (1999) *Headteachers and Leadership in Special Education*. London: Cassell.

Reay, D. (1995) They employ cleaners to do that? Habitus in the primary classroom, *British Journal of Sociology of Education*, 16(3): 353–71.

Reay, D. (1998a) Setting the agenda: the growing impact of market forces on pupil grouping in British secondary schooling, *Journal of Curriculum Studies*, 30(5): 545–58.

Reay, D. (1998b) Micro-politics in the 1990s: staff relationships in secondary schooling, *Journal of Educational Policy*, 13(2): 179–86.

Reay, D. and Ball, S. (1997) 'Spoilt for choice': the working classes and educational markets, in G. Walford (ed.) *Oxford Review of Education, Special Issue on Choice, Diversity and Equity in Secondary Education*, 23(1): 89–101.

Reeves, J., Moos, L. and Forrest, J. (1998) The school leader's view, in J. MacBeath (ed.) *Effective School Leadership: Responding to Change*. London: PCP.

Reyes, P., Scribner, J.D. and Scribner, A.P. (1999) *Lessons From High-performing Hispanic Schools: Creating Learning Communities*. New York: Teachers College Press.

Reynolds, D. and Teddlie, C. (2001) Reflections on the critics, and beyond them, *School Effectiveness and School Improvement*, 12(1): 99–113.

Reynolds, D. and Sullivan, M. with Murgatroyd, S. (1987) *The Comprehensive Expirement*. London: Falmer Press.

Ribbins, P. (1993) Conversations with a *condottiere* of administrative value, *Journal of Educational Administration and Foundations*, 8(1).

Ribbins, P. (1994a) Editorial: In praise of travel or in search of Maurice Zapp?, *Educational Management and Administration*, 22(1): 2–4.

Ribbins, P. (1994b) Editorial: Towards decentralisation – an editorial in search of a title, *Educational Management and Administration*, 22(2): 74–5.

Ribbins, P. (1999) Understanding leadership: developing headteachers, in T. Bush, L. Bell, R. Bolam, R. Glatter and P. Ribbins (eds) *Educational Management, Redefining Theory, Policy and Practice*. London: Paul Chapman.

Riches, C. (1997) Managing for people and performance, in T. Bush and D. Middlewood (eds) *Managing People in Education*. London: Paul Chapman.

Riley, K.A. and Seashore-Louis, K. (eds) (2000) *Leadership for Change and School Reform: International Perspectives*. London : Routledge.

Ritzer, G. (1993) *The McDonaldization of Society: An Investigation into the Changing Character of Contemporary Social Life*. London: Sage.

Robertson, S. (2000) *A Class Act: Changing Teachers' Work, the State and Globalisation*. London: Falmer Press.

Robinson, P. (1997) *Literacy, Numeracy and Economic Performance*. London: CEP/ London School of Economics.

Sammons, P., Hillman, J. and Mortimore, P. (1995) *Key Characteristics of Effective Schools: A Review of School Effectiveness Research*. London: Ofsted.

Sayer, A. (1995) *Radical Political Economy: A Critique*. Oxford: Blackwell.

Sayer, A. (2000) *Realism and Social Science*. London: Sage.

Schön, D.A. (1987) *Educating the Reflective Practitioner*. San Francisco: Jossey Bass.

Seifert, R. (1996) *Human Resource Management in Schools*. London: Pitman.

Sergiovanni, T.J. (1992) *Moral Leadership: Getting to the Heart of School Improvement*. San Francisco: Jossey Bass.

Sergiovanni, T.J. (1996) *Leadership for the Schoolhouse: How is it Different? Why is it Important?* San Francisco: Jossey Bass.

Sergiovanni, T.J. (1999) *Building Community in Schools*. San Francisco: Jossey Bass.

Sergiovanni, T.J. (2000) *The Lifeworld of Leadership*. San Francisco: Jossey Bass.

Sergiovanni, T.J. (2001a) *The Principalship: A Reflective Practice Perspective*, 4th edition. Boston: Allyn & Bacon.

Sergiovanni, T.J. (2001b) *Leadership: What's in it for Schools?* London: Routledge Falmer.

Sievers, B. (1986) Beyond the surrogate of motivation, *Organization Studies*, 7: 335–51.

Silver, H. (1994) *Good Schools, Effective Schools; Judgements and their Histories*. London: Cassell.

Skelton, M., Reeves, G. and Playfoot, D. (1991) *Development Planning for Primary Schools*. Walton-on-Thames: NFER-Nelson.

Slee, R. and Weiner, G. (1998) Introduction: school effectiveness for whom?, in R. Slee, S. Tomlinson with G. Weiner (eds) *School Effectiveness for Whom?* London: Falmer Press.

Slee, R., Weiner, G. with Tomlinson, S. (eds) (1998) *School Effectiveness for Whom?* London: Falmer Press.

Smith, P. (2001) Mentors as gate-keepers: an exploration of professional formation, *Educational Review*, 53: 313–24.

Smyth, J. (1989) *Critical Perspectives on Educational Leadership.* London: Falmer Press.

Smyth, J. (ed.) (1993) *A Socially Critical View of the Self-managing School.* London: Falmer Press.

Smyth, J. (1996) The socially just alternative to the self-managing school, in K. Leithwood, C. Chapman, D. Corson, P. Hallinger and A. Hart (eds) *International Handbook of Educational Leadership and Administration.* Dordrecht: Kluwer.

Smyth, J. and Dow, A. (1998) What's wrong with outcomes? Spotter planes, action plans, and steerage of the educational workplace, *British Journal of Sociology of Education*, 19: 291–303.

Smyth, J. and Shacklock, G. (1998) *Remaking Teaching: Ideology, Policy and Practice.* London: Routledge.

Snook, I. (1998) Teacher education: preparation for a learned profession?, *Delta*, 50(2): 135–48.

Southworth, G. (1998) *Leading Improving Primary Schools.* London: Falmer Press.

Southworth, G. and Conner, C. (1999) *Managing Improving Primary Schools.* London: Falmer Press.

Southworth, G. and Lincoln, P. (1999) *Supporting Improving Primary Schools*: London: Falmer Press.

Stacey, R. (1996a) *Strategic Management and Organizational Dynamics*, 2nd edition. London: Pitman.

Stacey, R. (1996b) *Complexity and Creativity in Organizations.* San Francisco: Berrett-Koehler.

Stoll, L. and Fink, D. (1996) *Changing Our Schools.* Buckingham: Open University Press.

Stoll, L. and Fink, D. (1998) The cruising school: the unidentified ineffective school, in L. Stoll and K. Myers (eds) *No Quick Fixes: Perspectives on Schools in Difficulty.* London: Falmer Press.

Stoll, L. and Myers, K. (eds) (1998) *No Quick Fixes: Perspectives in Schools in Difficulty.* London: Falmer Press.

Stoll, L., MacBeath, J., Smith, I. and Robertson, P. (2001a) The change equation: capacity for improvement, in J. MacBeath and P. Mortimore (eds) *Improving School Effectiveness.* Buckingham: Open University Press.

Stoll, L., MacBeath, J. and Mortimore, P. (2001b) Beyond 2000: where next for effectiveness and improvement, in J. MacBeath and P. Mortimore (eds) *Improving School Effectiveness.* Buckingham: Open University Press.

Stringfield, S. (1995) Attempting to enhance students' learning through innovative programs: the case for schools evolving into high reliability organisations, *School Effectiveness and School Improvement*, 6(1): 67–96.

Stringfield, S. (2002) Science making a difference: let's be realistic!, *School Effectiveness and School Improvement*, 13(1): 15–29.

Sullivan, M. (1991) *Marketing your Primary School: A Handbook*. London: Longman.

Taylor, F. (1911) *Principles of Scientific Management*. New York: Norton.

Teddlie, C. and Reynolds, D. (eds) (2000) *International Handbook of School Effectiveness Research*. London: Falmer.

Teddlie, C. and Reynolds, D. (2001) Countering the critics: responses to recent criticisms of school effectiveness research, *School Effectiveness and School Improvement*, 12(1): 41–82.

Teddlie, C., Reynolds, D. and Sammons, P. (2000) The methodology and scientific properties of school effectiveness research, in C. Teddlie and D. Reynolds (eds) *International Handbook of School Effectiveness Research*. London: Falmer.

Thompson, P. (2000) Move over Rover: an essay/assay of the field of educational management in the UK, *Journal of Education Policy*, 15(6): 717–32.

Thornton, K. (2002) Headships go out of fashion, *Times Educational Supplement*, 17 May.

Thrupp, M. (1998) The politics of blame: how can teacher education best respond?, *Delta*, 50(2): 163–86.

Thrupp, M. (1999) *Schools Making a Difference: Let's be Realistic!* Buckingham: Open University Press.

Thrupp, M. (2000) Review of Joyce, Bruce, Calhoun, E, and Hopkins, D. (1999) "The new structure of school improvement: inquiring schools and achieving students." *Journal of Education Policy*, 15(2): 258–9.

Thrupp, M. (2001a) Sociological and political concerns about school effectiveness research: time for a new research agenda, *School Effectiveness and School Improvement*, 12(1): 7–40.

Thrupp, M. (2001b) School quasi-markets in England and Wales: best understood as a class strategy? Paper presented to the BERA Annual Conference, Leeds, 13–15 August.

Thrupp, M. (2001c) New Labour and 'failing' schools: policies, claims and evidence. Paper presented to the SCSE Annual Conference 'Education, Education, Education: A Commitment Renewed'. London: Institute of Education, 15 November.

Thrupp, M. (2001d) Recent school effectiveness counter-critiques: problems and possibilities, *British Educational Research Journal*, 27(4): 443–57.

Thrupp, M. (2002) Why 'meddling' is necessary: a response to Teddlie, Reynolds, Townsend, Scheerens, Bosker and Creemers, *School Effectiveness and School Improvement*, 13(1): 1–14.

Thrupp, M., Harold, B., Mansell, H. and Hawksworth, L. (2000) *Mapping the Cumulative Impact of Educational Reform: A Study of Seven New Zealand Schools*. Hamilton: University of Waikato.

Thrupp, M., Lauder, H. and Robinson, T. (forthcoming) School composition and peer effects, *International Journal of Educational Research*.

Tomlinson, H. (1992) *Performance-related Pay in Education*. London: Routledge.

Tomlinson, H., Gunter, H. and Smith, P. (1999) *Living Headship*. London: Paul Chapman.

Tomlinson, S. (2001) *Education in a Post-welfare Society*. Buckingham: Open University Press.

Townsend, T. (2001) Satan or saviour? An analysis of two decades of school effectiveness research, *School Effectiveness and School Improvement*, 12(1): 115–29.

Troman, G. and Woods, P. (2001) *Primary Teachers' Stress*. London: RoutledgeFalmer.

Vincent, C. (2000) *Including Parents? Education, Citizenship and Parental Agency*. Buckingham: Open University Press.

Vincent, C. (2001) Social class and parental agency, *Journal of Education Policy*, 16(4): 347–64.

Waite, D. (1998) Editorial, *International Journal of Leadership in Education*, 1(1): 91–3.

Walford, G (1993) Self-managing schools, choice and equity, in J. Smyth (ed.) *A Socially Critical View of the Self-managing School*. London: Falmer Press.

Wallace, W. (2001a) Death of a school, *Times Educational Supplement*, 16 February.

Wallace, W. (2001b) Is that better? *Times Educational Supplement*, 2 February.

Walsh, M. (1999) *Building a Successful School*. London: Kogan Page.

Whitaker, P. (1993) *Managing Change in Schools*. Buckingham: Open University Press.

Whitty, G., Power, S. and Halpin, D. (1998) *Devolution and Choice in Education*. Buckingham: Open University Press.

Wiliam, D. (2001) *Level Best? Levels of Attainment in National Curriculum Assessment*. London: Association of Teachers and Lecturers.

Willmott, R. (1999) School effectiveness research: an ideological commitment?, *Journal of Philosophy of Education*, 33(2): 253–68.

Willmott, R. (2002a) *Education Policy and Realist Social Theory*. London: Routledge.

Willmott R. (2002b) Symposium review of H. Gunter (2001) Leaders and Leadership in Education, *Educational Management and Administration*, 30(3): 327–50.

Wilson, F. (1999) *Organizational Behaviour: A Critical Introduction*. Oxford: Oxford University Press.

Wolf, A. (2002) *Does Education Matter? Myths about Education and Economic Growth*. London: Penguin.

Wong, K. and Evers, C. (2001) *Leadership for Quality Schooling: International Perspectives*. London: RoutledgeFalmer.

Woods, P., Jeffrey, B., Troman, G. and Boyle, M. (1997) *Restructuring Schools, Reconstructing Teachers*. Buckingham: Open University Press.

Woods, P., Bagley, C. and Glatter, R. (1998) *School Choice and Competition: Markets in the Public Interest?* London: Routledge.

Woods, P., Jeffrey, B. and Troman, J. (2001) The impact of New Labour's educational policy on primary schools, in M. Fielding (ed.) *Taking Education Really Seriously: Four Years' Hard Labour*. London:RoutledgeFalmer.

Young, B.M. (1990) *Television Advertising and Children*. Oxford: Clarendon Press.

Index

EDUCATION IN A POST-WELFARE SOCIETY

Sally Tomlinson

This book provides a context for understanding educational policies which is currently missing from education and social policy courses. It should be compulsory reading.

Len Barton, University of Sheffield

- What have been the positive and negative effects of education reforms in recent years?
- Why are the moderate successes of state education unrecognized and education portrayed as 'failing' or in crisis?
- How has the reproduction of privilege by education persisted despite a rhetoric of equality and inclusion?

Education in a Post-Welfare Society provides a concise and critical overview of education policy, as government in Britain has moved from creating a welfare state to promoting a post-welfare society dominated by private enterprise and competitive markets. Concentrating particularly on the past twenty years, Sally Tomlinson places in context the avalanche of legislation and documentation that has re-formed education into a competitive enterprise in which young people 'learn to compete'. She also demonstrates how a relatively decentralized education system became a system in which funding, teaching and curriculum were centrally controlled, and education narrowed to an economic function. Chronologies of education acts, reports and initiatives are provided at the beginning of the first six chapters. Major legislation is summarized, and an extensive bibliography and annotated suggestions for further reading provide additional guidance. The result is an invaluable resource for students of social policy and education, as well as educational researchers and professionals.

Contents

224pp   0 335 20288 8 (Paperback)   0 335 20289 6 (Hardback)

ENGAGING TEACHERS
TOWARDS A RADICAL DEMOCRATIC AGENDA FOR SCHOOLING

Trevor Gale and Kathleen Densmore

Engaging Teachers reclaims the education discourse captured by new right politics and connects it with a radical democratic agenda for schooling. The authors concentrate on five areas central to schooling:

- Markets in education
- Education policy
- Leadership
- Professionalism
- Communities

By engaging with these topics, teachers are invited to become involved in reconstructing schooling in democratic ways for socially just purposes. This is not simply a matter of acquiescence or of resistance but a demonstration of the benefits that can result when teachers, students and parents work collectively to make things happen rather than having things done to them. This book is key reading for advanced undergraduate and masters students of education, teacher educators and policymakers.

Contents
Foreword by Simon Marginson – Introduction: to a politics of engagement – Markets: an increasingly visible hand – Policy: the authoritative allocation of values – Leadership: taking a radical democratic stance – Professionalism: a framework for just social relations – Community: reconnecting school and society – References – Index.

144pp   0 335 21026 0 (Paperback)   0 335 21027 9 (Hardback)